Contents at a Glance

Table of Contents

Part VII: Appendixes

About the Author

Michael Moncur is a freelance webmaster and author. He runs a network of websites, including the Web's oldest site about famous quotations, online since 1994. He wrote *Sams Teach Yourself DHTML in 24 Hours*, and has also written several bestselling books about networking, certification programs, and databases. He lives with his wife in Salt Lake City, Utah.

Dedication

To my family, and especially Laura. Thanks for all your love and support.

Acknowledgments

I'd like to thank everyone at Sams for their help with this book, and for the opportunity to write it. In particular, Betsy Brown got this edition started and kept it moving. Songlin Qiu managed the development of the book. Project editor Matt Purcell handled the editing process, and the copy editor, Jessica McCarty, saved me from many embarrassing errors. The technical reviewer, Jim O'Donnell, painstakingly tested the scripts and helped keep the writing grounded in reality.

I am grateful to everyone involved with previous editions of this book, including Scott Meyers, David Mayhew, Sean Medlock, Susan Hobbs, Michelle Wyner, Jeff Schultz, Amy Patton, George Nedeff, and Phil Karras. I'd also like to thank Neil Salkind and the rest of the team at Studio B for their help throughout this project.

Finally, personal thanks go to my wife, Laura; my parents, Gary and Susan Moncur; the rest of the family; and my friends, particularly Chuck Perkins, Matt Strebe, Cory Storm, Robert Parsons, Dylan Winslow, Ray Jones, Tyson Jensen, Curt Siffert, Richard Easlick, and Henry J. Tillman. I couldn't have done it without your support.

We Want to Hear from You!

As the reader of this book, *you* are our most important critic and commentator. We value your opinion and want to know what we're doing right, what we could do better, what areas you'd like to see us publish in, and any other words of wisdom you're willing to pass our way.

You can email or write me directly to let me know what you did or didn't like about this book—as well as what we can do to make our books stronger.

Please note that I cannot help you with technical problems related to the topic of this book, and that due to the high volume of mail I receive, I might not be able to reply to every message.

When you write, please be sure to include this book's title and author as well as your name and phone or email address. I will carefully review your comments and share them with the author and editors who worked on the book.

Email: webdev@samspublishing.com

Mail: Mark Taber
            Associate Publisher
            Sams Publishing
            800 East 96th Street
            Indianapolis, IN 46240 USA

Reader Services

Visit our website and register this book at www.samspublishing.com/register for convenient access to any updates, downloads, or errata that might be available for this book.

Introduction

The World Wide Web began as a simple repository for information, but it has grown into much more—it entertains, teaches, advertises, and communicates. As the Web has evolved, the tools have also evolved. Simple markup tools such as HTML have been joined by true programming languages—including JavaScript.

Now don't let the word "programming" scare you. For many, the term conjures up images of long nights staring at the screen, trying to remember which sequence of punctuation marks will produce the effect you need. (Don't get me wrong—some of us enjoy that sort of thing.)

Although JavaScript is programming, it's a very simple language. As a matter of fact, if you haven't programmed before, it makes a great introduction to programming. It requires very little knowledge to start programming with JavaScript—you'll write your first program in Hour 2, "Creating Simple Scripts."

If you can create a web page with HTML, you can easily use JavaScript to improve a page. JavaScript programs can range from a single line to a full-scale application. In this book, you'll start with simple scripts, and proceed to complex applications, such as a card game. You'll also explore some of the most recent uses of JavaScript, such as AJAX remote scripting.

If you've spent much time developing pages for the Web, you know that the Web is constantly changing, and it can be hard to keep up with the latest languages and tools. This book will help you add JavaScript to your web development toolbox, and I think you'll enjoy learning it.

JavaScript and Web Standards

When JavaScript first appeared in browsers, it had rather limited capabilities, and JavaScript programmers have always pushed the envelope to take maximum advantage of what the language was capable of. Unfortunately, this resulted in some bad practices, such as scripts that only worked in one browser, and JavaScript gained a bit of a bad reputation.

Now, thanks to wide browser support for standards established by the W3C (World Wide Web Consortium) and new technologies such as AJAX, JavaScript's future is looking brighter than ever, and a new, more responsible style of scripting is gaining favor. Unobtrusive scripting focuses on adding interactive features while keeping the HTML simple and standards-compliant.

Throughout this book, you'll learn the best practices for using JavaScript responsibly and following web standards. All of the examples in this book avoid browser-specific techniques in favor of standard techniques, and all of the examples will work in most modern browsers.

How to Use This Book

This book is divided into 24 lessons. Each covers a single JavaScript topic, and should take about an hour to complete. The lessons start with the basics of JavaScript, and continue with more advanced topics. You can study an hour a day, or whatever pace suits you. (If you choose to forego sleep and do your studying in a single 24-hour period, you might have what it takes to be a computer book author.)

Organization of This Book

This book is divided into six parts, each focusing on one area of JavaScript:

- ▶ Part I, "Introducing the Concept of Web Scripting and the JavaScript Language," introduces JavaScript, describes how it fits in with other languages, and explains the basic language features of JavaScript. It also introduces the DOM (Document Object Model), which connects JavaScript to web documents.

- ▶ Part II, "Learning JavaScript Basics," covers the fundamentals of the JavaScript language: variables, functions, objects, loops and conditions, and built-in functions. You'll also learn about third-party libraries that add functionality to JavaScript.

- ▶ Part III, "Learning More About the DOM," digs deeper into the DOM objects you'll use in nearly every JavaScript program. It covers events, windows, and web forms. You'll also learn about CSS style sheets, and the DOM features that enable you to change styles. Finally, you'll learn about the W3C DOM, which enables you to modify any part of a page using JavaScript.

- ▶ Part IV, "Working with Advanced JavaScript Features," begins with a look at unobtrusive scripting techniques to keep JavaScript from intruding on the functionality and validity of HTML documents. You'll also learn how to debug JavaScript applications, and finally take a look at two cutting-edge JavaScript features: AJAX and Greasemonkey.

- ▶ Part V, "Building Multimedia Applications with JavaScript," describes JavaScript's features for working with graphics, animation, sound, and browser plug-ins.

- ▶ Part VI, "Creating Complex Scripts," focuses on helping you create complete JavaScript applications. You'll learn how to create drop-down menus, a card game written in JavaScript, and other examples. In the last hour, you'll learn about what's in store for JavaScript and what other languages you might want to learn next.

Conventions Used in This Book

This book contains special elements as described by the following:

> These boxes highlight information that can make your JavaScript programming more efficient and effective.

Did you Know?

> These boxes provide additional information related to material you just read.

By the Way

> These boxes focus your attention on problems or side effects that can occur in specific situations.

Watch Out!

A special `monospace` font is used on programming-related terms and language.

Try It Yourself ▼

The Try It Yourself section at the end of each chapter guides you through the process of creating your own script or applying the techniques learned throughout the hour. This will help you create practical applications of JavaScript based on what you've learned. ▲

Q&A, Quiz, and Exercises

At the end of each hour's lesson, you'll find three final sections. Q&A answers a few of the most common questions about the hour's topic. The Quiz tests your knowledge of the skills you learned in that hour, and the Exercises offer ways for you to gain more experience with the techniques the hour covers.

This Book's Website

Because JavaScript and the Web are constantly changing, you'll need to stay up-to-date after reading this book. This book's website includes the latest updates as well as download-able versions of the listings and graphics for the examples used in this book. To access the book's website, register your book at http://www.samspublishing.com/register.

The Author's Website

The author of this book, Michael Moncur, maintains a website about JavaScript at http://www.jsworkshop.com/. There you'll find regular updates on the JavaScript language and the DOM, links to script examples, and detailed tutorial articles.

If you have questions or comments about this book, have noticed an error, or have trouble getting one of the scripts to work, you can also reach the author by email at js4@starlingtech.com. (Please check the website first to see if your question has been answered.)

PART I:

Introducing the Concept of Web scripting and the JavaScript Language

HOUR 1

Understanding JavaScript

What You'll Learn in This Hour:

▶ What web scripting is and what it's good for
▶ How scripting and programming are different (and similar)
▶ What JavaScript is and where it came from
▶ How to include JavaScript commands in a web page
▶ How different browsers handle JavaScript
▶ What JavaScript can do for your web pages
▶ How to choose between JavaScript and alternative languages

The World Wide Web (WWW) began as a text-only medium—the first browsers didn't even support images within web pages. Although it's still not quite ready to give television a run for its money, the Web has come a long way since then.

Today's websites can include a wealth of features: graphics, sounds, animation, video, and occasionally useful content. Web scripting languages, such as JavaScript, are one of the easiest ways to spice up a web page and to interact with users in new ways.

The first hour of this book introduces the concept of web scripting and the JavaScript language. It also describes how JavaScript fits in with other web languages.

Learning Web Scripting Basics

In the world of science fiction movies (and many other movies that have no excuse), computers are often seen obeying commands in English. Although this might indeed happen in the near future, computers currently find it easier to understand languages such as BASIC, C, and Java.

If you know how to use HTML (Hypertext Markup Language) to create a web document, you've already worked with one computer language. You use HTML tags to describe how

you want your document formatted, and the browser obeys your commands and shows the formatted document to the user.

Because HTML is a simple text markup language, it can't respond to the user, make decisions, or automate repetitive tasks. Interactive tasks such as these require a more sophisticated language: a programming language, or a *scripting* language.

Although many programming languages are complex, scripting languages are generally simple. They have a simple syntax, can perform tasks with a minimum of commands, and are easy to learn. Web scripting languages enable you to combine scripting with HTML to create interactive web pages.

Scripts and Programs

A movie or a play follows a script—a list of actions (or lines) for the actors to perform. A web script provides the same type of instructions for the web browser. A script in JavaScript can range from a single line to a full-scale application. (In either case, JavaScript scripts usually run within a browser.)

By the Way

> Is JavaScript a scripting language or a programming language? It depends on who you ask. We'll refer to scripting throughout this book, but feel free to include JavaScript programming on your résumé after you've finished this book.

Some programming languages must be *compiled*, or translated, into machine code before they can be executed. JavaScript, on the other hand, is an *interpreted* language: The browser executes each line of script as it comes to it.

There is one main advantage to interpreted languages: Writing or changing a script is very simple. Changing a JavaScript script is as easy as changing a typical HTML document, and the change is enacted as soon as you reload the document in the browser.

By the Way

> Interpreted languages have their disadvantages—they can't execute really quickly, so they're not ideally suited for complicated work, such as graphics. Also, they require the interpreter (in JavaScript's case, usually a browser) in order to work.

Introducing JavaScript

JavaScript was developed by Netscape Communications Corporation, the maker of the Netscape web browser. JavaScript was the first web scripting language to be supported by browsers, and it is still by far the most popular.

By the Way

A bit of history: JavaScript was originally called LiveScript and was first introduced in Netscape Navigator 2.0 in 1995. It was soon renamed JavaScript to indicate a marketing relationship with Sun's Java language.

JavaScript is almost as easy to learn as HTML, and it can be included directly in HTML documents. Here are a few of the things you can do with JavaScript:

▶ Display messages to the user as part of a web page, in the browser's status line, or in alert boxes

▶ Validate the contents of a form and make calculations (for example, an order form can automatically display a running total as you enter item quantities)

▶ Animate images or create images that change when you move the mouse over them

▶ Create ad banners that interact with the user, rather than simply displaying a graphic

▶ Detect the browser in use or its features and perform advanced functions only on browsers that support them

▶ Detect installed plug-ins and notify the user if a plug-in is required

▶ Modify all or part of a web page without requiring the user to reload it

▶ Display or interact with data retrieved from a remote server

You can do all this and more with JavaScript, including creating entire applications. We'll explore the uses of JavaScript throughout this book.

How JavaScript Fits into a Web Page

As you hopefully already know, HTML is the language you use to create web documents. To refresh your memory, Listing 1.1 shows a short but sadly typical web document.

LISTING 1.1   A Simple HTML Document

```
<html>
<head>
<title>Our Home Page</title>
</head>
<body>
<h1>The American Eggplant Society</h1>
<p>Welcome to our Web page. Unfortunately,
it's still under construction.</p>
</body>
</html>
```

This document consists of a header within the <head> tags and the body of the page within the <body> tags. To add JavaScript to a page, you'll use a similar tag: <script>.

The <script> tag tag>>tells the browser to start treating the text as a script, and the closing </script> tag tells the browser to return to HTML mode. In most cases, you can't use JavaScript statements in an HTML document except within <script> tags. The exception is event handlers, described later in this hour.

JavaScript and HTML

Using the <script> tag>>tag, you can add a short script (in this case, just one line) to a web document, as shown in Listing 1.2.

LISTING 1.2   A Simple HTML Document with a Simple Script

```
<html>
<head>
<title>Our Home Page</title>
</head>
<body>
<h1>The American Eggplant Society</h1>
<p>Welcome to our Web page. Unfortunately,
it's still under construction.
We last worked on it on this date:
<script language="JavaScript" type="text/javascript">
document.write(document.lastModified);
</script>
</p>
</body>
</html>
```

JavaScript's document.write statement, which you'll learn more about later, sends output as part of the web document. In this case, it displays the modification date of the document.

In this example, we placed the script within the body of the HTML document. There are actually four different places where you might use scripts:

▶ **In the body of the page**—In this case, the script's output is displayed as part of the HTML document when the browser loads the page.

▶ **In the header of the page between the `<head>` tags**—Scripts in the header don't immediately affect the HTML document, but can be referred to by other scripts. The header is often used for functions—groups of JavaScript statements that can be used as a single unit. You will learn more about functions in Hour 3, "Getting Started with JavaScript Programming."

▶ **Within an HTML tag, such as `<body>` or `<form>`**—This is called an *event handler* and enables the script to work with HTML elements. When using JavaScript in event handlers, you don't need to use the `<script>` tag. You'll learn more about event handlers in Hour 3.

▶ **In a separate file entirely**—JavaScript supports the use of files with the `.js` extension containing scripts; these can be included by specifying a file in the `<script>` tag.

Using Separate JavaScript Files

When you create more complicated scripts, you'll quickly find your HTML documents become large and confusing. To avoid this, you can use one or more external JavaScript files. These are files with the `.js` extension that contain JavaScript statements.

External scripts are supported by all modern browsers. To use an external script, you specify its filename in the `<script>` tag:

```
<script language="JavaScript" type="text/javascript" src="filename.js">
</script>
```

Because you'll be placing the JavaScript statements in a separate file, you don't need anything between the opening and closing `<script>` tags—in fact, anything between them will be ignored by the browser.

You can create the `.js` file using a text editor. It should contain one or more JavaScript commands, and only JavaScript—don't include `<script>` tags, other HTML tags, or HTML comments. Save the `.js` file in the same directory as the HTML documents that refer to it. See the Try It Yourself section of Hour 2 for an example of separate HTML and script files.

External JavaScript files have a distinct advantage: You can link to the same `.js` file from two or more HTML documents. Because the browser stores this file in its cache, this can reduce the time it takes your web pages to display.

Did you Know?

Events

Many of the useful things you can do with JavaScript involve interacting with the user, and that means responding to *events*—for example, a link or a button being clicked. You can define event handlers within HTML tags to tell the browser how to respond to an event. For example, Listing 1.3 defines a button that displays a message when clicked.

LISTING 1.3   A Simple Event Handler

```
<html>
<head>
<title>Event Test</title>
</head>
<body>
<h1>Event Test</h1>
<button onclick="alert('You clicked the button.')">
</body>
</html>
```

In Hour 9, "Responding to Events," you'll learn more about JavaScript's event model and creating simple and complex event handlers.

> You can also use an external script to define event handlers. This is a good practice because it lets you keep all of your JavaScript in one place, rather than scattered across the HTML document. See Hour 9 for details.

Browsers and JavaScript

Like HTML, JavaScript requires a web browser to be displayed, and different browsers may display it differently. Unlike HTML, the results of a browser incompatibility with JavaScript are more drastic: Rather than simply displaying your text incorrectly, the script may not execute at all, may display an error message, or may even crash the browser.

We'll take a quick look at the way different browsers—and different versions of the same browser—treat JavaScript in the following sections.

The DOM (Document Object Model)

Let's start with one reason you shouldn't have to think too much about different browsers. Almost everything you do with JavaScript involves working with the Document Object Model (DOM)—a standardized set of objects that represent a web document.

The DOM includes objects that enable you to work with all aspects of the current document. For example, you can read the value the user types in a form field, or the filename of the current page.

The DOM is defined by the W3C (World Wide Web Consortium) and the latest browsers support DOM levels 1 and 2, which enable you to control all parts of a web page with JavaScript.

> Early versions of the DOM only allowed JavaScript to manipulate certain parts of a page—such as form elements and links. The new DOM enables you to work with every element defined in HTML.

Internet Explorer

Microsoft's Internet Explorer (IE) browser was a latecomer to the Internet, but has now become the most popular browser. The latest versions of IE support most of JavaScript 1.5 and the W3C DOM.

At this writing, IE 6.0 is the latest released version, and IE 7.0 is in beta. Although most of the examples in this book will work in IE 5.0 and later, I recommend testing your scripts with the latest browsers.

Netscape and Firefox

Netscape, which for a time made the Web's most popular browser, established the Mozilla Foundation to maintain an open-source version of the browser. This led to the Mozilla browser and more recently, Firefox, a streamlined browser based on the Mozilla engine.

Firefox has recently begun to challenge Microsoft's browser dominance, with an estimated 10% of web users. That might not sound like many, but ignoring Firefox means ignoring at least 10% of your audience, and on many sites the percentage is much higher.

Firefox is available for Windows, Macintosh, and Linux platforms and is free, open-source software. You can download Firefox from the Mozilla website at http://www.mozilla.org/.

At this writing, the current version of Firefox is 1.5. Most of the scripts in this book will work with Firefox 1.0 or later, as well as versions 6 and 7 of the Netscape browser.

Netscape 4.0 and Internet Explorer 4.0 supported incompatible versions of Dynamic HTML (DHTML)—an attempt to overcome the limits of the current DOM. The new W3C DOM eliminates the need for these proprietary models, and you can now write standard code that will work on most modern browsers.

Other Browsers

Although Internet Explorer and Firefox are the most popular browsers, there are many other browsers. Here are two less-common browsers you'll probably hear about:

▶ Safari, Apple's browser, is included with MacOS and is the default browser on most Macintosh computers.

▶ Opera, from Opera Software, is an alternative browser notable for its support of many platforms, including mobile phones. The latest version of Opera, 8.0, supports the W3C DOM and JavaScript 1.5, and should work with most scripts in this book.

There are many other browsers out there, but you don't need to know all of them to create working scripts—as long as you follow the standards, your scripts will work on browsers that support JavaScript almost every time. This book will focus on teaching standards-based scripting that will work in all modern browsers.

Versions of JavaScript

The JavaScript language has evolved since its original release in Netscape 2.0. There have been several versions of JavaScript:

▶ JavaScript 1.0, the original version, is supported by Netscape 2.0 and Internet Explorer 3.0.

▶ JavaScript 1.1 is supported by Netscape 3.0 and mostly supported by Internet Explorer 4.0.

▶ JavaScript 1.2 is supported by Netscape 4.0 and partially supported by Internet Explorer 4.0.

▶ JavaScript 1.3 is supported by Netscape 4.5 and Internet Explorer 5.0 and 6.0.

▶ JavaScript 1.5 is partially supported by Internet Explorer 6.0, and supported by Netscape 6.0 and Firefox 1.0.

▶ JavaScript 1.6 is currently supported by Firefox 1.5.

Each of these versions is an improvement over the previous version and includes a number of new features. With rare exception, browsers that support the new version will also support scripts written for earlier versions.

The European Computer Manufacturing Association (ECMA) has finalized the ECMA-262 specification for ECMAScript, a standardized version of JavaScript. JavaScript 1.3 follows the ECMA-262 standard, and JavaScript 1.5 follows ECMA-262 revision 3.

> Another language you might hear of is JScript. This is how Microsoft refers to its implementation of JavaScript, which is generally compatible with the standard version.

By the Way

The Mozilla Foundation, the open-source offshoot of Netscape that develops the Firefox browser, is also working with ECMA on JavaScript 2.0, a future version that will correspond with the fourth edition of the ECMAScript standard. JavaScript 2.0 will improve upon earlier versions with a more modular approach, better object support, and features to make JavaScript useful as a general-purpose scripting language as well as a web language.

Specifying JavaScript Versions

As mentioned earlier in this hour, you can specify a version of JavaScript in the `<script>` tag. For example, this tag specifies JavaScript version 1.3:

```
<script language="JavaScript1.3" type="text/javascript">
```

There are two ways of specifying the JavaScript language in the `<script>` tag. The old method uses the `language` attribute, and the new method recommended by the HTML 4.0 specification uses the `type` attribute. To maintain compatibility with older browsers, you can use both attributes.

When you specify a version number in the `language` attribute, this allows your script to execute only if the browser supports the version you specified or a later version.

When the `<script>` tag doesn't specify a version number, all browsers that support JavaScript will run the script. Because most of the JavaScript language has remained the same since version 1.0, you will rarely need to worry about JavaScript versions.

> In most cases, you shouldn't specify a JavaScript version at all. This allows your script to run on all of the browsers that support JavaScript. You should only specify a particular version when your script uses features unique to a specific version.

Did you Know?

JavaScript Beyond the Browser

Although JavaScript programs traditionally run within a web browser, and web-based JavaScript is the focus of this book, JavaScript is becoming increasingly popular in other applications. Here are a few examples:

▶ Adobe Dreamweaver and Flash, used for web applications and multimedia, can be extended with JavaScript.

▶ Several server-side versions of JavaScript are available. These run within a web server rather than a browser.

▶ Microsoft's Windows Scripting Host (WSH) supports JScript, Microsoft's implementation of JavaScript, as a general-purpose scripting language for Windows. Unfortunately, the most popular applications developed for WSH so far have been email viruses.

▶ Microsoft's Common Language Runtime (CLR), part of the .NET framework, supports JavaScript.

Along with these examples, many of the changes in the upcoming JavaScript 2.0 are designed to make it more suitable as a general-purpose scripting language.

Exploring JavaScript's Capabilities

If you've spent any time browsing the Web, you've undoubtedly seen lots of examples of JavaScript in action. Here are some brief descriptions of typical applications for JavaScript, all of which you'll explore further, later in this book.

Improving Navigation

Some of the most common uses of JavaScript are in navigation systems for websites. You can use JavaScript to create a navigation tool—for example, a drop-down menu to select the next page to read, or a submenu that pops up when you hover over a navigation link.

When it's done right, this kind of JavaScript interactivity can make a site easier to use, while remaining usable for browsers that don't support JavaScript.

Validating Forms

Form validation is another common use of JavaScript. A simple script can read values the user types into a form and make sure they're in the right format, such as with ZIP Codes or phone numbers. This allows users to notice common errors and

fix them without waiting for a response from the web server. You'll learn how to write form validation scripts in Hour 11, "Getting Data with Forms."

Special Effects

One of the earliest and most annoying uses of JavaScript was to create attention-getting special effects—for example, scrolling a message in the browser's status line or flashing the background color of a page.

These techniques have fortunately fallen out of style, but thanks to the W3C DOM and the latest browsers, some more impressive effects are possible with JavaScript—for example, creating objects that can be dragged and dropped on a page, or creating fading transitions between images in a slideshow.

Remote Scripting (AJAX)

For a long time, the biggest limitation of JavaScript was that there was no way for it to communicate with a web server. For example, you could use it to verify that a phone number had the right number of digits, but not to look up the user's location in a database based on the number.

Now that some of JavaScript's advanced features are supported by most browsers, this is no longer the case. Your scripts can get data from a server without loading a page, or send data back to be saved. These features are collectively known as AJAX (Asynchronous JavaScript And XML), or *remote scripting*. You'll learn how to develop AJAX scripts in Hour 17, "AJAX: Remote Scripting."

You've seen AJAX in action if you've used Google's Gmail mail application, or recent versions of Yahoo! Mail or Microsoft Hotmail. All of these use remote scripting to present you with a responsive user interface that works with a server in the background.

Alternatives to JavaScript

JavaScript is not the only language used on the Web, and in some cases, it may not be the right tool for the job. Other languages, such as Java, can do some things better than JavaScript. In the following sections, we'll look at a few other commonly used web languages and their advantages.

Java

Java is a programming language developed by Sun Microsystems that can be used to create *applets*, or programs that execute within a web page.

Java is a compiled language, but the compiler produces code for a *virtual machine* rather than a real computer. The virtual machine is a set of rules for bytecodes and their meanings, with capabilities that fit well into the scope of a web browser.

The virtual machine code is then interpreted by a web browser. This allows the same Java applet to execute the same way on PCs, Macintoshes, and UNIX machines, and on different browsers.

> Java is also a densely populated island in Indonesia and a slang term for coffee. This has resulted in a widespread invasion of coffee-related terms in computer literature.

At this point, we need to make one thing clear: Java is a fine language, but you won't be learning it in this book. Although their names and some of their commands are similar, JavaScript and Java are entirely different languages.

ActiveX

ActiveX is a specification developed by Microsoft that enables ordinary Windows programs to be run within a web page. ActiveX programs can be written in languages such as Visual C++ and Visual Basic, and they are compiled before being placed on the web server.

ActiveX applications, called *controls*, are downloaded and executed by the web browser, like Java applets. Unlike Java applets, controls can be installed permanently when they are downloaded, eliminating the need to download them again.

ActiveX's main advantage is that it can do just about anything. This can also be a disadvantage: Several enterprising programmers have already used ActiveX to bring exciting new capabilities to web pages, such as "the web page that turns off your computer" and "the web page that formats your disk drive."

Fortunately, ActiveX includes a signature feature that identifies the source of the control and prevents controls from being modified. Although this won't prevent a control from damaging your system, you can specify which sources of controls you trust.

ActiveX has two main disadvantages: First, it isn't as easy to program as a scripting language or Java. Second, ActiveX is proprietary—it works only in Microsoft Internet Explorer, and only under Windows platforms.

VBScript

VBScript, sometimes known as Visual Basic Scripting Edition, is Microsoft's answer to JavaScript. Just as JavaScript's syntax is loosely based on Java, VBScript's syntax is

loosely based on Microsoft Visual Basic, a popular programming language for Windows machines.

Like JavaScript, VBScript is a simple scripting language, and you can include VBScript statements within an HTML document. VBScript can work with the DOM in the same way as JavaScript. To begin a VBScript script, you use the `<script LAN-GUAGE="VBScript">` tag.

VBScript can do many of the same things as JavaScript, and it even looks similar in some cases. It has two main advantages:

▶ For those who already know Visual Basic, it may be easier to learn than JavaScript.

▶ It is closely integrated with ActiveX, Microsoft's standard for web-embedded applications.

VBScript's main disadvantage is that it is supported only by Microsoft Internet Explorer. JavaScript, on the other hand, is supported by Netscape, Internet Explorer, and several other browsers. JavaScript is a much more popular language, and you can see it in use all over the Web.

CGI and Server-Side Scripting

CGI (Common Gateway Interface) is not really a language, but a specification that enables programs to run on web servers. CGI programs can be written in any number of languages, including Perl, C, and Visual Basic.

Along with traditional CGI, scripting languages such as Microsoft's Active Server Pages, Java Server Pages, Cold Fusion, and PHP are often used on web servers. A server-side implementation of JavaScript is also available.

Server-side programs are heavily used on the Web. Almost every time you type information into a form and press a button to send it to a website, the data is processed by a server-side application.

The main difference between JavaScript and server-side languages is that JavaScript applications execute on the client (the web browser) and server-side applications execute on the web server. The main disadvantage of this approach is that, because the data must be sent to the web server and back, response time might be slow.

On the other hand, CGI can do things JavaScript can't do. In particular, it can read and write files on the server and interact with other server components, such as databases. Although a client-side JavaScript program can read information from a form and then manipulate it, it can't store the data on the web server.

JavaScript is often used in conjunction with server-side languages. In its simplest form, this means JavaScript handles client-side chores such as form validation, whereas a server-side language receives data and stores it in a database. Using AJAX, this interaction can be instantaneous and does not even require loading a new page.

> CGI and server-side programming are outside the focus of this book. You can learn more about these technologies with other Sams books, including *Teach Yourself CGI Programming in 24 Hours*, *Teach Yourself Perl in 24 Hours*, and *Teach Yourself PHP in 24 Hours*. See Appendix A, "Other JavaScript Resources," for more sources of information.

Summary

During this hour, you've learned what web scripting is and what JavaScript is. You've also learned how to insert a script into an HTML document or refer to an external JavaScript file, what sorts of things JavaScript can do, and how JavaScript differs from other web languages.

If you're waiting for some real JavaScript code, look no further. The next hour, "Creating Simple Scripts," guides you through the process of creating several working JavaScript examples. You'll also learn about the tools you'll need to work with JavaScript.

Q&A

Q. *Do I need to test my JavaScript on more than one browser?*

A. In an ideal world, any script you write that follows the standards for JavaScript will work in all browsers, and 90% of the time that's true in the real world. But browsers do have their quirks, and you should test your scripts on Internet Explorer and Firefox at a minimum.

Q. *If I plan to learn Java or CGI anyway, will I have any use for JavaScript?*

A. Certainly. JavaScript is the ideal tool for many applications, such as form validation. Although Java and CGI have their uses, they can't do all that JavaScript can do.

Q. *Are there browsers out there that don't support JavaScript?*

A. Yes. A few niche browsers, such as text-based browsers and tools for blind users, have partial JavaScript support or no support. Mobile phone browsers

often support little or no JavaScript. Finally, many users of Internet Explorer or Firefox have JavaScript support turned off, and some corporate firewalls and ad-blocking software block JavaScript. Hour 2 describes how to account for browsers that don't support JavaScript.

Quiz Questions

Test your knowledge of JavaScript by answering the following questions:

1. Why do JavaScript and Java have similar names?

    a. JavaScript is a stripped-down version of Java.

    b. Netscape's marketing department wanted them to sound related.

    c. They both originated on the island of Java.

2. When a user views a page containing a JavaScript program, which machine actually executes the script?

    a. The user's machine running a web browser

    b. The web server

    c. A central machine deep within Netscape's corporate offices

3. Which of the following languages is supported by both Microsoft Internet Explorer and Netscape?

    a. VBScript

    b. ActiveX

    c. JavaScript

Quiz Answers

1. b. Although some of the syntax is similar, JavaScript got its Java-based name mostly because of a marketing relationship.

2. a. JavaScript programs execute on the web browser. (There is actually a server-side version of JavaScript, but that's another story.)

3. c. JavaScript is supported by both Netscape and Internet Explorer, although the implementations are not identical.

Exercises

If you want to learn a bit about JavaScript or check out the latest developments before you proceed with the next hour, perform these activities:

▶ Visit this book's website to check for news about JavaScript and updates to the scripts in this book.

▶ View some of the examples on this book's website to see JavaScript in action.

Creating Simple Scripts

What You'll Learn in This Hour:

▶ The software tools you will need to create and test scripts
▶ Beginning and ending scripts
▶ Formatting JavaScript statements
▶ How a script can display a result
▶ Including a script within a web document
▶ Testing a script using browsers
▶ Modifying a script
▶ Dealing with errors in scripts
▶ Moving scripts into separate files

As you learned in Hour 1, "Understanding JavaScript," JavaScript is a scripting language for web pages. You can include JavaScript commands directly in the HTML document, and the script will be executed when the page is viewed in a browser.

During this hour, you will create a simple script, edit it, and test it using a web browser. Along the way you'll learn the basic tasks involved in creating and using scripts.

Tools for Scripting

Unlike many programming languages, you won't need any special software to create JavaScript scripts. In fact, you probably already have everything you need.

Text Editors

The first tool you'll need to work with JavaScript is a *text editor*. JavaScript scripts are stored in simple text files, usually as part of HTML documents. Any editor that can store ASCII text files will work.

You can choose from a wide range of editors, from simple text editors to word processors. If you don't have a favorite editor already, a simple editor is most likely included with your computer. For Windows computers, the Notepad accessory will work just fine.

Watch Out!

> If you use a word processor to create JavaScript programs, be sure you save the files as ASCII text rather than as word processing documents. Otherwise, the browser might not recognize them.

A variety of dedicated HTML editors is also available and will work with JavaScript. In fact, many include features specifically for JavaScript—for example, color-coding the various JavaScript statements to indicate their purposes, or even creating simple scripts automatically.

For Windows computers, here are a few recommended editors:

▶ **HomeSite**—An excellent HTML editor that includes JavaScript support. HomeSite is included as part of Adobe Dreamweaver and is also available separately.

▶ **Microsoft FrontPage 2003**—Microsoft's visual HTML editor. The Script Builder component enables you to easily create simple scripts.

▶ **TextPad**—A powerful text editor that includes a number of features missing from Notepad. TextPad's view of a JavaScript document is shown in Figure 2.1.

FIGURE 2.1
A text editor (TextPad) with a JavaScript document.

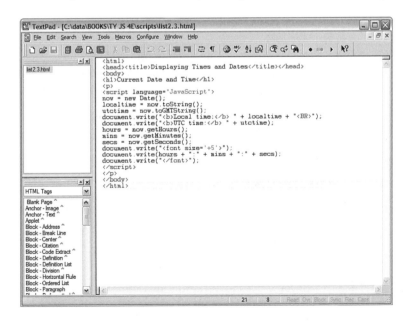

The following editors are available for both Windows and Macintosh:

▶ **Adobe Dreamweaver**—A visually oriented editor that works with HTML, JavaScript, and Macromedia's Flash plug-in.

▶ **Adobe GoLive**—A visual and HTML editor that also includes features for designing and organizing the structure of large sites.

Additionally for the Macintosh, BBEdit, TextWrangler, and Alpha are good HTML editors that you can use to create web pages and scripts.

> Appendix B, "Tools for JavaScript Developers," includes web addresses to download these and other HTML and JavaScript editors.

By the Way

Browsers

You'll need two other things to work with JavaScript: a web browser and a computer to run it on. Because this book covers new features introduced up to JavaScript 1.5 and the latest W3C DOM, I recommend that you use the latest version of Mozilla Firefox or Microsoft Internet Explorer. See the Mozilla (http://www.mozilla.com) or Microsoft (http://www.microsoft.com) website to download a copy.

At a minimum, you should have Firefox 1.0, Netscape 7.0, or Internet Explorer 6.0 or later. Although Netscape 4.x and Internet Explorer 4 will run many of the scripts in this book, they don't support a lot of the latest features you'll learn about.

You can choose whichever browser you like for your web browsing, but for developing JavaScript you should have more than one browser—at a minimum, Firefox and Internet Explorer. This will allow you to test your scripts in the common browsers users will employ on your site.

> If you plan on making your scripts available over the Internet, you'll also need a web server, or access to one. However, you can use most of the JavaScript examples in this book directly from your computer's hard disk.

By the Way

Displaying Time with JavaScript

One common and easy use for JavaScript is to display dates and times. Because JavaScript runs on the browser, the times it displays will be in the user's current time zone. However, you can also use JavaScript to calculate "universal" (UTC) time.

> UTC stands for Universal Time (Coordinated), and is the atomic time standard based on the old GMT (Greenwich Mean Time) standard. This is the time at the Prime Meridian, which runs through Greenwich, London, England.

As a basic introduction to JavaScript, you will now create a simple script that displays the current time and the UTC time within a web page.

Beginning the Script

Your script, like most JavaScript programs, begins with the HTML `<script>` tag. As you learned in Hour 1, you use the `<script>` and `</script>` tags to enclose a script within the HTML document.

> Remember to include only valid JavaScript statements between the starting and ending `<script>` tags. If the browser finds anything but valid JavaScript statements within the `<script>` tags, it will display a JavaScript error message.

To begin creating the script, open your favorite text editor and type the beginning and ending `<script>` tags as shown.

```
<script LANGUAGE="JavaScript" type="text/javascript">
</script>
```

Because this script does not use any of the new features of JavaScript 1.1 or later, you won't need to specify a version number in the `<script>` tag. This script should work with all browsers going back to Netscape 2.0 or Internet Explorer 3.0.

Adding JavaScript Statements

Your script now needs to determine the local and UTC times, and then display them to the browser. Fortunately, all of the hard parts, such as converting between date formats, are built in to the JavaScript interpreter.

Storing Data in Variables

To begin the script, you will use a *variable* to store the current date. You will learn more about variables in Hour 5, "Using Variables, Strings, and Arrays." A variable is a container that can hold a value—a number, some text, or in this case, a date.

To start writing the script, add the following line after the first `<script>` tag. Be sure to use the same combination of capital and lowercase letters in your version because JavaScript commands and variable names are case sensitive.

```
now = new Date();
```

This statement creates a variable called now and stores the current date and time in it. This statement and the others you will use in this script use JavaScript's built-in Date object, which enables you to conveniently handle dates and times. You'll learn more about working with dates in Hour 8, "Using Built-in Functions and Libraries."

Notice the semicolon at the end of the previous statement. This tells the browser that it has reached the end of a statement. Semicolons are optional, but using them helps you avoid some common errors. We'll use them throughout this book for clarity.

Calculating the Results

Internally, JavaScript stores dates as the number of milliseconds since January 1, 1970. Fortunately, JavaScript includes a number of functions to convert dates and times in various ways, so you don't have to figure out how to convert milliseconds to day, date, and time.

To continue your script, add the following two statements before the final </script> tag:

```
localtime = now.toString();
utctime = now.toGMTString();
```

These statements create two new variables: localtime, containing the current time and date in a nice readable format, and utctime, containing the UTC equivalent.

The localtime and utctime variables store a piece of text, such as January 1, 2001 12:00 PM. In programming parlance, a piece of text is called a *string*. You will learn more about strings in Hour 5.

Creating Output

You now have two variables—localtime and utctime—which contain the results we want from our script. Of course, these variables don't do us much good unless we can see them. JavaScript includes a number of ways to display information, and one of the simplest is the document.write statement.

The document.write statement displays a text string, a number, or anything else you throw at it. Because your JavaScript program will be used within a web page, the output will be displayed as part of the page. To display the result, add these statements before the final </script> tag:

```
document.write("<b>Local time:</b> " + localtime + "<br>");
document.write("<b>UTC time:</b> " + utctime);
```

These statements tell the browser to add some text to the web page containing your script. The output will include some brief strings introducing the results, and the contents of the localtime and utctime variables.

Notice the HTML tags, such as <b>, within the quotation marks—because JavaScript's output appears within a web page, it needs to be formatted using HTML. The <br> tag in the first line ensures that the two times will be displayed on separate lines.

> Notice the plus signs (+) used between the text and variables in the previous statements. In this case, it tells the browser to combine the values into one string of text. If you use the plus sign between two numbers, they are added together.

Adding the Script to a Web Page

You should now have a complete script that calculates a result and displays it. Your listing should match Listing 2.1.

LISTING 2.1   The Complete Date and Time Script

```
<script language="JavaScript" type="text/javascript">
now = new Date();
localtime = now.toString();
utctime = now.toGMTString();
document.write("<b>Local time:</b> " + localtime + "<BR>");
document.write("<b>UTC time:</b> " + utctime);
</script>
```

To use your script, you'll need to add it to an HTML document. In its most basic form, the HTML document should include opening and closing <html> tags, <head> tags, and <body> tags.

If you add these tags to the document containing your script along with a descriptive heading, you should end up with something like Listing 2.2.

LISTING 2.2   The Date and Time Script in an HTML Document

```
<html>
<head><title>Displaying Times and Dates</title></head>
<body>
<h1>Current Date and Time</h1>
<p>
<script language="JavaScript" type="text/javascript">
now = new Date();
localtime = now.toString();
utctime = now.toGMTString();
document.write("<b>Local time:</b> " + localtime + "<BR>");
```

```
document.write("<b>UTC time:</b> " + utctime);
</script>
</p>
</body>
</html>
```

Now that you have a complete HTML document, save it with the `.htm` or `.html` extension.

By the Way

Testing the Script

To test your script, you simply need to load the HTML document you created in a web browser. Start Netscape or Internet Explorer and select Open from the File menu. Click the Choose File or Browse button, and then find your HTML file. After you've selected it, click the Open button to view the page.

If you typed the script correctly, your browser should display the result of the script, as shown in Figure 2.2. (Of course, your result won't be the same as mine, but it should be the same as the setting of your computer's clock.)

A note about Internet Explorer 6.0 and above: Depending on your security settings, the script might not execute, and a yellow highlighted bar on the top of the browser might display a security warning. In this case, click the yellow bar and select Allow Blocked Content to allow your script to run. (This happens because the default security settings allow JavaScript in online documents, but not in local files.)

FIGURE 2.2
Firefox displays the results of the Date and Time script.

You can download the HTML document for this hour from this book's website. If the version you type doesn't work, try downloading the online version.

Did you Know?

Modifying the Script

Although the current script does indeed display the current date and time, its display isn't nearly as attractive as the clock on your wall or desk. To remedy that, you can use some additional JavaScript features and a bit of HTML to display a large clock.

To display a large clock, we need the hours, minutes, and seconds in separate variables. Once again, JavaScript has built-in functions to do most of the work:

```
hours = now.getHours();
mins = now.getMinutes();
secs = now.getSeconds();
```

These statements load the hours, mins, and secs variables with the components of the time using JavaScript's built-in date functions.

After the hours, minutes, and seconds are in separate variables, you can create doc-ument.write statements to display them:

```
document.write("<h1>");
document.write(hours + ":" + mins + ":" + secs);
document.write("</h1>");
```

The first statement displays an HTML <h1> header tag to display the clock in a large typeface. The second statement displays the hours, mins, and secs variables, sepa-rated by colons, and the third adds the closing </h1> tag.

You can add the preceding statements to the original date and time script to add the large clock display. Listing 2.3 shows the complete modified version of the script.

LISTING 2.3   The Date and Time Script with Large Clock Display

```
<html>
<head><title>Displaying Times and Dates</title></head>
<body>
<h1>Current Date and Time</h1>
<p>
<script language="JavaScript">
now = new Date();
localtime = now.toString();
utctime = now.toGMTString();
document.write("<b>Local time:</b> " + localtime + "<BR>");
document.write("<b>UTC time:</b> " + utctime);
hours = now.getHours();
mins = now.getMinutes();
secs = now.getSeconds();
document.write("<h1>");
document.write(hours + ":" + mins + ":" + secs);
document.write("</h1>");
</script>
</p>
</body>
</html>
```

Now that you have modified the script, save the HTML file and open the modified file in your browser. If you left the browser running, you can simply use the Reload button to load the new version of the script. Try it and verify that the same time is displayed in both the upper portion of the window and the new large clock. Figure 2.3 shows the results.

FIGURE 2.3
Internet Explorer displays the modified Date and Time script.

> The time formatting produced by this script isn't perfect: Hours after noon are in 24-hour time, and there are no leading zeroes, so 12:04 is displayed as 12:4. See Hour 8, "Using Built-in Functions and Libraries," for solutions to these issues.

By the Way

Dealing with JavaScript Errors

As you develop more complex JavaScript applications, you're going to run into errors from time to time. JavaScript errors are usually caused by mistyped JavaScript statements.

To see an example of a JavaScript error message, modify the statement you added in the previous section. We'll use a common error: omitting one of the parentheses. Change the last `document.write` statement in Listing 2.3 to read

```
document.write("</h1>";
```

Save your HTML document again and load the document into the browser. Depending on the browser version you're using, one of two things will happen: Either an error message will be displayed, or the script will simply fail to execute.

If an error message is displayed, you're halfway to fixing the problem by adding the missing parenthesis. If no error was displayed, you should configure your browser to display error messages so that you can diagnose future problems:

▶ In Netscape or Firefox, type **javascript:** into the browser's Location field to display the JavaScript Console. In Firefox, you can also select Tools, JavaScript Console from the menu. The console is shown in Figure 2.4, displaying the error message you created in this example.

▶ In Internet Explorer, select Tools, Internet Options. On the Advanced page, uncheck the Disable Script Debugging box and check the Display a Notification About Every Script Error box. (If this is disabled, a yellow icon in the status bar will still notify you of errors.)

By the Way

Notice the field at the top of the JavaScript Console. This enables you to type a JavaScript statement, which will be executed immediately. This is a handy way to test JavaScript's features.

FIGURE 2.4
Firefox's
JavaScript
Console dis-
plays an error
message.

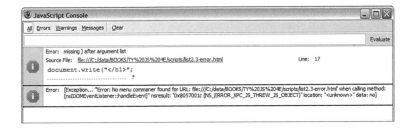

The error we get in this case is `missing ) after argument list` (Firefox) or `Expected ')'` (Internet Explorer), which turns out to be exactly the problem. Be warned, however, that error messages aren't always this enlightening.

While Internet Explorer displays error dialog boxes for each error, Firefox's JavaScript Console displays a single list of errors and allows you to test commands. For this reason, you might find it useful to install Firefox for debugging and testing JavaScript, even if Internet Explorer is your primary browser.

Did you Know?

As you develop larger JavaScript applications, finding and fixing errors becomes more important. You'll learn more about dealing with JavaScript errors in Hour 16, "Debugging JavaScript Applications."

▼ **Try It Yourself**

Using a Separate JavaScript File

Although simple scripts like this one can be embedded in an HTML file, as in the previous example, it's good practice to separate the HTML and JavaScript by using a separate JavaScript file. This has a few advantages:

▶ Browsers with JavaScript disabled, or older browsers that don't support it, will ignore the script.

▶ When multiple pages on your site use the same script, the browser only has to load the JavaScript file once, and use a cached copy on other pages.

▶ It's easier to maintain the HTML and JavaScript code when they're separated, especially if different people are working on the design and the scripting.

We'll also be using separate JavaScript files for most of the examples in this book, so you should be familiar with this technique.

To use a separate JavaScript file with the date and time example, you will need two files. A quick way to create them is to save the combined HTML/JavaScript file in Listing 2.3 to two files, and then edit them.

The first file, datetime.html, will be the HTML file. Remove everything between the <script> tags, and add the src="datetime.js" attribute to the opening <script> tag. The resulting file is shown in Listing 2.4.

LISTING 2.4   HTML File for the Date and Time Script (datetime.html)

```
<html>
<head><title>Displaying Times and Dates</title></head>
<body>
<h1>Current Date and Time</h1>
<p>
<script language="JavaScript" type="text/javascript"
 src = "datetime.js">
</script>
</p>
</body>
</html>
```

The second file, datetime.js, will contain only JavaScript commands—the same ones you removed from the HTML file. This file should *not* include <script> tags, or any HTML tags. The JavaScript file is shown in Listing 2.5.

LISTING 2.5   The Date and Time Script (datetime.js)

```
now = new Date();
localtime = now.toString();
utctime = now.toGMTString();
document.write("<b>Local time:</b> " + localtime + "<BR>");
document.write("<b>UTC time:</b> " + utctime);
hours = now.getHours();
mins = now.getMinutes();
secs = now.getSeconds();
document.write("<h1>");
document.write(hours + ":" + mins + ":" + secs);
document.write("</h1>");
```

> If Internet Explorer displays a warning message in a yellow bar at the top of the browser window instead of executing your script, simply click the bar and select Allow Blocked Content.

As you create larger scripts, you'll find it far less confusing to keep the HTML and JavaScript in separate files. The next hour discusses this and other best practices for JavaScript.

Summary

During this hour, you wrote a simple JavaScript program and tested it using a browser. You learned about the tools you need to work with JavaScript—basically, an editor and a browser. You also learned how to modify and test scripts, and what happens when a JavaScript program runs into an error. Finally, you learned how to use scripts in separate JavaScript files.

In the process of writing this script, you have used some of JavaScript's basic features: variables, the `document.write` statement, and functions for working with dates and times.

Now that you've learned a bit of JavaScript syntax, you're ready to learn more of the details. You'll do that in Hour 3, "Getting Started with JavaScript Programming."

Q&A

Q. *Why do I need more than one browser to test scripts? Won't JavaScript behave the same way on both browsers?*

A. Although JavaScript is standardized, the browsers don't interpret it in exactly the same way. Your script might have minor flaws that have no effect in one browser but cause an error in another. Also, as you move on to more advanced features of JavaScript, you'll need to deal with browsers in different ways, as described in Hour 15, "Unobtrusive Scripting," and you'll need to test each one.

Q. *When I try to run my script, the browser displays the actual script in the browser window instead of executing it. What did I do wrong?*

A. This is most likely caused by one of three errors. First, you might be missing the beginning or ending `<script>` tags. Check them, and verify that the first reads `<script LANGUAGE="JavaScript" type="text/javascript">`. Second, your file might have been saved with a `.txt` extension, causing the browser to treat it as a text file. Rename it to `.htm` or `.html` to fix the problem. Third, make sure your browser supports JavaScript, and that it is not disabled in the Preferences dialog.

Q. *Why are the `<b>` and `<br>` tags allowed in the statements to print the time? I thought HTML tags weren't allowed within the `<script>` tags.*

A. Because this particular tag is inside quotation marks, it's considered a valid part of the script. The script's output, including any HTML tags, is interpreted and displayed by the browser. You can use other HTML tags within quotation marks to add formatting, such as the `<h1>` tags we added for the large clock display.

Quiz Questions

Test your knowledge of JavaScript by answering the following questions:

1. What software do you use to create and edit JavaScript programs?

   a. A browser

   b. A text editor

   c. A pencil and a piece of paper

2. What are variables used for in JavaScript programs?

   a. Storing numbers, dates, or other values

   b. Varying randomly

   c. Causing high school algebra flashbacks

3. What should appear at the very end of a JavaScript script embedded in an HTML file?

   a. The `<script LANGUAGE="JavaScript">` tag

   b. The `</script>` tag

   c. The `END` statement

Quiz Answers

1. b. Any text editor can be used to create scripts. You can also use a word processor if you're careful to save the document as a text file with the `.html` or `.htm` extension.

2. a. Variables are used to store numbers, dates, or other values.

3. b. Your script should end with the `</script>` tag.

Exercises

To further your knowledge of JavaScript, perform the following exercises:

▶ Add a millisecond field to the large clock. You can use the `getMilliseconds` function, which works just like `getSeconds` but returns milliseconds.

▶ Modify the script to display the time, including milliseconds, twice. Notice whether any time passes between the two time displays when you load the page.

HOUR 3

Getting Started with JavaScript Programming

What You'll Learn in This Hour:

▶ Organizing scripts using functions

▶ What objects are and how JavaScript uses them

▶ How JavaScript can respond to events

▶ An introduction to conditional statements and loops

▶ How browsers execute scripts in the proper order

▶ Syntax rules for avoiding JavaScript errors

▶ Adding comments to document your JavaScript code

You've reached the halfway point of Part I of this book. In the first couple of hours, you've learned what JavaScript is, learned the variety of things JavaScript can do, and created a simple script.

In this hour, you'll learn a few basic concepts and script components that you'll use in just about every script you write. This will prepare you for the remaining hours of this book, in which you'll explore specific JavaScript functions and features.

Basic Concepts

There are a few basic concepts and terms you'll run into throughout this book. In the following sections, you'll learn about the basic building blocks of JavaScript.

Statements

Statements are the basic units of a JavaScript program. A statement is a section of code that performs a single action. For example, the following three statements are from the date and time example in Hour 2, "Creating Simple Scripts":

```
hours = now.getHours();
mins = now.getMinutes();
secs = now.getSeconds();
```

Although a statement is typically a single line of JavaScript, this is not a rule—it's possible to break a statement across multiple lines, or to include more than one statement in a single line.

A semicolon marks the end of a statement. You can also omit the semicolon if you start a new line after the statement. If you combine statements into a single line, you must use semicolons to separate them.

Combining Tasks with Functions

In the basic scripts you've examined so far, you've seen some JavaScript statements that have a section in parentheses, like this:

```
document.write("Testing.");
```

This is an example of a *function*. Functions provide a simple way to handle a task, such as adding output to a web page. JavaScript includes a wide variety of built-in functions, which you will learn about throughout this book. A statement that uses a function, as in the preceding example, is referred to as a *function call*.

Functions take parameters (the expression inside the parentheses) to tell them what to do. Additionally, a function can return a value to a waiting variable. For example, the following function call prompts the user for a response and stores it in the text variable:

```
text = prompt("Enter some text.")
```

You can also create your own functions. This is useful for two main reasons: First, you can separate logical portions of your script to make it easier to understand. Second, and more importantly, you can use the function several times or with different data to avoid repeating script statements.

You will learn how to define, call, and return values from your own functions in Hour 6, "Using Functions and Objects."

Variables

In Hour 2, you learned that variables are containers that can store a number, a string of text, or another value. For example, the following statement creates a variable called fred and assigns it the value 27:

```
var fred = 27;
```

JavaScript variables can contain numbers, text strings, and other values. You'll learn more about them in Hour 5, "Using Variables, Strings, and Arrays."

Understanding Objects

JavaScript also supports *objects*. Like variables, objects can store data—but they can store two or more pieces of data at once.

The items of data stored in an object are called the *properties* of the object. For example, you could use objects to store information about people such as in an address book. The properties of each person object might include a name, an address, and a telephone number.

JavaScript uses periods to separate object names and property names. For example, for a person object called Bob, the properties might include Bob.address and Bob.phone.

Objects can also include *methods*. These are functions that work with the object's data. For example, our person object for the address book might include a display() method to display the person's information. In JavaScript terminology, the statement Bob.display() would display Bob's details.

The document.write function we discussed earlier this hour is actually the write method of the document object. You will learn more about this object in Hour 4, "Working with the Document Object Model (DOM)."

By the Way

Don't worry if this sounds confusing—you'll be exploring objects in much more detail later in this book. For now, you just need to know the basics. JavaScript supports three kinds of objects:

▶ *Built-in objects* are built in to the JavaScript language. You've already encountered one of these, Date, in Hour 2. Other built-in objects include Array and String, which you'll explore in Hour 5, and Math, which is explained in Hour 8, "Using Built-in Functions and Libraries."

▶ *DOM (Document Object Model) objects* represent various components of the browser and the current HTML document. For example, the alert() function

you used earlier in this hour is actually a method of the window object. You'll explore these in more detail in Hour 4.

▶ *Custom objects* are objects you create yourself. For example, you could create a person object, as in the examples in this section. You'll learn to use custom objects in Hour 6.

Conditionals

Although event handlers notify your script when something happens, you might want to check certain conditions yourself. For example, did the user enter a valid email address?

JavaScript supports *conditional statements*, which enable you to answer questions like this. A typical conditional uses the if statement, as in this example:

```
if (count==1) alert("The countdown has reached 1.");
```

This compares the variable count with the constant 1, and displays an alert message to the user if they are the same. You will use conditional statements like this in most of your scripts.

By the Way

> You'll learn more about conditionals in Hour 7, "Controlling Flow with Conditions and Loops."

Loops

Another useful feature of JavaScript—and most other programming languages—is the capability to create *loops*, or groups of statements that repeat a certain number of times. For example, these statements display the same alert 10 times, greatly annoying the user:

```
for (i=1; i<=10; i++) {
   Alert("Yes, it's yet another alert!");
}
```

The for statement is one of several statements JavaScript uses for loops. This is the sort of thing computers are supposed to be good at: performing repetitive tasks. You will use loops in many of your scripts, in much more useful ways than this example.

By the Way

> Loops are covered in detail in Hour 7.

Event Handlers

As mentioned in Hour 1, "Understanding JavaScript," not all scripts are located within `<script>` tags. You can also use scripts as *event handlers*. Although this might sound like a complex programming term, it actually means exactly what it says: Event handlers are scripts that handle events.

In real life, an event is something that happens to you. For example, the things you write on your calendar are events: "Dentist appointment" or "Fred's birthday." You also encounter unscheduled events in your life: for example, a traffic ticket, an IRS audit, or an unexpected visit from relatives.

Whether events are scheduled or unscheduled, you probably have normal ways of handling them. Your event handlers might include things such as *When Fred's birthday arrives, send him a present* or *When relatives visit unexpectedly, turn out the lights and pretend nobody is home.*

Event handlers in JavaScript are similar: They tell the browser what to do when a certain event occurs. The events JavaScript deals with aren't as exciting as the ones you deal with—they include such events as *When the mouse button clicks* and *When this page is finished loading*. Nevertheless, they're a very useful part of JavaScript.

Many JavaScript events (such as mouse clicks) are caused by the user. Rather than doing things in a set order, your script can respond to the user's actions. Other events don't involve the user directly—for example, an event is triggered when an HTML document finishes loading.

Each event handler is associated with a particular browser object, and you can specify the event handler in the tag that defines the object. For example, images and text links have an event, onMouseOver, that happens when the mouse pointer moves over the object. Here is a typical HTML image tag with an event handler:

```
<img src="button.gif" onMouseOver="highlight();">
```

You specify the event handler as an attribute to the HTML tag and include the JavaScript statement to handle the event within the quotation marks. This is an ideal use for functions because function names are short and to the point and can refer to a whole series of statements.

See the Try It Yourself section at the end of this hour for a complete example of an event handler within an HTML document.

> **By the Way**
>
> You can also define event handlers within JavaScript without using HTML attributes. You'll learn this technique, and more about event handlers, in Hour 9, "Responding to Events."

Which Script Runs First?

You can actually have several scripts within a web document: one or more sets of <script> tags, external JavaScript files, and any number of event handlers. With all of these scripts, you might wonder how the browser knows which to execute first. Fortunately, this is done in a logical fashion:

▶ Sets of <script> tags within the <head> section of an HTML document are handled first, whether they include embedded code or refer to a JavaScript file. Because these scripts cannot create output in the web page, it's a good place to define functions for use later.

▶ Sets of <script> tags within the <body> section of the HTML document are executed after those in the <head> section, while the web page loads and displays. If there is more than one script in the body, they are executed in order.

▶ Event handlers are executed when their events happen. For example, the onLoad event handler is executed when the body of a web page loads. Because the <head> section is loaded before any events, you can define functions there and use them in event handlers.

JavaScript Syntax Rules

JavaScript is a simple language, but you do need to be careful to use its *syntax*—the rules that define how you use the language—correctly. The rest of this book covers many aspects of JavaScript syntax, but there are a few basic rules you should understand to avoid errors.

Case Sensitivity

Almost everything in JavaScript is *case sensitive*: you cannot use lowercase and capital letters interchangeably. Here are a few general rules:

▶ JavaScript keywords, such as for and if, are always lowercase.

▶ Built-in objects such as Math and Date are capitalized.

▶ DOM object names are usually lowercase, but their methods are often a combination of capitals and lowercase. Usually capitals are used for all but the first word, as in toLowerCase and getElementById.

When in doubt, follow the exact case used in this book or another JavaScript reference. If you use the wrong case, the browser will usually display an error message.

Variable, Object, and Function Names

When you define your own variables, objects, or functions, you can choose their names. Names can include uppercase letters, lowercase letters, numbers, and the underscore (_) character. Names must begin with a letter or underscore.

You can choose whether to use capitals or lowercase in your variable names, but remember that JavaScript is case sensitive: score, Score, and SCORE would be considered three different variables. Be sure to use the same name each time you refer to a variable.

Reserved Words

One more rule for variable names—they must not be *reserved words*. These include the words that make up the JavaScript language, such as if and for, DOM object names such as window and document, and built-in object names such as Math and Date. A complete list of reserved words is included in Appendix D, "JavaScript Quick Reference."

Spacing

Blank space (known as *whitespace* by programmers) is ignored by JavaScript. You can include spaces and tabs within a line, or blank lines, without causing an error. Blank space often makes the script more readable.

Using Comments

JavaScript *comments* enable you to include documentation within your script. This will be useful if someone else tries to understand the script, or even if you try to understand it after a long break. To include comments in a JavaScript program, begin a line with two slashes, as in this example:

```
//this is a comment.
```

You can also begin a comment with two slashes in the middle of a line, which is useful for documenting a script. In this case, everything on the line after the slashes is treated as a comment and ignored by the browser. For example,

```
a = a + 1; // add one to the value of a
```

JavaScript also supports C-style comments, which begin with /* and end with */. These comments can extend across more than one line, as the following example demonstrates:

```
/*This script includes a variety
of features, including this comment. */
```

Because JavaScript statements within a comment are ignored, C-style comments are often used for *commenting out* sections of code. If you have some lines of JavaScript that you want to temporarily take out of the picture while you debug a script, you can add /* at the beginning of the section and */ at the end.

> Because these comments are part of JavaScript syntax, they are only valid inside `<script>` tags or within an external JavaScript file.

Best Practices for JavaScript

You should now be familiar with the basic rules for writing valid JavaScript. Along with following the rules, it's also a good idea to follow *best practices*. The following practices may not be required, but you'll save yourself and others some headaches if you follow them.

▶ **Use comments liberally**—These make your code easier for others to understand, and also easier for you to understand when you edit them later. They are also useful for marking the major divisions of a script.

▶ **Use a semicolon at the end of each statement, and only use one statement per line**—This will make your scripts easier to debug.

▶ **Use separate JavaScript files whenever possible**—This separates JavaScript from HTML and makes debugging easier, and also encourages you to write modular scripts that can be reused.

▶ **Avoid being browser-specific**—As you learn more about JavaScript, you'll learn some features that only work in one browser. Avoid them unless absolutely necessary, and always test your code in more than one browser.

▶ **Keep JavaScript optional**—Don't use JavaScript to perform an essential function on your site—for example, the primary navigation links. Whenever possible, users without JavaScript should be able to use your site, although it may not be quite as attractive or convenient. This strategy is known as *progressive enhancement*.

There are many more best practices involving more advanced aspects of JavaScript. These are covered in detail in Hour 15, "Unobtrusive Scripting."

Try It Yourself ▼

Using an Event Handler

To conclude this hour, here's a simple example of an event handler. This will demonstrate how you set up an event, which you'll use throughout this book, and how JavaScript works without `<script>` tags. Listing 3.1 shows an HTML document that includes a simple event handler.

LISTING 3.1 An HTML Document with a Simple Event Handler

```
<html>
<head>
<title>Event Handler Example</title>
</head>
<body>
<h1>Event Handler Example</h1>
<p>
<a href="http://www.jsworkshop.com/"
onClick="alert('Aha! An Event!');">Click this link</a>
to test an event handler.
</p>
</body>
</html>
```

The event handler is defined with the following `onClick` attribute within the `<a>` tag that defines a link:

```
onClick="alert('Aha! An Event!');"
```

This event handler uses the built-in `alert()` function to display a message when you click on the link. In more complex scripts, you will usually define your own function to act as an event handler. Figure 3.1 shows this example in action.

You'll use other event handlers similar to this in the next hour, and events will be covered in more detail in Hour 9.

> Notice that after you click the OK button on the alert, the browser follows the link defined in the `<a>` tag. Your event handler could also stop the browser from following the link, as described in Hour 9.

Did you Know?

FIGURE 3.1
The browser displays an alert when you click the link.

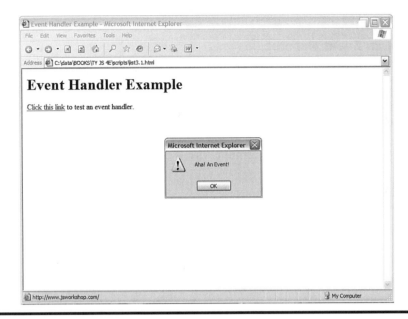

Summary

During this hour, you've been introduced to several components of JavaScript programming and syntax: functions, objects, event handlers, conditions, and loops. You also learned how to use JavaScript comments to make your script easier to read, and looked at a simple example of an event handler.

In the next hour, you'll look at the Document Object Model (DOM) and learn how you can use the objects within the DOM to work with web pages and interact with users.

Q&A

Q. *I've heard the term* object-oriented *applied to languages such as C++ and Java. If JavaScript supports objects, is it an object-oriented language?*

A. Yes, although it might not fit some people's strict definitions. JavaScript objects do not support all of the features that languages such as C++ and Java support, although the latest versions of JavaScript have added more object-oriented features.

Q. *Having several scripts that execute at different times seems confusing. Why would I want to use event handlers?*

A. Event handlers are the ideal way (and in JavaScript, the only way) to handle gadgets within the web page, such as buttons, check boxes, and text fields. It's actually more convenient to handle them this way. Rather than writing a script that sits and waits for a button to be pushed, you can simply create an event handler and let the browser do the waiting for you.

Q. *Some examples in other books suggest enclosing scripts in HTML comments (<!-- and -->) to hide the script from older browsers. Is this necessary?*

A. This technique was only necessary for supporting very old browsers, such as Netscape 2.0. I no longer recommend this because all modern browsers handle JavaScript correctly. If you are still concerned about non-JavaScript browsers, the best way to hide your script is to use an external JavaScript file, as described in Hour 2.

Quiz Questions

Test your knowledge of JavaScript by answering the following questions:

1. A script that executes when the user clicks the mouse button is an example of what?

   a. An object

   b. An event handler

   c. An impossibility

2. Which of the following are capabilities of functions in JavaScript?

   a. Accept parameters

   b. Return a value

   c. Both of the above

3. Which of the following is executed first by a browser?

   a. A script in the <head> section

   b. A script in the <body> section

   c. An event handler for a button

Quiz Answers

1. b. A script that executes when the user clicks the mouse button is an event handler.

2. c. Functions can accept both parameters and return values.

3. a. Scripts defined in the <head> section of an HTML document are executed first by the browser.

Exercises

To further explore the JavaScript features you learned about in this hour, you can perform the following exercises:

▶ Examine the Date and Time script you created in Hour 2 and find any examples of functions and objects being used.

▶ Add JavaScript comments to the Date and Time script to make it more clear what each line does. Verify that the script still runs properly.

Working with the Document Object Model (DOM)

What You'll Learn in This Hour:

▶ How to access the various objects in the DOM

▶ Working with windows using the window object

▶ Working with web documents using the document object

▶ Using objects for links and anchors

▶ Using the location object to work with URLs

▶ Creating JavaScript-based Back and Forward buttons

You've reached the end of Part I. In this hour, you'll be introduced to one of the most important tools you'll use with JavaScript: the Document Object Model (DOM), which lets your scripts manipulate web pages, windows, and documents.

Without the DOM, JavaScript would be just another scripting language—with the DOM, it becomes a powerful tool for making pages dynamic. This hour will introduce the idea of the DOM and some of the objects you'll use most often.

Understanding the Document Object Model (DOM)

One advantage that JavaScript has over basic HTML is that scripts can manipulate the web document and its contents. Your script can load a new page into the browser, work with parts of the browser window and document, open new windows, and even modify text within the page dynamically.

To work with the browser and documents, JavaScript uses a hierarchy of parent and child objects called the Document Object Model (DOM). These objects are organized into a tree-like structure, and represent all of the content and components of a web document.

By the Way

> The DOM is not part of the JavaScript language—rather, it's an API (application programming interface) built in to the browser. While the DOM is most often used with JavaScript, it can also be used by other languages, such as VBScript and Java.

The objects in the DOM have *properties*—variables that describe the web page or document, and *methods*—functions that enable you to work with parts of the web page.

When you refer to an object, you use the parent object name followed by the child object name or names, separated by periods. For example, JavaScript stores objects to represent images in a document as children of the document object. The following refers to the image9 object, a child of the document object, which is a child of the window object:

```
window.document.image9
```

The window object is the parent object for all of the objects we will be looking at in this hour. Figure 4.1 shows this section of the DOM object hierarchy and a variety of its objects.

FIGURE 4.1
The DOM object hierarchy.

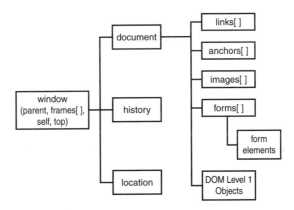

By the Way

> This diagram only includes the basic browser objects that will be covered in this hour. These are actually a small part of the DOM, which you'll learn more about in Part III, "Learning More About the DOM."

History of the DOM

Starting with the introduction of JavaScript 1.0 in Netscape 2.0, browsers have included objects that represent parts of a web document and other browser features. However, there was never a true standard. While both Netscape and Microsoft Internet

Explorer included many of the same objects, there was no guarantee that the same objects would work the same way in both browsers, let alone in less common browsers.

The bad news is that there are still differences between the browsers—but here's the good news. Since the release of Netscape 3.0 and Internet Explorer 4.0, all of the basic objects (those covered in this hour) are supported in much the same way in both browsers. With more recent browser releases, a much more advanced DOM is supported.

DOM Levels

The W3C (World Wide Web Consortium) developed the DOM level 1 recommendation. This is a standard that defines not only basic objects, but an entire set of objects that encompass all parts of an HTML document. A level 2 DOM standard has also been released, and level 3 is under development.

Netscape 4 and Internet Explorer 4 supported their own DOMs that allowed more control over documents, but weren't standardized. Fortunately, starting with Internet Explorer 5 and Netscape 6, both support the W3C DOM, so you can support both browsers with simple, standards-compliant code. All of today's current browsers support the W3C DOM.

The basic object hierarchy described in this hour is informally referred to as DOM level 0, and the objects are included in the DOM level 1 standard. You'll learn how to use the W3C DOM to work with any part of a web document later in this book.

> The W3C DOM allows you to modify a web page in real time after it has loaded. You'll learn how to do this in Part III.

Did you Know?

Using window Objects

At the top of the browser object hierarchy is the window object, which represents a browser window. You've already used at least one method of the window object: the window.alert() method, or simply alert(), displays a message in an alert box.

There can be several window objects at a time, each representing an open browser window. Frames are also represented by window objects. You'll learn more about windows and frames in Hour 10, "Using Windows and Frames."

> Layers, which enable you to include, modify, and position dynamic content within a web document, are also similar to window objects. These are explained in Hour 13, "Using the W3C DOM."

By the Way

Working with Web Documents

The document object represents a web document, or page. Web documents are displayed within browser windows, so it shouldn't surprise you to learn that the document object is a child of the window object.

Because the window object always represents the current window (the one containing the script), you can use window.document to refer to the current document. You can also simply refer to document, which automatically refers to the current window.

You've already used the document.write method to display text within a web document. The examples in earlier hours only used a single window and document, so it was unnecessary to use window.document.write—but this longer syntax would have worked equally well.

If multiple windows or frames are in use, there might be several window objects, each with its own document object. To use one of these document objects, you use the name of the window and the name of the document.

In the following sections, you will look at some of the properties and methods of the document object that will be useful in your scripting.

Getting Information About the Document

Several properties of the document object include information about the current document in general:

▶ document.URL specifies the document's URL. This is a simple text field. You can't change this property. If you need to send the user to a different location, use the window.location object, described later in this hour.

▶ document.title lists the title of the current page, defined by the HTML <title> tag.

▶ document.referrer is the URL of the page the user was viewing prior to the current page—usually, the page with a link to the current page.

▶ document.lastModified is the date the document was last modified. This date is sent from the server along with the page.

▶ document.bgColor and document.fgColor are the background and foreground (text) colors for the document, corresponding to the BGCOLOR and TEXT attributes of the <body> tag.

▶ document.linkColor, document.alinkColor, and document.vlinkColor are the colors for links within the document. These correspond to the LINK, ALINK, and VLINK attributes of the <body> tag.

▶ document.cookie enables you to read or set a cookie for the document. See http://www.jsworkshop.com/cookies.html for information about cookies.

As an example of a document property, Listing 4.1 shows a short HTML document that displays its last modified date using JavaScript.

LISTING 4.1   Displaying the Last Modified Date

```html
<html><head><title>Test Document</title></head>
<body>
<p>This page was last modified on:
<script language="JavaScript" type="text/javascript">
document.write(document.lastModified);
</script>
</p>
</body>
</html>
```

This can tell the user when the page was last changed. If you use JavaScript, you don't have to remember to update the date each time you modify the page. (You could also use the script to always print the current date instead of the last modified date, but that would be cheating.)

> You might find that the document.lastModified property doesn't work on your web pages, or returns the wrong value. The date is received from the web server, and some servers do not maintain modification dates correctly.

By the Way

Writing Text in a Document

The simplest document object methods are also the ones you will use most often. In fact, you've used one of them already. The document.write method prints text as part of the HTML page in a document window. This statement is used whenever you need to include output in a web page.

An alternative statement, document.writeln, also prints text, but it also includes a newline (\n) character at the end. This is handy when you want your text to be the last thing on the line.

> Bear in mind that the newline character is displayed as a space by the browser, except inside a <pre> container. You will need to use the <br> tag if you want an actual line break.

Watch Out!

You can use these methods only within the body of the web page, so they will be executed when the page loads. You can't use these methods to add to a page that has already loaded without reloading it.

You can also directly modify the text of a web page on newer browsers using the features of the new DOM. You'll learn these techniques in Hour 14.

The document.write method can be used within a <script> tag in the body of an HTML document. You can also use it in a function, provided you include a call to the function within the body of the document.

Using Links and Anchors

Another child of the document object is the link object. Actually, there can be multiple link objects in a document. Each one includes information about a link to another location or an anchor.

Anchors are named places in an HTML document that can be jumped to directly. You define them with a tag like this: <a name="part2">. You can then link to them: <a href="#part2">.

You can access link objects with the links array. Each member of the array is one of the link objects in the current page. A property of the array, document.links.length, indicates the number of links in the page.

Each link object (or member of the links array) has a list of properties defining the URL. The href property contains the entire URL, and other properties define portions of it. These are the same properties as the location object, defined later in this hour.

You can refer to a property by indicating the link number and property name. For example, the following statement assigns the entire URL of the first link to the variable link1:

```
link1 = links[0].href;
```

The anchor objects are also children of the document object. Each anchor object represents an anchor in the current document—a particular location that can be jumped to directly.

Like links, you can access anchors with an array: anchors. Each element of this array is an anchor object. The document.anchors.length property gives you the number of elements in the anchors array.

Accessing Browser History

The history object is another child (property) of the window object. This object holds information about the URLs that have been visited before and after the current one, and it includes methods to go to previous or next locations.

The history object has one property you can access:

▶ history.length keeps track of the length of the history list—in other words, the number of different locations that the user has visited.

The history object has three methods you can use to move through the history list:

▶ history.go() opens a URL from the history list. To use this method, specify a positive or negative number in parentheses. For example, history.go(-2) is equivalent to pressing the Back button twice.

▶ history.back() loads the previous URL in the history list—equivalent to pressing the Back button.

▶ history.forward() loads the next URL in the history list, if available. This is equivalent to pressing the Forward button.

You'll use these methods in the Try It Yourself section at the end of this hour.

Working with the location Object

A third child of the window object is the location object. This object stores information about the current URL stored in the window. For example, the following statement loads a URL into the current window:

```
window.location.href="http://www.starlingtech.com";
```

The href property used in this statement contains the entire URL of the window's current location. You can also access portions of the URL with various properties of the location object. To explain these properties, consider the following URL:

```
http://www.jsworkshop.com:80/test.cgi?lines=1#anchor
```

The following properties represent parts of the URL:

- ▶ location.protocol is the protocol part of the URL (http: in the example).

- ▶ location.hostname is the host name of the URL (www.jsworkshop.com in the example).

- ▶ location.port is the port number of the URL (80 in the example).

- ▶ location.pathname is the filename part of the URL (test.cgi in the example).

- ▶ location.search is the query portion of the URL, if any (lines=1 in the example). Queries are used mostly by CGI scripts.

- ▶ location.hash is the anchor name used in the URL, if any (#anchor in the example).

The link object, introduced earlier this hour, also includes this list of properties for accessing portions of the URL.

> Although the location.href property usually contains the same URL as the document.URL property described earlier in this hour, you can't change the document.URL property. Always use location.href to load a new page.

The location object has two methods:

- ▶ location.reload() reloads the current document. This is the same as the Reload button on the browser's toolbar. If you optionally include the true parameter, it will ignore the browser's cache and force a reload whether the document has changed or not.

- ▶ location.replace() replaces the current location with a new one. This is similar to setting the location object's properties yourself. The difference is that the replace method does not affect the browser's history. In other words, the Back button can't be used to go to the previous location. This is useful for splash screens or temporary pages that it would be useless to return to.

▼ **Try It Yourself**

Creating Back and Forward Buttons

You can use the back and forward methods of the history object to add your own Back and Forward buttons to a web document. The browser already has Back and Forward buttons, of course, but it's occasionally useful to include your own links that serve the same purpose.

You will now create a script that displays Back and Forward buttons and use these methods to navigate the browser. Here's the code that will create the Back button:

```
<input type="button"
    onClick="history.back();" value="<-- Back">
```

The <input> tag defines a button labeled Back. The onClick event handler uses the history.back() method to go to the previous page in history. The code for the Forward button is similar:

```
<input type="button"
    onClick="history.forward();" value="Forward -->">
```

With these out of the way, you just need to build the rest of the HTML document. Listing 4.2 shows the complete HTML document, and Figure 4.2 shows a browser's display of the document. After you load this document into a browser, visit other URLs and make sure the Back and Forward buttons work.

LISTING 4.2   A Web Page That Uses JavaScript to Include Back and Forward Buttons

```
<html>
<head><title>Back and Forward Buttons</title>
</head>
<body>
<h1>Back and Forward Buttons</h1>
<p>This page allows you to go back or forward to pages in the history list.
These should be equivalent to the back and forward arrow buttons in the
browser's toolbar.</p>
<p>
<input type="button"
    onClick="history.back();" value="<-- Back">
<input type="button"
    onClick="history.forward();" value="Forward -->">
</p>
</body>
</html>
```

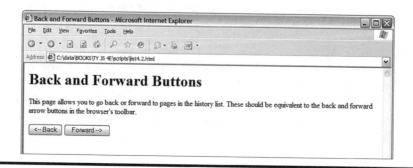

FIGURE 4.2
The Back and Forward buttons in Internet Explorer.

Summary

In this hour, you've learned about the Document Object Model (DOM), JavaScript's hierarchy of web page objects. You've learned how you can use the document object to work with documents, and used the history and location objects to control the current URL displayed in the browser.

You should now have a basic understanding of the DOM and some of its objects—you'll learn about more of the objects throughout this book.

Congratulations! You've reached the end of Part I of this book. In Part II, you'll get back to learning the JavaScript language, starting with Hour 5, "Using Variables, Strings, and Arrays."

Q&A

Q. *I can use history and document instead of window.history and window.document. Can I leave out the window object in other cases?*

A. Yes. For example, you can use alert instead of window.alert to display a message. The window object contains the current script, so it's treated as a default object. However, be warned that you shouldn't omit the window object's name when you're using frames, layers, or multiple windows, or in an event handler.

Q. *I used the document.lastModified method to display a modification date for my page, but it displays a date in 1970, or a date that I know is incorrect. What's wrong?*

A. This function depends on the server sending the last modified date of the document to the browser. Some web servers don't do this properly, or require specific file attributes in order for this to work.

Q. *Can I change history entries, or prevent the user from using the Back and Forward buttons?*

A. You can't change the history entries. You can't prevent the use of the Back and Forward buttons, but you can use the location.replace() method to load a series of pages that don't appear in the history. There are a few tricks for preventing the Back button from working properly, but I don't recommend them—that's the sort of thing that gives JavaScript a bad name.

Quiz Questions

Test your knowledge of JavaScript by answering the following questions:

1. Which of the following objects can be used to load a new URL into the browser window?

   a. `document.url`

   b. `window.location`

   c. `window.url`

2. Which object contains the `alert()` method?

   a. `window`

   b. `document`

   c. `location`

3. Which of the following DOM levels describes the objects described in this hour?

   a. `DOM level 0`

   b. `DOM level 1`

   c. `DOM level 2`

Quiz Answers

1. b. The `window.location` object can be used to send the browser to a new URL.

2. a. The `window` object contains the `alert()` method.

3. a. The objects described in this hour fall under the informal DOM level 0 specification.

Exercises

To further explore the JavaScript features you learned about in this hour, you can perform the following exercises:

▶ Modify the Back and Forward example in Listing 4.2 to include a Reload button along with the Back and Forward buttons. (This button would trigger the `location.reload()` method.)

▶ Modify the Back and Forward example to display the current number of history entries.

PART II:

Learning JavaScript Basics

HOUR 5

Using Variables, Strings, and Arrays

What You'll Learn in This Hour:

▶ Naming and declaring variables

▶ Choosing whether to use local or global variables

▶ Assigning values to variables

▶ How to convert between different data types

▶ Using variables and literals in expressions

▶ How strings are stored in `String` objects

▶ Creating and using `String` objects

▶ Creating and using arrays of numbers and strings

Welcome to the beginning of Part II of this book. Now that you have learned some of the fundamentals of JavaScript and the DOM, it's time to dig into more details of the JavaScript language.

In this hour, you'll learn three tools for storing data in JavaScript: variables, which store numbers or text; strings, which are special variables for working with text; and arrays, which are multiple variables you can refer to by number.

Using Variables

Unless you skipped the first few hours of this book, you've already used a few variables. You probably can also figure out how to use a few more without any help. Nevertheless, there are some aspects of variables you haven't learned yet. We will now look at some of the details.

Choosing Variable Names

Variables are named containers that can store data (for example, a number, a text string, or an object). As you learned earlier in this book, each variable has a name. There are specific rules you must follow when choosing a variable name:

▶ Variable names can include letters of the alphabet, both upper- and lowercase. They can also include the digits 0–9 and the underscore (_) character.

▶ Variable names cannot include spaces or any other punctuation characters.

▶ The first character of the variable name must be either a letter or an underscore.

▶ Variable names are case sensitive—totalnum, Totalnum, and TotalNum are separate variable names.

▶ There is no official limit on the length of variable names, but they must fit within one line.

Using these rules, the following are examples of valid variable names:

```
total_number_of_fish
LastInvoiceNumber
temp1
a
_var39
```

You can choose to use either friendly, easy-to-read names or completely cryptic ones. Do yourself a favor: use longer, friendly names whenever possible. Although you might remember the difference between a, b, x, and x1 right now, you might not after a good night's sleep.

Using Local and Global Variables

Some computer languages require you to declare a variable before you use it. JavaScript includes the var keyword, which can be used to declare a variable. You can omit var in many cases; the variable is still declared the first time you assign a value to it.

To understand where to declare a variable, you will need to understand the concept of *scope*. A variable's scope is the area of the script in which that variable can be used. There are two types of variables:

▶ *Global variables* have the entire script (and other scripts in the same HTML document) as their scope. They can be used anywhere, even within functions.

▶ *Local variables* have a single function as their scope. They can be used only within the function they are created in.

To create a global variable, you declare it in the main script, outside any functions. You can use the var keyword to declare the variable, as in this example:

```
var students = 25;
```

This statement declares a variable called students and assigns it a value of 25. If this statement is used outside functions, it creates a global variable. The var keyword is optional in this case, so this statement is equivalent to the previous one:

```
students = 25;
```

Before you get in the habit of omitting the var keyword, be sure you understand exactly when it's required. It's actually a good idea to always use the var keyword— you'll avoid errors and make your script easier to read, and it won't usually cause any trouble.

For the most part, the variables you've used in earlier hours of this book have been global.

By the Way

A local variable belongs to a particular function. Any variable you declare with the var keyword in a function is a local variable. Additionally, the variables in the function's parameter list are always local variables.

To create a local variable within a function, you must use the var keyword. This forces JavaScript to create a local variable, even if there is a global variable with the same name.

You should now understand the difference between local and global variables. If you're still a bit confused, don't worry—if you use the var keyword every time, you'll usually end up with the right type of variable.

Assigning Values to Variables

As you learned in Hour 2, "Creating a Simple Script," you can use the equal sign to assign a value to a variable. For example, this statement assigns the value 40 to the variable lines:

```
lines = 40;
```

You can use any expression to the right of the equal sign, including other variables. You have used this syntax earlier to add one to a variable:

```
lines = lines + 1;
```

Because incrementing or decrementing variables is quite common, JavaScript includes two types of shorthand for this syntax. The first is the += operator, which enables you to create the following shorter version of the preceding example:

```
lines += 1;
```

Similarly, you can subtract a number from a variable using the -= operator:

```
lines -= 1;
```

If you still think that's too much to type, JavaScript also includes the increment and decrement operators, ++ and - -. This statement adds one to the value of lines:

```
lines++;
```

Similarly, this statement subtracts one from the value of lines:

```
lines--;
```

You can alternately use the ++ or - - operators before a variable name, as in ++lines. However, these are not identical. The difference is when the increment or decrement happens:

▶ If the operator is after the variable name, the increment or decrement happens *after* the current expression is evaluated.

▶ If the operator is before the variable name, the increment or decrement happens *before* the current expression is evaluated.

This difference is only an issue when you use the variable in an expression and increment or decrement it in the same statement. As an example, suppose you have assigned the lines variable the value 40. The following two statements have different effects:

```
alert(lines++);
alert(++lines);
```

The first statement displays an alert with the value 40, and then increments lines to 41. The second statement first increments lines to 41, then displays an alert with the value 41.

These operators are strictly for your convenience. If it makes more sense to you to stick to lines = lines + 1, do it—your script won't suffer.

Understanding Expressions and Operators

An *expression* is a combination of variables and values that the JavaScript inter-preter can evaluate to a single value. The characters that are used to combine these values, such as + and /, are called *operators*.

Along with variables and constant values, you can also use calls to functions that return results within an expression.

Did you Know?

Using JavaScript Operators

You've already used some operators, such as the + sign (addition) and the increment and decrement operators. Table 5.1 lists some of the most important operators you can use in JavaScript expressions.

TABLE 5.1 Common JavaScript Operators

Operator	Description	Example
+	Concatenate (combine) strings	`message="this is" + " a test";`
+	Add	`result = 5 + 7;`
-	Subtract	`score = score - 1;`
*	Multiply	`total = quantity * price;`
/	Divide	`average = sum / 4;`
%	Modulo (remainder)	`remainder = sum % 4;`
++	Increment	`tries++;`
- -	Decrement	`total--;`

Along with these, there are also many other operators used in conditional statements—you'll learn about these in Hour 7, "Controlling Flow with Conditions and Loops."

Operator Precedence

When you use more than one operator in an expression, JavaScript uses rules of *operator precedence* to decide how to calculate the value. Table 5.1 lists the operators from lowest to highest precedence, and operators with highest precedence are evalu-ated first. For example, consider this statement:

```
result = 4 + 5 * 3;
```

If you try to calculate this result, there are two ways to do it. You could multiply 5 * 3 first and then add 4 (result: 19) or add 4 + 5 first and then multiply by 3 (result: 27). JavaScript solves this dilemma by following the precedence rules: Because multiplication has a higher precedence than addition, it first multiplies 5 * 3 and then adds 4, producing a result of 19.

By the Way

> If you're familiar with any other programming languages, you'll find that the operators and precedence in JavaScript work, for the most part, the same way as those in C, C++, and Java.

Sometimes operator precedence doesn't produce the result you want. For example, consider this statement:

```
result = a + b + c + d / 4;
```

This is an attempt to average four numbers by adding them all together and then dividing by four. However, because JavaScript gives division a higher precedence than addition, it will divide the d variable by 4 before adding the other numbers, producing an incorrect result.

You can control precedence by using parentheses. Here's the working statement to calculate an average:

```
result = (a + b + c + d) / 4;
```

The parentheses ensure that the four variables are added first, and then the sum is divided by four.

Did you Know?

> If you're unsure about operator precedence, you can use parentheses to make sure things work the way you expect and to make your script more readable.

Data Types in JavaScript

In some computer languages, you have to specify the type of data a variable will store: for example, a number or a string. In JavaScript, you don't need to specify a data type in most cases. However, you should know the types of data JavaScript can deal with.

These are the basic JavaScript data types:

▶ *Numbers*, such as 3, 25, or 1.4142138. JavaScript supports both integers and floating-point numbers.

▶ *Boolean*, or logical values. These can have one of two values: `true` or `false`. These are useful for indicating whether a certain condition is true.

You'll learn more about Boolean values, and about using conditions in JavaScript, in Hour 7.

▶ *Strings*, such as `"I am a jelly doughnut"`. These consist of one or more characters of text. (Strictly speaking, these are `String` objects, which you'll learn about later in this hour.)

▶ *The null value*, represented by the keyword `null`. This is the value of an undefined variable. For example, the statement `document.write(fig)` will result in this value (and an error message) if the variable `fig` has not been previously used or defined.

Although JavaScript keeps track of the data type currently stored in each variable, it doesn't restrict you from changing types midstream. For example, suppose you declared a variable by assigning it a value:

```
total = 31;
```

This statement declares a variable called `total` and assigns it the value of 31. This is a numeric variable. Now suppose you changed the value of `total`:

```
total = "albatross";
```

This assigns a string value to `total`, replacing the numeric value. JavaScript will not display an error when this statement executes; it's perfectly valid, although it's probably not a very useful total.

Although this feature of JavaScript is convenient and powerful, it can also make it easy to make a mistake. For example, if the `total` variable was later used in a mathematical calculation, the result would be invalid—but JavaScript does not warn you that you've made this mistake.

Converting Between Data Types

JavaScript handles conversions between data types for you whenever it can. For example, you've already used statements like this:

```
document.write("The total is " + total);
```

This statement prints out a message such as "The total is 40". Because the document.write function works with strings, the JavaScript interpreter automatically converts any nonstrings in the expression (in this case, the value of total) to strings before performing the function.

This works equally well with floating-point and Boolean values. However, there are some situations where it won't work. For example, the following statement will work fine if the value of total is 40:

```
average = total / 3;
```

However, the total variable could also contain a string; in this case, the preceding statement would result in an error.

In some situations, you might end up with a string containing a number, and need to convert it to a regular numeric variable. JavaScript includes two functions for this purpose:

▶ parseInt()—Converts a string to an integer number.

▶ parseFloat()—Converts a string to a floating-point number.

Both of these functions will read a number from the beginning of the string and return a numeric version. For example, these statements convert the string "30 angry polar bears" to a number:

```
stringvar = "30 angry polar bears";
numvar = parseInt(stringvar);
```

After these statements execute, the numvar variable contains the number 30. The nonnumeric portion of the string is ignored.

By the Way

These functions look for a number of the appropriate type at the beginning of the string. If a valid number is not found, the function will return the special value NaN, meaning *not a number*.

Using String **Objects**

You've already used several strings during the first few hours of this book. Strings store a group of text characters, and are named similarly to other variables. As a simple example, this statement assigns the string This is a test to a string variable called test:

```
test = "This is a test";
```

Creating a `String` Object

JavaScript stores strings as `String` objects. You usually don't need to worry about this, but it will explain some of the techniques for working with strings, which use methods (built-in functions) of the `String` object.

There are two ways to create a new `String` object. The first is the one you've already used, whereas the second uses object-oriented syntax. The following two statements create the same string:

```
test = "This is a test";
test = new String("This is a test");
```

The second statement uses the new keyword, which you use to create objects. This tells the browser to create a new `String` object containing the text This is a test, and assigns it to the variable test.

> Although you can create a string using object-oriented syntax, the standard JavaScript syntax is simpler, and there is no difference in the strings created by these two methods.

By the Way

Assigning a Value

You can assign a value to a string in the same way as any other variable. Both of the examples in the previous section assigned an initial value to the string. You can also assign a value after the string has already been created. For example, the following statement replaces the contents of the test variable with a new string:

```
test = "This is only a test.";
```

You can also use the concatenation operator (+) to combine the values of two strings. Listing 5.1 shows a simple example of assigning and combining the values of strings.

LISTING 5.1   Assigning Values to Strings and Combining Them

```
<html>
<head>
<title>String Test</title>
</head>
<body>
<h1>String Test</h1>
<script language="JavaScript" type="text/javascript">;
test1 = "This is a test. ";
test2 = "This is only a test.";
both = test1 + test2;
alert(both);
</script>
</body>
</html>
```

This script assigns values to two string variables, `test1` and `test2`, and then displays an alert with their combined value. If you load this HTML document in a browser, your output should resemble Figure 5.1.

FIGURE 5.1
The output of the string example script.

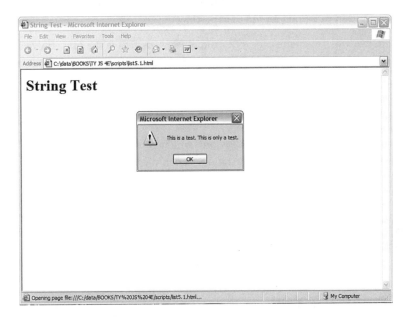

In addition to using the + operator to concatenate two strings, you can use the += operator to add text to a string. For example, this statement adds a period to the current contents of the string `sentence`:

```
sentence += ".";
```

By the Way

> The plus sign (+) is also used to add numbers in JavaScript. The browser knows whether to use addition or concatenation based on the types of data you use with the plus sign. If you use it between a number and a string, the number is converted to a string and concatenated.

Calculating the String's Length

From time to time, you might find it useful to know how many characters a string variable contains. You can do this with the `length` property of `String` objects, which you can use with any string. To use this property, type the string's name followed by `.length`.

For example, `test.length` refers to the length of the `test` string. Here is an example of this property:

```
test = "This is a test.";
document.write(test.length);
```

The first statement assigns the string `This is a test` to the `test` variable. The second statement displays the length of the string—in this case, 15 characters. The `length` property is a read-only property, so you cannot assign a value to it to change a string's length.

> Remember that although `test` refers to a string variable, the value of `test.length` is a number and can be used in any numeric expression.

By the Way

Converting the String's Case

Two methods of the `String` object enable you to convert the contents of a string to all uppercase or all lowercase:

- ▶ `toUpperCase()`—Converts all characters in the string to uppercase.

- ▶ `toLowerCase()`—Converts all characters in the string to lowercase.

For example, the following statement displays the value of the `test` string variable in lowercase:

```
document.write(test.toLowerCase());
```

Assuming that this variable contained the text `This Is A Test`, the result would be the following string:

```
this is a test
```

Note that the statement doesn't change the value of the `text` variable. These methods return the upper- or lowercase version of the string, but they don't change the string itself. If you want to change the string's value, you can use a statement like this:

```
test = test.toLowerCase();
```

> Note that the syntax for these methods is similar to the `length` property introduced earlier. The difference is that methods always use parentheses, whereas properties don't. The `toUpperCase` and `toLowerCase` methods do not take any parameters, but you still need to use the parentheses.

By the Way

Working with Substrings

So far, you've worked with entire strings. JavaScript also enables you to work with *substrings*, or portions of a string. You can use the substring method to retrieve a portion of a string, or the charAt method to get a single character. These are explained in the following sections.

Using Part of a String

The substring method returns a string consisting of a portion of the original string between two index values, which you must specify in parentheses. For example, the following statement displays the fourth through sixth characters of the text string:

```
document.write(text.substring(3,6));
```

At this point, you're probably wondering where the 3 and the 6 come from. There are three things you need to understand about the index parameters:

▶ Indexing starts with 0 for the first character of the string, so the fourth character is actually index 3.

▶ The second index is noninclusive. A second index of 6 includes up to index 5 (the sixth character).

▶ You can specify the two indexes in either order. The smaller one will be assumed to be the first index. In the previous example, (6,3) would have produced the same result. Of course, there is rarely a reason to use the reverse order.

As another example, suppose you defined a string called alpha to hold the alphabet:

```
alpha = "ABCDEFGHIJKLMNOPQRSTUVWXYZ";
```

The following are examples of the substring() method using this string:

▶ alpha.substring(0,4) returns ABCD.

▶ alpha.substring(10,12) returns KL.

▶ alpha.substring(12,10) also returns KL. Because it's smaller, 10 is used as the first index.

▶ alpha.substring(6,7) returns G.

▶ alpha.substring(24,26) returns YZ.

▶ alpha.substring(0,26) returns the entire alphabet.

▶ alpha.substring(6,6) returns the null value, an empty string. This is true whenever the two index values are the same.

Getting a Single Character

The charAt method is a simple way to grab a single character from a string. You specify the character's index, or position, in parentheses. The indexes begin at 0 for the first character. Here are a few examples using the alpha string:

- ▶ alpha.charAt(0) returns A.

- ▶ alpha.charAt(12) returns M.

- ▶ alpha.charAt(25) returns Z.

- ▶ alpha.charAt(27) returns an empty string because there is no character at that position.

Finding a Substring

Another use for substrings is to find a string within another string. One way to do this is with the indexOf method. To use this method, add indexOf to the string you want to search, and specify the string to search for in the parentheses. This example searches for "this" in the test string:

```
loc = test.indexOf("this");
```

As with most JavaScript methods and property names, indexOf is case sensitive. Make sure you type it exactly as shown here when you use it in scripts.

By the Way

The value returned in the loc variable is an index into the string, similar to the first index in the substring method. The first character of the string is index 0.

You can specify an optional second parameter to indicate the index value to begin the search. For example, this statement searches for the word fish in the temp string, starting with the 20th character:

```
location = temp.indexOf("fish",19);
```

One use for the second parameter is to search for multiple occurrences of a string. After finding the first occurrence, you search starting with that location for the second one, and so on.

By the Way

A second method, lastIndexOf(), works the same way, but finds the *last* occurrence of the string. It searches the string backwards, starting with the last character. For example, this statement finds the last occurrence of Fred in the names string:

```
location = names.lastIndexOf("Fred");
```

As with `indexOf()`, you can specify a location to search from as the second parameter. In this case, the string will be searched backward starting at that location.

Using Numeric Arrays

An array is a numbered group of data items that you can treat as a single unit. For example, you might use an array called `scores` to store several scores for a game. Arrays can contain strings, numbers, objects, or other types of data. Each item in an array is called an *element* of the array.

Creating a Numeric Array

Unlike most other types of JavaScript variables, you typically need to declare an array before you use it. The following example creates an array with four elements:

```
scores = new Array(4);
```

To assign a value to the array, you use an *index* in brackets. Indexes begin with 0, so the elements of the array in this example would be numbered 0 to 3. These statements assign values to the four elements of the array:

```
scores[0] = 39;
scores[1] = 40;
scores[2] = 100;
scores[3] = 49;
```

You can also declare an array and specify values for elements at the same time. This statement creates the same `scores` array in a single line:

```
scores = new Array(39,40,100,49);
```

In JavaScript 1.2 and later, you can also use a shorthand syntax to declare an array and specify its contents. The following statement is an alternative way to create the `scores` array:

```
scores = [39,40,100,49];
```

Did you Know?

Remember to use parentheses when declaring an array with the new keyword, as in a=new Array(3,4,5), and use brackets when declaring an array without new, as in a=[3,4,5]. Otherwise, you'll run into JavaScript errors.

Understanding Array Length

Like strings, arrays have a length property. This tells you the number of elements in the array. If you specified the length when creating the array, this value becomes the length property's value. For example, these statements would print the number 30:

```
scores = new Array(30);
document.write(scores.length);
```

You can declare an array without a specific length, and change the length later by assigning values to elements or changing the length property. For example, these statements create a new array and assign values to two of its elements:

```
test = new Array();
test[0]=21;
test[5]=22;
```

In this example, because the largest index number assigned so far is 5, the array has a length property of 6—remember, elements are numbered starting at 0.

Accessing Array Elements

You can read the contents of an array using the same notation you used when assigning values. For example, the following statements would display the values of the first three elements of the scores array:

```
scoredisp = "Scores: " + scores[0] + "," + scores[1] + "," + scores[2];
document.write(scoredisp);
```

Looking at this example, you might imagine it would be inconvenient to display all the elements of a large array. This is an ideal job for loops, which enable you to perform the same statements several times with different values. You'll learn all about loops in Hour 7.

Did you Know?

Using String Arrays

So far, you've used arrays of numbers. JavaScript also allows you to use *string arrays*, or arrays of strings. This is a powerful feature that enables you to work with a large number of strings at the same time.

Creating a String Array

You declare a string array in the same way as a numeric array—in fact, JavaScript does not make a distinction between them:

```
names = new Array(30);
```

You can then assign string values to the array elements:

```
names[0] = "Henry J. Tillman";
names[1] = "Sherlock Holmes";
```

As with numeric arrays, you can also specify a string array's contents when you create it. Either of the following statements would create the same string array as the preceding example:

```
names = new Array("Henry J. Tillman", "Sherlock Holmes");
names = ["Henry J. Tillman", "Sherlock Holmes"];
```

You can use string array elements anywhere you would use a string. You can even use the string methods introduced earlier. For example, the following statement prints the first five characters of the first element of the names array, resulting in Henry:

```
document.write(names[0].substring(0,5));
```

Splitting a String

JavaScript includes a string method called split, which splits a string into its component parts. To use this method, specify the string to split and a character to divide the parts:

```
test = "John Q. Public";
parts = test.split(" ");
```

In this example, the test string contains the name John Q. Public. The split method in the second statement splits the name string at each space, resulting in three strings. These are stored in a string array called parts. After the example statements execute, the elements of parts contain the following:

▶ parts[0] = "John"

▶ parts[1] = "Q."

▶ parts[2] = "Public"

JavaScript also includes an array method, join, which performs the opposite function. This statement reassembles the parts array into a string:

```
fullname = parts.join(" ");
```

The value in the parentheses specifies a character to separate the parts of the array. In this case, a space is used, resulting in the final string John Q. Public. If you do not specify a character, commas are used.

Sorting a String Array

JavaScript also includes a sort method for arrays, which returns an alphabetically sorted version of the array. For example, the following statements initialize an array of four names and sort it:

```
names[0] = "Public, John Q.";
names[1] = "Tillman, Henry J.";
names[2] = "Bush, George W.";
names[3] = "Mouse, Mickey";
sortednames = names.sort();
```

The last statement sorts the names array and stores the result in a new array, sort-ednames.

Sorting a Numeric Array

Because the sort method sorts alphabetically, it won't work with a numeric array—at least not the way you'd expect. If an array contains the numbers 4, 10, 30, and 200, for example, it would sort them as 10, 200, 30, 4—not even close. Fortunately, there's a solution: You can specify a function in the sort method's parameters, and that function will be used to compare the numbers. The following code sorts a numeric array correctly:

```
function numcompare(a,b) {
    return a-b;
}
nums = new Array(30, 10, 200, 4);
sortednums = nums.sort(numcompare);
```

This example defines a simple function, numcompare, which subtracts the two numbers. After you specify this function in the sort method, the array is sorted in the correct numeric order: 4, 10, 30, 200.

JavaScript expects the comparison function to return a negative number if a belongs before b, 0 if they are the same, or a positive number if a belongs after b. This is why a-b is all you need for the function to sort numerically.

By the Way

▼   **Try It Yourself**

Sorting and Displaying Names

To gain more experience working with JavaScript's string and array features, you can create a script that enables the user to enter a list of names, and displays the list in sorted form.

Because this will be a larger script, you will create separate HTML and JavaScript files, as described in Hour 3, "Getting Started with JavaScript Programming." First, the sort.html file will contain the HTML structure and form fields for the script to work with. Listing 5.2 shows the HTML document.

LISTING 5.2   The HTML Document for the Sorting Example

```
<html>
<head>
<title>Array Sorting Example</title>
<script type="text/javascript" language="javascript" src="sort.js">
</script>
</head>
<body>
<h1>Sorting String Arrays</h1>
<p>Enter two or more names in the field below,
and the sorted list of names will appear in the
text area.</p>
<form name="theform">
Name:
<input type="text" name="newname" size="20">
<input type="button" name="addname" value="Add"
onclick="SortNames();">
<br>
<h2>Sorted Names</h2>
<textarea cols="60" rows="10" name="sorted">
The sorted names will appear here.
</textarea>
</form>
</body>
</html>
```

Because the script will be in a separate document, the <script> tag in the header of this document uses the src attribute to include a JavaScript file called sort.js. You will create this file next.

This document defines a form named theform, a text field named newname, an addname button, and a textarea named sorted. Your script will use these form fields as its user interface. Listing 5.3 shows the JavaScript file.

LISTING 5.3   The JavaScript File for the Sorting Example

```
// initialize the counter and the array
var numnames=0;
var names = new Array();
function SortNames() {
```

LISTING 5.3   Continued

```
    // Get the name from the text field
    thename=document.theform.newname.value;
    // Add the name to the array
    names[numnames]=thename;
    // Increment the counter
    numnames++;
    // Sort the array
    names.sort();
    document.theform.sorted.value=names.join("\n");
}
```

The script begins by defining two variables with the var keyword: numnames will be a counter that increments as each name is added, and the names array will store the names.

When you type a name into the text field and click the button, the onclick event handler calls the SortNames function. This function stores the text field value in a variable, thename, and then adds the name to the names array using numnames as the index. It then increments numnames to prepare for the next name.

The final section of the script sorts the names and displays them. First, the sort() method is used to sort the names array. Next, the join() method is used to combine the names, separating them with line breaks, and display them in the textarea.

To test the script, save it as sort.js, and then load the sort.html file you created previously into a browser. You can then add some names and test the script. Figure 5.2 shows the result after sorting several names.

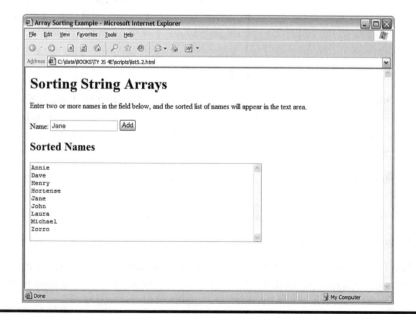

FIGURE 5.2
The output of the name-sorting example.

Summary

During this hour, you've focused on variables and how JavaScript handles them. You've learned how to name variables, how to declare them, and the differences between local and global variables. You also explored the data types supported by JavaScript and how to convert between them.

You also learned about JavaScript's more complex variables, strings and arrays, and looked at the features that enable you to perform operations on them, such as converting strings to uppercase or sorting arrays.

In the next hour, you'll continue your JavaScript education by learning more about two additional key features: functions and objects.

Q&A

Q. *What is the importance of the* `var` *keyword? Should I always use it to declare variables?*

A. You only need to use var to define a local variable in a function. However, if you're unsure at all, it's always safe to use var. Using it consistently will help you keep your scripts organized and error free.

Q. *Is there any reason I would want to use the* `var` *keyword to create a local variable with the same name as a global one?*

A. Not on purpose. The main reason to use var is to avoid conflicts with global variables you might not know about. For example, you might add a global variable in the future, or you might add another script to the page that uses a similar variable name. This is more of an issue with large, complex scripts.

Q. *What good are Boolean variables?*

A. Often in scripts you'll need a variable to indicate whether something has happened—for example, whether a phone number the user has entered is in the right format. Boolean variables are ideal for this; they're also useful in working with conditions, as you'll see in Hour 7.

Q. *Can I store other types of data in an array? For example, can I have an array of dates?*

A. Absolutely. JavaScript allows you to store any data type in an array.

Q. *What about two-dimensional arrays?*

A. These are arrays with two indexes (such as columns and rows). JavaScript does not directly support this type of array, but you can use objects to achieve the same effect. You will learn more about objects in the next hour.

Quiz Questions

Test your knowledge of JavaScript by answering the following questions:

1. Which of the following is *not* a valid JavaScript variable name?

   a. `2names`

   b. `first_and_last_names`

   c. `FirstAndLast`

2. If the statement `var fig=2` appears in a function, which type of variable does it declare?

   a. A global variable

   b. A local variable

   c. A constant variable

3. If the string `test` contains the value `The eagle has landed.`, what would be the value of `test.length`?

   a. 4

   b. 21

   c. The

4. Using the same example string, which of these statements would return the word `eagle`?

   a. `test.substring(4,9)`

   b. `test.substring(5,9)`

   c. `test.substring("eagle")`

5. What will be the result of the JavaScript expression `31 + " angry polar bears"`?

   a. An error message

   b. 32

   c. "31 angry polar bears"

Quiz Answers

1. a. 2names is an invalid JavaScript variable name because it begins with a number. The others are valid, although they're probably not ideal choices for names.

2. b. Because the variable is declared in a function, it is a local variable. The var keyword ensures that a local variable is created.

3. b. The length of the string is 21 characters.

4. a. The correct statement is test.substring(4,9). Remember that the indexes start with 0, and that the second index is noninclusive.

5. c. JavaScript converts the whole expression to the string "31 angry polar bears". (No offense to polar bears, who are seldom angry and rarely seen in groups this large.)

Exercises

To further explore JavaScript variables, strings, and arrays, you can perform the following exercises:

▶ Modify the sorting example in Listing 5.3 to convert the names to all uppercase before sorting and displaying them.

▶ Modify Listing 5.3 to display a numbered list of names in the textarea.

HOUR 6

Using Functions and Objects

What You'll Learn in This Hour:

▶ Defining and calling functions
▶ Returning values from functions
▶ Understanding JavaScript objects
▶ Defining custom objects
▶ Working with object properties and values
▶ Defining and using object methods
▶ Using objects to store data and related functions

In this hour, you'll learn about two more key JavaScript concepts that you'll use throughout the rest of this book. First, you'll learn the details of using functions, which enable you to group any number of statements into a block. This is useful for repeating sections of code, and you can also create functions that accept parameters and return values for later use.

Whereas functions enable you to group sections of code, objects enable you to group data—you can use them to combine related data items and functions for working with the data.

Using Functions

The scripts you've seen so far are simple lists of instructions. The browser begins with the first statement after the `<script>` tag and follows each instruction in order until it reaches the closing `</script>` tag (or encounters an error).

Although this is a straightforward approach for short scripts, it can be confusing to read a longer script written in this fashion. To make it easier for you to organize your scripts, JavaScript supports functions, which you learned about in Hour 3, "Getting Started with JavaScript Programming." In this section, you will learn how to define and use functions.

Defining a Function

Functions are groups of JavaScript statements that can be treated as a single unit. To use a function, you must first define it. Here is a simple example of a function definition:

```
function Greet() {
    alert("Greetings.");
}
```

This defines a function that displays an alert message to the user. This begins with the `function` keyword. The function's name is `Greet`. Notice the parentheses after the function's name. As you'll learn next, the space between them is not always empty.

The first and last lines of the function definition include braces ({ and }). You use these to enclose all of the statements in the function. The browser uses the braces to determine where the function begins and ends.

Between the braces, this particular function contains a single line. This uses the built-in `alert()` function, which displays an alert message. The message will contain the text "Greetings."

By the Way

> Function names are case sensitive. If you define a function such as `Greet()` with a capital letter, be sure you use the identical name when you call the function.

Now, about those parentheses. The current `Greet()` function always does the same thing: Each time you use it, it displays the same message. Although this avoids a bit of typing, it doesn't really provide much of an advantage.

To make your function more flexible, you can add *parameters*, also known as *arguments*. These are variables that are received by the function each time it is called. For example, you can add a parameter called who that tells the function the name of the person to greet. Here is the modified `Greet()` function:

```
function Greet(who) {
    alert("Greetings, " + who);
}
```

Of course, to use this function, you should include it in an HTML document. Traditionally, the best place for a function definition is within the <head> section of the document. Because the statements in the <head> section are executed first, this ensures that the function is defined before it is used.

Listing 6.1 shows the `Greet()` function embedded in the header section of an HTML document.

LISTING 6.1 The `Greet()` Function in an HTML Document

```
<html>
<head>
<title>Functions</title>
<script language="JavaScript" type="text/javascript">
function Greet(who) {
    alert("Greetings, " + who);
}
</script>
</head>
<body>
This is the body of the page.
</body>
</html>
```

As usual, you can download the listings for this hour or view them online at this book's website.

By the Way

Calling the Function

You have now defined a function and placed it in an HTML document. However, if you load Listing 6.1 into a browser, you'll notice that it does absolutely nothing. This is because the function is defined—ready to be used—but we haven't used it yet.

Making use of a function is referred to as *calling* the function. To call a function, use the function's name as a statement in a script. You will need to include the parentheses and the values for the function's parameters. For example, here's a statement that calls the Greet function:

```
Greet("Fred");
```

This tells the JavaScript interpreter to transfer control to the first statement in the Greet function. It also passes the parameter "Fred" to the function. This value will be assigned to the who variable inside the function.

Functions can have more than one parameter. To define a function with multiple parameters, list a variable name for each parameter, separated by commas. To call the function, specify values for each parameter separated by commas.

By the Way

Listing 6.2 shows a complete HTML document that includes the function definition and a second script in the body of the page that actually calls the function. To demonstrate the usefulness of functions, we'll call it twice to greet two different people.

LISTING 6.2   The Complete Function Example

```html
<html>
<head>
<title>Functions</title>
<script language="JavaScript" type="text/javascript">
function Greet(who) {
    alert("Greetings, " + who);
}
</script>
</head>
<body>
<h1>Function Example</h1>
<p>Prepare to be greeted twice.</p>
<script language="JavaScript" type="text/javascript">
Greet("Fred");
Greet("Ethel");
</script>
</body>
</html>>
```

This listing includes a second set of `<script>` tags in the body of the page. The second script includes two function calls to the `Greet` function, each with a different name.

Now that you have a script that actually does something, try loading it into a browser. You should see something like Figure 6.1, which shows the Greeting script running in Firefox.

FIGURE 6.1
The output of the Greeting example.

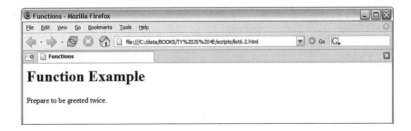

 By the Way

> Notice that the second alert message isn't displayed until you press the OK button on the first alert. This is because JavaScript processing is halted while alerts are displayed.

Returning a Value

The function you just created displays a message to the user, but functions can also return a value to the script that called them. This allows you to use functions to calculate values. As an example, you can create a function that averages four numbers.

Your function should begin with the `function` keyword, the function's name, and the parameters it accepts. We will use the variable names a, b, c, and d for the four numbers to average. Here is the first line of the function:

```
function Average(a,b,c,d) {
```

> I've also included the opening brace ({) on the first line of the function. This is a common style, but you can also place the brace on the next line, or on a line by itself.

Next, the function needs to calculate the average of the four parameters. You can calculate this by adding them, and then dividing by the number of parameters (in this case, 4). Thus, here is the next line of the function:

```
result = (a + b + c + d) / 4;
```

This statement creates a variable called `result` and calculates the result by adding the four numbers, and then dividing by 4. (The parentheses are necessary to tell JavaScript to perform the addition before the division.)

To send this result back to the script that called the function, you use the `return` keyword. Here is the last part of the function:

```
return result;
}
```

Listing 6.3 shows the complete `Average()` function in an HTML document. This HTML document also includes a small script in the <body> section that calls the `Average()` function and displays the result.

LISTING 6.3   The `Average()` **Function in an HTML Document**

```
<html>_
<head>
<title>Function Example</title>
<script language="JavaScript" type="text/javascript">
function Average(a,b,c,d) {
result = (a + b + c + d) / 4;
return result;
}
</script>
</head>
<body>
<p>The following is the result of the function call.</p>
<script LANGUAGE="JavaScript" type="text/javascript">
score = Average(3,4,5,6);
document.write("The average is: " + score);
</script>_
</body>
</html>
```

You can use a variable with the function call, as shown in this listing. This statement averages the numbers 3, 4, 5, and 6 and stores the result in a variable called score:

```
score = Average(3,4,5,6);
```

> You can also use the function call directly in an expression. For example, you could use the alert statement to display the result of the function:
> `alert(Average(1,2,3,4)) .`

Introducing Objects

In the previous hour, you learned how to use variables to represent different kinds of data in JavaScript. JavaScript also supports *objects*, a more complex kind of variable that can store multiple data items and functions.

Although a variable can have only one value at a time, an object can contain multiple values, as well as functions for working with the values. This allows you to group related data items and the functions that deal with them into a single object.

In this hour, you'll learn how to define and use your own objects. You've already worked with some objects:

- ▶ **DOM objects**—Allow your scripts to interact with web pages. You learned about these in Hour 4, "Working with the Document Object Model (DOM)."

- ▶ **Built-in objects**—Include strings and arrays, which you learned about in Hour 5, "Using Variables, Strings, and Arrays."

The syntax for working with all three types of objects—DOM objects, built-in objects, and custom objects—is the same, so even if you don't end up creating your own objects, you should have a good understanding of JavaScript's object terminology and syntax.

Creating Objects

When you created an array in the previous hour, you used the following JavaScript statement:

```
scores = new Array(4);
```

The new keyword tells the JavaScript interpreter to use a function—in this case, the built-in Array function—to create an object. You'll create a function for a custom object later in this hour.

Object Properties and Values

Each object has one or more *properties*—essentially, variables that will be stored within the object. For example, in Hour 4, you learned that the `location.href` property gives you the URL of the current document. The `href` property is one of the properties of the `location` object in the DOM.

You've also used the `length` property of `String` objects, as in the following example from the previous hour:

```
test = "This is a test.";
document.write(test.length);
```

Like variables, each object property has a *value*. To read a property's value, you simply include the object name and property name, separated by a period, in any expression, as in `test.length` previously. You can change a property's value using the = operator, just like a variable. The following example sends the browser to a new URL by changing the `location.href` property:

```
location.href="http://www.jsworkshop.com/";
```

> An object can also be a property of another object. This is referred to as a *child object*.

By the Way

Understanding Methods

Along with properties, each object can have one or more *methods*. These are functions that work with the object's data. For example, the following JavaScript statement reloads the current document, as you learned in Hour 4:

```
location.reload();
```

When you use `reload()`, you're using a method of the `location` object. Like normal functions, methods can accept arguments in parentheses, and can return values.

Using Objects to Simplify Scripting

Although JavaScript's variables and arrays are versatile ways to store data, sometimes you need a more complicated structure. For example, suppose you are creating a script to work with a business card database that contains names, addresses, and phone numbers for a variety of people.

If you were using regular variables, you would need several separate variables for each person in the database: a name variable, an address variable, and so on. This would be very confusing.

Arrays would improve things slightly. You could have a names array, an addresses array, and a phone number array. Each person in the database would have an entry in each array. This would be more convenient, but still not perfect.

With objects, you can make the variables that store the database as logical as business cards. Each person is represented by a `Card` object, which has properties for name, address, and phone number. You can even add methods to the object to display or work with the information.

In the following sections, you'll use JavaScript to actually create the `Card` object and its properties and methods. Later in this hour, you'll use the `Card` object in a script to display information for several members of the database.

Defining an Object

The first step in creating an object is to name it and its properties. We've already decided to call the object a `Card` object. Each object will have the following properties:

► name

► address

► workphone

► homephone

The first step in using this object in a JavaScript program is to create a function to make new `Card` objects. This function is called the *constructor* for an object. Here is the constructor function for the `Card` object:

```
function Card(name,address,work,home) {
   this.name = name;
   this.address = address;
   this.workphone = work;
   this.homephone = home;
}
```

The constructor is a simple function that accepts parameters to initialize a new object and assigns them to the corresponding properties. This function accepts several parameters from the statement that calls the function, and then assigns them as properties of an object. Because the function is called `Card`, the object is the `Card` object.

Notice the `this` keyword. You'll use it anytime you create an object definition. Use `this` to refer to the current object—the one that is being created by the function.

Defining an Object Method

Next, you will create a method to work with the Card object. Because all Card objects will have the same properties, it might be handy to have a function that prints out the properties in a neat format. Let's call this function PrintCard().

Your PrintCard() function will be used as a method for Card objects, so you don't need to ask for parameters. Instead, you can use the this keyword again to refer to the current object's properties. Here is a function definition for the PrintCard() function:

```
function PrintCard() {
   line1 = "Name: " + this.name + "<br>\n";
   line2 = "Address: " + this.address + "<br>\n";
   line3 = "Work Phone: " + this.workphone + "<br>\n";
   line4 = "Home Phone: " + this.homephone + "<hr>\n";
   document.write(line1, line2, line3, line4);
}
```

This function simply reads the properties from the current object (this), prints each one with a caption, and skips to a new line.

You now have a function that prints a card, but it isn't officially a method of the Card object. The last thing you need to do is make PrintCard() part of the function definition for Card objects. Here is the modified function definition:

```
function Card(name,address,work,home) {
   this.name = name;
   this.address = address;
   this.workphone = work;
   this.homephone = home;
   this.PrintCard = PrintCard;
}
```

The added statement looks just like another property definition, but it refers to the PrintCard() function. This will work so long as the PrintCard() function is defined with its own function definition. Methods are essentially properties that define a function rather than a simple value.

> The previous example uses lowercase names such as workphone for properties, and an uppercase name (PrintCard) for the method. You can use any case for property and method names, but this is one way to make it clear that PrintCard is a method rather than an ordinary property.

Creating an Object Instance

Now let's use the object definition and method you just created. To use an object definition, you create a new object. This is done with the new keyword. This is the same keyword you've already used to create Date and Array objects.

The following statement creates a new `Card` object called `tom`:

```
tom = new Card("Tom Jones", "123 Elm Street", "555-1234", "555-9876");
```

As you can see, creating an object is easy. All you do is call the `Card()` function (the object definition) and give it the required attributes, in the same order as the definition.

After this statement executes, a new object is created to hold Tom's information. This is called an *instance* of the `Card` object. Just as there can be several string variables in a program, there can be several instances of an object you define.

Rather than specify all the information for a card with the new keyword, you can assign them after the fact. For example, the following script creates an empty `Card` object called `holmes`, and then assigns its properties:

```
holmes = new Card();
holmes.name = "Sherlock Holmes";
holmes.address = "221B Baker Street";
holmes.workphone = "555-2345";
holmes.homephone = "555-3456";
```

After you've created an instance of the `Card` object using either of these methods, you can use the `PrintCard()` method to display its information. For example, this statement displays the properties of the `tom` card:

```
tom.PrintCard();
```

Extending Built-in Objects

JavaScript includes a feature that enables you to extend the definitions of built-in objects. For example, if you think the `String` object doesn't quite fit your needs, you can extend it, adding a new property or method. This might be very useful if you were creating a large script that used many strings.

You can add both properties and methods to an existing object by using the `prototype` keyword. (A *prototype* is another name for an object's definition, or constructor function.) The `prototype` keyword enables you to change the definition of an object outside its constructor function.

As an example, let's add a method to the `String` object definition. You will create a method called `heading`, which converts a string into an HTML heading. The following statement defines a string called `title`:

```
title = "Fred's Home Page";
```

This statement would output the contents of the `title` string as an HTML level 1 heading:

```
document.write(title.heading(1));
```

Listing 6.4 adds a heading method to the String object definition that will display the string as a heading, and then displays three headings using the method.

LISTING 6.4   Adding a Method to the String Object

```
<html>
<head><title>Test of heading method</title>
</head>
<body>
<script LANGUAGE="JavaScript" type="text/javascript">
function addhead (level) {
   html = "H" + level;
   text = this.toString();
   start = "<" + html + ">";
   stop = "</" + html + ">";
   return start + text + stop;
}
String.prototype.heading = addhead;
document.write ("This is a heading 1".heading(1));
document.write ("This is a heading 2".heading(2));
document.write ("This is a heading 3".heading(3));
</script>
</body>
</html>
```

First, you define the addhead() function, which will serve as the new string method. It accepts a number to specify the heading level. The start and stop variables are used to store the HTML "begin header" and "end header" tags, such as <h1> and </h1>.

After the function is defined, use the prototype keyword to add it as a method of the String object. You can then use this method on any String object or, in fact, any JavaScript string. This is demonstrated by the last three statements, which display quoted text strings as level 1, 2, and 3 headers.

Try It Yourself   ▼

Storing Data in Objects

Now you've created a new object to store business cards and a method to print them out. As a final demonstration of objects, properties, functions, and methods, you will now use this object in a web page to display data for several cards.

Your script will need to include the function definition for PrintCard(), along with the function definition for the Card object. You will then create three cards and print them out in the body of the document. We will use separate HTML and JavaScript files for this example. Listing 6.5 shows the complete script.

LISTING 6.5   An Example Script That Uses the `Card` Object

```
// define the functions
function PrintCard() {
line1 = "<b>Name: </b>" + this.name + "<br>\n";
line2 = "<b>Address: </b>" + this.address + "<br>\n";
line3 = "<b>Work Phone: </b>" + this.workphone + "<br>\n";
line4 = "<b>Home Phone: </b>" + this.homephone + "<hr>\n";
document.write(line1, line2, line3, line4);
}
function Card(name,address,work,home) {
   this.name = name;
   this.address = address;
   this.workphone = work;
   this.homephone = home;
   this.PrintCard = PrintCard;
}
// Create the objects
sue = new Card("Sue Suthers", "123 Elm Street", "555-1234", "555-9876");
phred = new Card("Phred Madsen", "233 Oak Lane", "555-2222", "555-4444");
henry = new Card("Henry Tillman", "233 Walnut Circle", "555-1299", "555-1344");
// And print them
sue.PrintCard();
phred.PrintCard();
henry.PrintCard();
```

Notice that the `PrintCard()` function has been modified slightly to make things look good with the captions in boldface. To use this script, save it as `cardtest.js`. Next, you'll need to include the script in a simple HTML document. Listing 6.6 shows the HTML document for this example.

LISTING 6.6   The HTML File for the `Card` Object Example

```
<html>
<head>
<title>JavaScript Business Cards</title>
</head>
<body>
<h1>JavaScript Business Card Test</h1>
<p>Script begins here.</p><hr>
<script language="JavaScript" type="text/javascript"
   src="cardtest.js">
</script>
<p>End of script.</p>
</body>
</html>
```

To test the script, save the HTML document in the same directory as the `cardtest.js` file you created earlier, and then load the HTML document into a browser. The browser's display of this example is shown in Figure 6.2.

This example isn't a very sophisticated database because you have to include the data for each person in the script. However, an object like this could be used to store a database record retrieved from a database server with thousands of records.

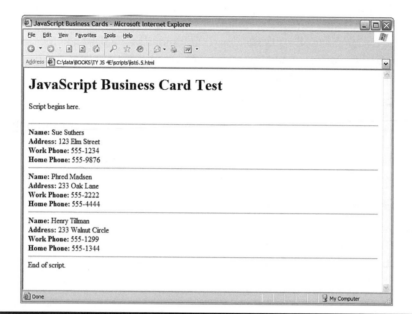

FIGURE 6.2
Internet Explorer displays the output of the business card example.

Summary

In this hour, you've looked at two important features of JavaScript. First, you learned how to use functions to group JavaScript statements, and how to call functions and use the values they return.

You also learned about JavaScript's object-oriented features—defining objects with constructor functions, creating object instances, and working with properties, property values, and methods.

In the next hour, you'll look at two more features you'll use in almost every script—conditions to let your scripts evaluate data, and loops to repeat sections of code.

Q&A

Q. *Many objects in JavaScript, such as DOM objects, include parent and child objects. Can I include child objects in my custom object definitions?*

A. Yes. Just create a constructor function for the child object, and then add a property to the parent object that corresponds to it. For example, if you created a `Nicknames` object to store several nicknames for a person in the card file example, you could add it as a child object in the `Card` object's constructor: `this.nick = new Nicknames();`.

Q. *Can I create an array of custom objects?*

A. Yes. First, create the object definition as usual and define an array with the required number of elements. Then assign a new object to each array element (for example, `cardarray[1] = new Card();`). You can use a loop, described in the next hour, to assign objects to an entire array at once.

Q. *Can I modify all properties of objects?*

A. With custom objects, yes—but this varies with built-in objects and DOM objects. For example, you can use the `length` property to find the length of a string, but it is a *read-only property* and cannot be modified.

Quiz Questions

Test your knowledge of JavaScript by answering the following questions:

1. What JavaScript keyword is used to create an instance of an object?

   a. `object`

   b. `new`

   c. `instance`

2. What is the meaning of the `this` keyword in JavaScript?

   a. The current object.

   b. The current script.

   c. It has no meaning.

3. What does the `prototype` keyword allow you to do in a script?

    a. Change the syntax of JavaScript commands.

    b. Modify the definitions of built-in objects.

    c. Modify the user's browser so only your scripts will work.

Quiz Answers

1. b. The `new` keyword creates an object instance.

2. a. The `this` keyword refers to the current object.

3. b. The `prototype` keyword allows you to modify the definitions of built-in objects.

Exercises

To further explore the JavaScript features you learned about in this hour, you can perform the following exercises:

▶ Modify the `Greet()` function to accept two parameters, `who1` and `who2`, and to include both names in a single greeting dialog. Modify Listing 6.2 to use a single function call to the new function.

▶ Modify the definition of the `Card` object to include a property called `email` for the person's email address. Modify the `PrintCard()` function in Listing 6.5 to include this property.

HOUR 7

Controlling Flow with Conditions and Loops

What You'll Learn in This Hour:

▶ Testing variables with the `if` statement

▶ Using various operators to compare values

▶ Using logical operators to combine conditions

▶ Using alternative conditions with `else`

▶ Creating expressions with conditional operators

▶ Testing for multiple conditions

▶ Performing repeated statements with the `for` loop

▶ Using `while` for a different type of loop

▶ Using `do...while` loops

▶ Creating infinite loops (and why you shouldn't)

▶ Escaping from loops and continuing loops

▶ Looping through an array's properties

Statements in a JavaScript program generally execute in the order in which they appear, one after the other. Because this isn't always practical, most programming languages provide *flow control* statements that let you control the order in which code is executed. Functions, which you learned about in the previous hour, are one type of flow control—although a function might be defined first thing in your code, its statements can be executed anywhere in the script.

In this hour, you'll look at two other types of flow control in JavaScript: conditions, which allow a choice of different options depending on a value, and loops, which allow repetitive statements.

The `if` **Statement**

One of the most important features of a computer language is the capability to test and compare values. This allows your scripts to behave differently based on the values of variables, or based on input from the user.

The `if` statement is the main conditional statement in JavaScript. This statement means much the same in JavaScript as it does in English—for example, here is a typical conditional statement in English:

If the phone rings, answer it.

This statement consists of two parts: a condition (*If the phone rings*) and an action (*answer it*). The `if` statement in JavaScript works much the same way. Here is an example of a basic `if` statement:

```
if (a == 1) window.alert("Found a 1!");
```

This statement includes a condition (if a equals 1) and an action (display a message). This statement checks the variable a and, if it has a value of 1, displays an alert message. Otherwise, it does nothing.

If you use an `if` statement like the preceding example, you can use a single statement as the action. You can also use multiple statements for the action by enclosing them in braces ({}), as shown here:

```
if (a == 1) {
   window.alert("Found a 1!");
   a = 0;
}
```

This block of statements checks the variable a once again. If it finds a value of 1, it displays a message and sets a back to 0.

Conditional Operators

The action part of an `if` statement can include any of the JavaScript statements you've already learned (and any others, for that matter), but the condition part of the statement uses its own syntax. This is called a *conditional expression*.

A conditional expression usually includes two values to be compared (in the preceding example, the values were a and 1). These values can be variables, constants, or even expressions in themselves.

Either side of the conditional expression can be a variable, a constant, or an expression. You can compare a variable and a value, or compare two variables. (You can compare two constants, but there's usually no reason to.)

Between the two values to be compared is a *conditional operator*. This operator tells JavaScript how to compare the two values. For instance, the == operator is used to test whether the two values are equal. A variety of conditional operators is available:

▶ == — Is equal to

▶ != — Is not equal to

▶ < — Is less than

▶ > — Is greater than

▶ >= — Is greater than or equal to

▶ <= — Is less than or equal to

By the Way

Be sure not to confuse the equality operator (==) with the assignment operator (=), even though they both might be read as "equals." Remember to use = when *assigning* a value to a variable, and == when *comparing* values. Confusing these two is one of the most common mistakes in JavaScript programming.

Combining Conditions with Logical Operators

Often, you'll want to check a variable for more than one possible value, or check more than one variable at once. JavaScript includes *logical operators*, also known as Boolean operators, for this purpose. For example, the following two statements check different conditions and use the same action:

```
if (phone == "") window.alert("error!");
if (email == "") window.alert("error!");
```

Using a logical operator, you can combine them into a single statement:

```
if (phone == "" || email == "") window.alert("Something's Missing!");
```

This statement uses the logical Or operator (||) to combine the conditions. Translated to English, this would be, "If the phone number is blank or the email address is blank, display an error message."

An additional logical operator is the And operator, &&. Consider this statement:

```
if (phone == "" && email == "") window.alert("Both are Missing!");
```

This statement uses && (And) instead of || (Or), so the error message will only be displayed if *both* the email address and phone number variables are blank. (In this particular case, Or is a better choice.)

> If the JavaScript interpreter discovers the answer to a conditional expression before reaching the end, it does not evaluate the rest of the condition. For example, if the first of two conditions separated by the && operator is false, the second is not evaluated. You can take advantage of this to improve the speed of your scripts.

The third logical operator is the exclamation mark (!), which means Not. It can be used to invert an expression—in other words, a true expression would become false, and a false one would become true. For example, here's a statement that uses the Not operator:

```
if (!($phone == "")) alert("phone is OK");
```

In this statement, the ! (Not) operator inverts the condition, so the action of the if statement is executed only if the phone number variable is *not* blank. The extra parentheses are necessary because all JavaScript conditions must be in parentheses. You could also use the != (Not equal) operator to simplify this statement:

```
if ($phone != "") alert("phone is OK");
```

As with the previous statement, this alerts you if the phone number field is not blank.

> The logical operators are powerful, but it's easy to accidentally create an impossible condition with them. For example, the condition (a < 10 && a > 20) might look correct at first glance. However, if you read it out loud, you get "If a is less than 10 and a is greater than 20"—an impossibility in our universe. In this case, Or (¦¦) should have been used.

The else **Keyword**

An additional feature of the if statement is the else keyword. Much like its English equivalent, else tells the JavaScript interpreter what to do if the condition isn't true. The following is a simple example of the else keyword in action:

```
if (a == 1) {
   alert("Found a 1!");
   a = 0;
}
else {
   alert("Incorrect value: " + a);
}
```

This is a modified version of the previous example. This displays a message and resets the variable a if the condition is met. If the condition is not met (if a is not 1), a different message is displayed.

> Like the `if` statement, `else` can be followed either by a single action statement or by a number of statements enclosed in braces.

Using Shorthand Conditional Expressions

In addition to the `if` statement, JavaScript provides a shorthand type of conditional expression that you can use to make quick decisions. This uses a peculiar syntax that is also found in other languages, such as C. A conditional expression looks like this:

```
variable = (condition) ? (true action) : (false action);
```

This assigns one of two values to the variable: one if the condition is true, and another if it is false. Here is an example of a conditional expression:

```
value = (a == 1) ? 1 : 0;
```

This statement might look confusing, but it is equivalent to the following `if` statement:

```
if (a == 1)
    value = 1;
else
    value = 0;
```

In other words, the value after the question mark (?) will be used if the condition is true, and the value after the colon (:) will be used if the condition is false. The colon represents the `else` portion of this statement and, like the `else` portion of the `if` statement, is optional.

These shorthand expressions can be used anywhere JavaScript expects a value. They provide an easy way to make simple decisions about values. As an example, here's an easy way to display a grammatically correct message about a variable:

```
document.write("Found " + counter + ((counter == 1) ? " word." : " words."));
```

This will print the message Found 1 word if the `counter` variable has a value of 1, and Found 2 words if its value is 2 or greater. This is one of the most common uses for a conditional expression.

Testing Multiple Conditions with `if` and `else`

You can now create an example script using `if` and `else`. In Hour 2, "Creating Simple Scripts," you created a script that displays the current date and time. This example will use conditions to display a greeting that depends on the time:

"Good morning," "Good Afternoon," "Good Evening," or "Good Day". To accomplish this, you can use a combination of several if statements:

```
if (hours < 10) document.write("Good morning.");
else if (hours >= 14 && hours <= 17) document.write("Good afternoon.");
else if (hours >= 17) document.write("Good evening.");
else document.write("Good day.");
```

The first statement checks the hours variable for a value less than 10—in other words, it checks whether the current time is before 10:00 a.m. If so, it displays the greeting "Good morning."

The second statement checks whether the time is between 2:00 p.m. and 5:00 p.m. and, if so, displays "Good afternoon." This statement uses else if to indicate that this condition will only be tested if the previous one failed—if it's morning, there's no need to check whether it's afternoon. Similarly, the third statement checks for times after 5:00 p.m. and displays "Good evening."

The final statement uses a simple else, meaning it will be executed if none of the previous conditions matched. This covers the times between 10:00 a.m. and 2:00 p.m. (neglected by the other statements) and displays "Good day."

The HTML File

To try this example in a browser, you'll need an HTML file. We will keep the JavaScript code separate, so Listing 7.1 is the complete HTML file. Save it as timegreet.html but don't load it into the browser until you've prepared the JavaScript file in the next section.

LISTING 7.1   The HTML File for the Time and Greeting Example

```
<html>
<head><title>if statement example</title></head>
<body>
<h1>Current Date and Time</h1>
<p>
<script language="JavaScript" type="text/javascript"
 src = "timegreet.js">
</script>
</p>
</body>
</html>
```

The JavaScript File

Listing 7.2 shows the complete JavaScript file for the time greeting example. This uses the built-in Date object functions to find the current date and store it in hours, mins,

and secs variables. Next, document.write statements display the current time, and the if and else statements introduced earlier display an appropriate greeting.

LISTING 7.2   A Script to Display the Current Time and a Greeting

```
// Get the current date
now = new Date();
// Split into hours, minutes, seconds
hours = now.getHours();
mins = now.getMinutes();
secs = now.getSeconds();
// Display the time
document.write("<h2>");
document.write(hours + ":" + mins + ":" + secs);
document.write("</h2>");
// Display a greeting
document.write("<p>");
if (hours < 10) document.write("Good morning.");
else if (hours >= 14 && hours <= 17) document.write("Good afternoon.");
else if (hours > 17) document.write("Good evening.");
else document.write("Good day.");
document.write("</p>");
```

To try this example, save this file as timegreet.js (or download it from this book's website) and then load the timegreet.html file into your browser. Figure 7.1 shows the results of this script.

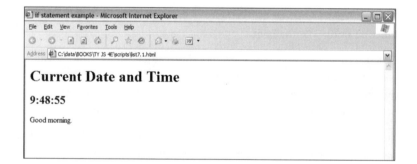

FIGURE 7.1
The output of the time greeting example, as shown by Internet Explorer.

Using Multiple Conditions with switch

In the previous example, you used several if statements in a row to test for different conditions. Here is another example of this technique:

```
if (button=="next") window.location="next.html";
else if (button=="previous") window.location="prev.html";
else if (button=="home") window.location="home.html";
else if (button=="back") window.location="menu.html";
```

Although this is a compact way of doing things, this method can get messy if each if statement has its own block of code with several statements. As an alternative, JavaScript includes the switch statement, which enables you to combine several tests of the same variable or expression into a single block of statements. The following shows the same example converted to use switch:

```
switch(button) {
    case "next":
        window.location="next.html";
        break;
    case "previous":
        window.location="prev.html";
        break;
    case "home":
        window.location="home.html";
        break;
    case "back":
        window.location="menu.html";
        break;
    default:
        window.alert("Wrong button.");
}
```

The switch statement has several components:

▶ The initial switch statement. This statement includes the value to test (in this case, button) in parentheses.

▶ Braces ({ and }) enclose the contents of the switch statement, similar to a function or an if statement.

▶ One or more case statements. Each of these statements specifies a value to compare with the value specified in the switch statement. If the values match, the statements after the case statement are executed. Otherwise, the next case is tried.

▶ The break statement is used to end each case. This skips to the end of the switch. If break is not included, statements in multiple cases might be executed whether they match or not.

▶ Optionally, the default case can be included and followed by one or more statements that are executed if none of the other cases were matched.

By the Way

You can use multiple statements after each case statement within the switch structure. You don't need to enclose them in braces. If the case matches, the JavaScript interpreter executes statements until it encounters a break or the next case.

Using for Loops

Loops are useful any time you need a section of code to execute more than once. The for keyword is the first tool to consider for creating loops. A for loop typically uses a variable (called a *counter* or an *index*) to keep track of how many times the loop has executed, and it stops when the counter reaches a certain number. A basic for statement looks like this:

```
for (var = 1; var < 10; var++) {
```

There are three parameters to the for loop, separated by semicolons:

- ▶ The first parameter (var = 1 in the example) specifies a variable and assigns an initial value to it. This is called the *initial expression* because it sets up the initial state for the loop.

- ▶ The second parameter (var < 10 in the example) is a condition that must remain true to keep the loop running. This is called the *condition* of the loop.

- ▶ The third parameter (var++ in the example) is a statement that executes with each iteration of the loop. This is called the *increment expression* because it is typically used to increment the counter. The increment expression executes at the end of each loop iteration.

After the three parameters are specified, a left brace ({) is used to signal the beginning of a block. A right brace (}) is used at the end of the block. All the statements between the braces will be executed with each iteration of the loop.

The parameters for a for loop may sound a bit confusing, but once you're used to it, you'll use for loops frequently. Here is a simple example of this type of loop:

```
for (i=0; i<10; i++) {
   document.write("This is line " + i + "<br>");
}
```

These statements define a loop that uses the variable i, initializes it with the value of zero, and loops as long as the value of i is less than 10. The increment expression, i++, adds one to the value of i with each iteration of the loop. Because this happens at the end of the loop, the output will list the numbers zero through nine.

When a loop includes only a single statement between the braces, as in this example, you can omit the braces if you want. The following statement defines the same loop without braces:

```
for (i=0; i<10; i++)
   document.write("This is line " + i + "<br>");
```

It's a good style convention to use braces with all loops whether they contain one statement or many. This makes it easy to add statements to the loop later without causing syntax errors.

The loop in this example contains a document.write statement that will be repeatedly executed. To see just what this loop does, you can add it to a <script> section of an HTML document as shown in Listing 7.3.

LISTING 7.3   A Loop Using the for Keyword

```html
<html>
<head>
<title>Using a for Loop</title>
</head>
<body>
<h1>"for" Loop Example</h1>
<p>The following is the output of the
<b>for</b> loop:</p>
<script language="JavaScript" type="text/javascript">
for (i=1;i<10;i++) {
   document.write("This is line " + i + "<br>");
}
</script>
</body>
</html>
```

This example displays a message with the loop's counter during each iteration. The output of Listing 7.3 is shown in Figure 7.2.

Notice that the loop was only executed nine times. This is because the conditional is i<10. When the counter (i) is incremented to 10, the expression is no longer true. If you need the loop to count to 10, you can change the conditional; either i<=10 or i<11 will work fine.

You might notice that the variable name i is often used as the counter in loops. This is a programming tradition that began with an ancient language called Forth. There's no need for you to follow this tradition, but it is a good idea to use one consistent variable for counters. (To learn more about Forth, see the Forth Interest Group's website at www.forth.org.)

The structure of the for loop in JavaScript is based on Java, which in turn is based on C. Although it is traditionally used to count from one number to another, you can use just about any statement for the initialization, condition, and increment. However, there's usually a better way to do other types of loops with the while keyword, described in the next section.

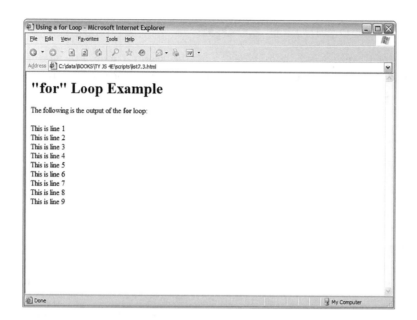

FIGURE 7.2
The results of
the for loop
example.

Using while **Loops**

Another keyword for loops in JavaScript is while. Unlike for loops, while loops don't necessarily use a variable to count. Instead, they execute as long as a condition is true. In fact, if the condition starts out as false, the statements won't execute at all.

The while statement includes the condition in parentheses, and it is followed by a block of statements within braces, just like a for loop. Here is a simple while loop:

```
while (total < 10) {
   n++;
   total += values[n];
}
```

This loop uses a counter, n, to iterate through the values array. Rather than stopping at a certain count, however, it stops when the total of the values reaches 10.

You might have noticed that you could have done the same thing with a for loop:

```
for (n=0;total < 10; n++) {
   total += values[n];
}
```

As a matter of fact, the for loop is nothing more than a special kind of while loop that handles an initialization and an increment for you. You can generally use while for any loop. However, it's best to choose whichever type of loop makes the most sense for the job, or that takes the least amount of typing.

Using do...while **Loops**

JavaScript 1.2 introduced a third type of loop: the do...while loop. This type of loop is similar to an ordinary while loop, with one difference: The condition is tested at the *end* of the loop rather than the beginning. Here is a typical do...while loop:

```
do {
    n++;
    total += values[n];
}
while (total < 10);
```

As you've probably noticed, this is basically an upside-down version of the previous while example. There is one difference: With the do loop, the condition is tested at the end of the loop. This means that the statements in the loop will always be executed at least once, even if the condition is never true.

> As with the for and while loops, the do loop can include a single statement without braces, or a number of statements enclosed in braces.

Working with Loops

Although you can use simple for and while loops for straightforward tasks, there are some considerations you should make when using more complicated loops. In the next sections, we'll look at infinite loops and the break and continue statements, which give you more control over your loops.

Creating an Infinite Loop

The for and while loops give you quite a bit of control over the loop. In some cases, this can cause problems if you're not careful. For example, look at the following loop code:

```
while (i < 10) {
    n++;
    values[n] = 0;
}
```

There's a mistake in this example. The condition of the while loop refers to the i variable, but that variable doesn't actually change during the loop. This creates an *infinite loop*. The loop will continue executing until the user stops it, or until it generates an error of some kind.

Infinite loops can't always be stopped by the user, except by quitting the browser—and some loops can even prevent the browser from quitting, or cause a crash.

Obviously, infinite loops are something to avoid. They can also be difficult to spot because JavaScript won't give you an error that actually tells you there is an infinite loop. Thus, each time you create a loop in a script, you should be careful to make sure there's a way out.

> Depending on the browser version in use, an infinite loop might even make the browser stop responding to the user. Be sure you provide an escape route from infinite loops, and save your script before you test it just in case.

By the Way

Occasionally, you might want to create an infinite loop deliberately. This might include situations when you want your program to execute until the user stops it, or if you are providing an escape route with the `break` statement, which is introduced in the next section. Here's an easy way to create an infinite loop:

```
while (true) {
```

Because the value `true` is the conditional, this loop will always find its condition to be true.

Escaping from a Loop

There is one way out of an infinite loop. You can use the `break` statement during a loop to exit it immediately and continue with the first statement after the loop. Here is a simple example of the use of `break`:

```
while (true) {
   n++;
   if (values[n] == 1) break;
}
```

Although the `while` statement is set up as an infinite loop, the `if` statement checks the corresponding value of an array. If it finds a value of 1, it exits the loop.

When the JavaScript interpreter encounters a `break` statement, it skips the rest of the loop and continues the script with the first statement after the right brace at the loop's end. You can use the `break` statement in any type of loop, whether infinite or not. This provides an easy way to exit if an error occurs, or if another condition is met.

Continuing a Loop

One more statement is available to help you control the execution of statements in a loop. The `continue` statement skips the rest of the loop but, unlike `break`, it continues with the next iteration of the loop. Here is a simple example:

```
for (i=1; i<21; i++) {
   if (score[i]==0) continue;
   document.write("Student number ",i, " Score: ", score[i], "\n");
}
```

This script uses a `for` loop to print out scores for 20 students, stored in the `score` array. The `if` statement is used to check for scores with a value of 0. The script assumes that a score of 0 means that the student didn't take the test, so it continues the loop without printing that score.

Looping Through Object Properties

A third type of loop is available in JavaScript. The `for...in` loop is not as flexible as an ordinary `for` or `while` loop. Instead, it is specifically designed to perform an operation on each property of an object.

For example, the `navigator` object contains properties that describe the user's browser, as you'll learn in Hour 15, "Unobtrusive Scripting." You can use `for...in` to display this object's properties:

```
for (i in navigator) {
   document.write("property: " + i);
   document.write(" value: " + navigator[i] + "<br>");
}
```

Like an ordinary `for` loop, this type of loop uses an index variable (i in the example). For each iteration of the loop, the variable is set to the next property of the object. This makes it easy when you need to check or modify each of an object's properties.

▼   **Try It Yourself**

Working with Arrays and Loops

To apply your knowledge of loops, you will now create a script that deals with arrays using loops. As you progress through this script, try to imagine how difficult it would be without JavaScript's looping features.

This simple script will prompt the user for a series of names. After all of the names have been entered, it will display the list of names in a numbered list. To begin the script, initialize some variables:

```
names = new Array();
i = 0;
```

The names array will store the names the user enters. You don't know how many names will be entered, so you don't need to specify a dimension for the array. The i variable will be used as a counter in the loops.

Next, use the prompt statement to prompt the user for a series of names. Use a loop to repeat the prompt for each name. You want the user to enter at least one name, so a do loop is ideal:

```
do {
    next = prompt("Enter the Next Name", "");
    if (next > " ") names[i] = next;
    i = i + 1;
    }
    while (next > " ");
```

If you're interested in making your scripts as short as possible, remember that you could use the increment (++) operator to combine the i = i + 1 statement with the previous statement: names[i++]=1.

Did you Know?

This loop prompts for a string called next. If a name was entered and isn't blank, it's stored as the next entry in the names array. The i counter is then incremented. The loop repeats until the user doesn't enter a name or clicks Cancel in the prompt dialog.

Next, your script can display the number of names that was entered:

```
document.write("<h2>" + (names.length) + " names entered.</h2>");
```

This statement displays the length property of the names array, surrounded by level 2 heading tags for emphasis.

Next, the script should display all the names in the order they were entered. Because the names are in an array, the for...in loop is a good choice:

```
document.write("<ol>");
for (i in names) {
    document.write("<li>" + names[i] + "<br>");
}
document.write("</ol>");
```

Here you have a for...in loop that loops through the names array, assigning the counter i to each index in turn. The script then prints the name with a <li> tag as an item in an ordered list. Before and after the loop, the script prints beginning and ending <ol> tags.

You now have everything you need for a working script. Listing 7.4 shows the HTML file for this example, and Listing 7.5 shows the JavaScript file.

LISTING 7.4   **A Script to Prompt for Names and Display Them (HTML)**

```
<html>
<head>
<title>Loops Example</title>
</head>
<body>
<h1>Loop Example</h1>
<p>Enter a series of names. I will then
display them in a nifty numbered list.</p>
<script language="JavaScript" type="text/javascript"
src="loops.js">
</script>
</body>
</html>
```

LISTING 7.5   **A Script to Prompt for Names and Display Them (JavaScript)**

```
// create the array
names = new Array();
i = 0;
// loop and prompt for names
do {
    next = window.prompt("Enter the Next Name", "");
    if (next > " ") names[i] = next;
    i = i + 1;
    } while (next > " ");
document.write("<h2>" + (names.length) + " names entered.</h2>");
// display all of the names
document.write("<ol>");
for (i in names) {
    document.write("<li>" + names[i] + "<br>");
}
document.write("</ol>");
```

To try this example, save the JavaScript file as loops.js and then load the HTML document into a browser. You'll be prompted for one name at a time. Enter several names, and then click Cancel to indicate that you're finished. Figure 7.3 shows what the final results should look like in a browser.

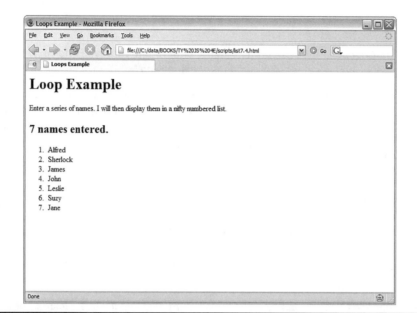

FIGURE 7.3
The output of
the names
example, as
shown by
Firefox.

Summary

In this hour, you've learned two ways to control the flow of your scripts. First, you learned how to use the `if` statement to evaluate conditional expressions and react to them. You also learned a shorthand form of conditional expression using the `?` operator, and the `switch` statement for working with multiple conditions.

You also learned about JavaScript's looping capabilities using `for`, `while`, and other loops, and how to control loops further using the `break` and `continue` statements. Lastly, you looked at the `for...in` loop for working with each property of an object.

In the next hour, you'll look at JavaScript's built-in functions, another essential tool for creating your own scripts. You'll also learn about third-party libraries that enable you to create complex effects with simple scripts.

Q&A

Q. *What happens if I compare two items of different data types (for example, a number and a string) in a conditional expression?*

A. The JavaScript interpreter does its best to make the values a common format and compare them. In this case, it would convert them both to strings before comparing. In JavaScript 1.3 and later, you can use the special equality operator === to compare two values and their types—using this operator, the expression will be true only if the expressions have the same value *and* the same data type.

Q. *Why would I use switch* if *using* if *and* else *is just as simple?*

A. Either one works, so it's your choice. Personally, I find switch statements confusing and prefer to use if. Your choice might also depend on what other programming languages you're familiar with because some support switch and others don't.

Q. *Why don't I get a friendly error message if I accidentally use = instead of ==?*

A. In some cases, this will result in an error. However, the incorrect version often appears to be a correct statement. For example, in the statement if (a=1), the variable a will be assigned the value 1. The if statement is considered true, and the value of a is lost.

Q. *It seems like I could use a* for *loop to replace any of the other loop methods (*while*,* do*, and so on). Why so many choices?*

A. You're right. In most cases, a for loop will work, and you can do all your loops that way if you want. For that matter, you can use while to replace a for loop. You can use whichever looping method makes the most sense for your application.

Quiz Questions

Test your knowledge of JavaScript conditions and loops by answering the following questions.

1. Which of the following operators means "is not equal to" in JavaScript?

    a. !

    b. !=

    c. <>

2. What does the `switch` statement do?

    a. Tests a variable for a number of different values

    b. Turns a variable on or off

    c. Makes ordinary `if` statements longer and more confusing

3. Which type of JavaScript loop checks the condition at the *end* of the loop?

    a. `for`

    b. `while`

    c. `do…while`

4. Within a loop, what does the `break` statement do?

    a. Crashes the browser

    b. Starts the loop over

    c. Escapes the loop entirely

5. The statement `while (3==3)` is an example of

    a. A typographical error

    b. An infinite loop

    c. An illegal JavaScript statement

Quiz Answers

1. b. The `!=` operator means *is not equal to.*

2. a. The `switch` statement can test the same variable or expression for a number of different values.

3. c. The `do…while` loop uses a condition at the end of the loop.

4. c. The `break` statement escapes the loop.

5. b. Because the condition `(3==3)` will always be true, this statement creates an infinite loop.

Exercises

To further explore the JavaScript features you learned about in this hour, you can perform the following exercises:

▶ Modify Listing 7.4 to sort the names in alphabetical order before displaying them. You can use the sort method of the Array object, described in Hour 5, "Using Variables, Strings, and Arrays."

▶ Modify Listing 7.4 to prompt for exactly 10 names. What happens if you click the Cancel button instead of entering a name?

HOUR 8

Using Built-in Functions and Libraries

What You'll Learn in This Hour:

▶ Using the Math object's methods
▶ Using the Date object to work with dates
▶ Creating an application using JavaScript math functions
▶ Using with to work with objects
▶ How third-party libraries make scripting easier
▶ Using third-party libraries in your scripts

You've nearly reached the end of Part II! In this hour, you'll learn the basics of objects in JavaScript and the details of using the Math and Date objects. You'll also look at some third-party libraries, which enable you to achieve amazing JavaScript effects with a few lines of code.

Using the Math Object

The Math object is a built-in JavaScript object that includes math constants and functions. You don't need to create a Math object; it exists automatically in any JavaScript program. The Math object's properties represent mathematical constants, and its methods are mathematical functions.

Rounding and Truncating

Three of the most useful methods of the Math object enable you to round decimal values up and down:

▶ `Math.ceil()` rounds a number up to the next integer.

▶ `Math.floor()` rounds a number down to the next integer.

▶ `Math.round()` rounds a number to the nearest integer.

All of these take the number to be rounded as their single parameter. You might notice one thing missing: the capability to round to a decimal place, such as for dollar amounts. Fortunately, you can easily simulate this. Here is a simple function that rounds numbers to two decimal places:

```
function round(num) {
    return Math.round(num * 100) / 100;
}
```

This function multiplies the value by 100 to move the decimal, and then rounds the number to the nearest integer. Finally, the value is divided by 100 to restore the decimal to its original position.

Generating Random Numbers

One of the most commonly used methods of the `Math` object is the `Math.random()` method, which generates a random number. This method doesn't require any parameters. The number it returns is a random decimal number between zero and one.

You'll usually want a random number between one and a value. You can do this with a general-purpose random number function. The following is a function that generates random numbers between one and the parameter you send it:

```
function rand(num) {
    return Math.floor(Math.random() * num) + 1;
}
```

This function multiplies a random number by the value specified in the num parameter, and then converts it to an integer between one and the number by using the `Math.floor()` method.

Other Math Functions

The `Math` object includes many functions beyond those you've looked at here. For example, `Math.sin()` and `Math.cos()` calculate sines and cosines. The `Math` object also includes properties for various mathematical constants, such as `Math.PI`. See Appendix D, "JavaScript Quick Reference," for a complete list of math functions and constants.

Working with Math Functions

The `Math.random()` method generates a random number between 0 and 1. However, it's very difficult for a computer to generate a truly random number. (It's also hard for a human being to do so—that's why dice were invented.)

Today's computers do reasonably well at generating random numbers, but just how good is JavaScript's `Math.random` function? One way to test it is to generate many random numbers and calculate the average of all of them.

In theory, the average should be somewhere near .5, halfway between 0 and 1. The more random values you generate, the closer the average should get to this middle ground.

As an example of the use of the `Math` object's methods, you can create a script that tests JavaScript's random number function. To do this, you'll generate 5,000 random numbers and calculate their average.

Rather than typing it in, you can download and try this hour's example at this book's website.

Did you Know?

In case you skipped Hour 7, "Controlling Flow with Conditions and Loops," and are getting out your calculator, don't worry—you'll use a loop to generate the random numbers. You'll be surprised how fast JavaScript can do this.

To begin your script, you will initialize a variable called `total`. This variable will store a running total of all of the random values, so it's important that it starts at 0:

```
total = 0;
```

Next, begin a loop that will execute 5,000 times. Use a `for` loop because you want it to execute a fixed number of times:

```
for (i=1; i<=5000; i++) {
```

Within the loop, you will need to create a random number and add its value to `total`. Here are the statements that do this and continue with the next iteration of the loop:

```
    num = Math.random();
    total += num;
}
```

Depending on the speed of your computer, it might take a few seconds to generate those 5,000 random numbers. Just to be sure something is happening, the script will display a status message after each 1,000 numbers:

```
if (i % 1000 == 0)
   document.write("Generated " + i + " numbers...<br>");
```

By the Way

The % symbol in the previous code is the *modulo operator*, which gives you the remainder after dividing one number by another. Here it is used to find even multiples of 1,000.

The final part of your script will calculate the average by dividing `total` by 5,000. Your script can also round the average to three decimal places, using the trick you learned earlier in this hour:

```
average = total / 5000;
average = Math.round(average * 1000) / 1000;
document.write("<H2>Average of 5000 numbers: " + average + "</H2>");
```

To test this script and see just how random those numbers are, combine the complete script with an HTML document and <script> tags. Listing 8.1 shows the complete random number testing script.

LISTING 8.1 A Script to Test JavaScript's Random Number Function

```
<html>
<head>
<title>Math Example</title>
</head>
<body>
<h1>Math Example</h1>
<p>How random are JavaScript's random numbers?
Let's generate 5000 of them and find out.</p>
<script language="JavaScript" type="text/javascript">
total = 0;
for (i=1; i<=5000; i++) {
    num = Math.random();
    total += num;
    if (i % 1000 == 0)
        document.write("Generated " + i + " numbers...<br>");
}
average = total / 5000;
average = Math.round(average * 1000) / 1000;
document.write("<H2>Average of 5000 numbers: " + average + "</H2>");
</script>
</body>
</html>
```

To test the script, load the HTML document into a browser. After a short delay, you should see a result. If it's close to .5, the numbers are reasonably random. My result was .502, as shown in Figure 8.1.

The average you've used here is called an *arithmetic mean*. This type of average isn't a perfect way to test randomness. Actually, all it tests is the distribution of the numbers above and below .5. For example, if the numbers turned out to be 2,500 .4s and 2,500 .6s, the average would be a perfect .5—but they wouldn't be very random numbers. (Thankfully, JavaScript's random numbers don't have this problem.)

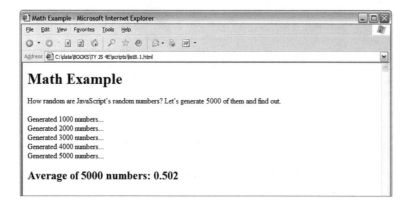

FIGURE 8.1
The random number testing script in action.

Using the with **Keyword**

The with keyword is one you haven't seen before. You can use it to make JavaScript programming easier—or at least easier to type.

The with keyword specifies an object, and it is followed by a block of statements enclosed in braces. For each statement in the block, any properties you mention without specifying an object are assumed to be for that object.

As an example, suppose you have a string called lastname. You can use with to perform string operations on it without specifying the name of the string every time:

```
with (lastname) {
   window.alert("length of last name: " + length);
   capname = toUpperCase();
}
```

In this example, the length property and the toUpperCase method refer to the lastname string, although it is only specified once with the with keyword.

Obviously, the with keyword only saves a bit of typing in situations like this. However, you might find it more useful when you're dealing with a DOM object throughout a large procedure, or when you are using a built-in object, such as the Math object, repeatedly.

Working with Dates

The Date object is a built-in JavaScript object that enables you to conveniently work with dates and times. You can create a Date object anytime you need to store a date, and use the Date object's methods to work with the date.

You encountered one example of a Date object in Hour 2, "Creating Simple Scripts," with the time/date script. The Date object has no properties. To set or obtain values from a Date object, you must use the methods described in the next section.

> JavaScript dates are stored as the number of milliseconds since midnight, January 1, 1970. This date is called the *epoch*. Dates before 1970 weren't allowed in early versions, but are now represented by negative numbers.

Creating a Date Object

You can create a Date object using the new keyword. You can also optionally specify the date to store in the object when you create it. You can use any of the following formats:

```
birthday = new Date();
birthday = new Date("June 20, 2003 08:00:00");
birthday = new Date(6, 20, 2003);
birthday = new Date(6, 20, 2003, 8, 0, 0);
```

You can choose any of these formats, depending on which values you wish to set. If you use no parameters, as in the first example, the current date is stored in the object. You can then set the values using the set methods, described in the next section.

Setting Date Values

A variety of set methods enable you to set components of a Date object to values:

- ▶ setDate() sets the day of the month.

- ▶ setMonth() sets the month. JavaScript numbers the months from 0 to 11, starting with January (0).

- ▶ setFullYear() sets the year.

- ▶ setTime() sets the time (and the date) by specifying the number of milliseconds since January 1, 1970.

- ▶ setHours(), setMinutes(), and setSeconds() set the time.

As an example, the following statement sets the year of a `Date` object called `holiday` to 2003:

```
holiday.setFullYear(2003);
```

Reading `Date` **Values**

You can use the `get` methods to get values from a `Date` object. This is the only way to obtain these values, because they are not available as properties. Here are the available `get` methods for dates:

- ▶ `getDate()` gets the day of the month.

- ▶ `getMonth()` gets the month.

- ▶ `getFullYear()` gets the year.

- ▶ `getTime()` gets the time (and the date) as the number of milliseconds since January 1, 1970.

- ▶ `getHours()`, `getMinutes()`, `getSeconds()`, and `getMilliseconds()` get the components of the time.

Along with `setFullYear` and `getFullYear`, which require four-digit years, JavaScript includes `setYear` and `getYear` methods, which use two-digit year values. You should always use the four-digit version to avoid Year 2000 issues.

By the
Way

Working with Time Zones

Finally, a few functions are available to help your `Date` objects work with local time values and time zones:

- ▶ `getTimeZoneOffset()` gives you the local time zone's offset from UTC (Coordinated Universal Time, based on the old Greenwich Mean Time standard). In this case, *local* refers to the location of the browser. (Of course, this only works if the user has set his or her system clock accurately.)

- ▶ `toUTCString()` converts the date object's time value to text, using UTC. This method was introduced in JavaScript 1.2 to replace the `toGMTString` method, which still works but should be avoided.

- ▶ `toLocalString()` converts the date object's time value to text, using local time.

Along with these basic functions, JavaScript 1.2 and later include UTC versions of several of the functions described previously. These are identical to the regular commands, but work with UTC instead of local time:

▶ `getUTCDate()` gets the day of the month in UTC time.

▶ `getUTCDay()` gets the day of the week in UTC time.

▶ `getUTCFullYear()` gets the four-digit year in UTC time.

▶ `getUTCMonth()` returns the month of the year in UTC time.

▶ `getUTCHours()`, `getUTCMinutes()`, `getUTCSeconds()`, and `getUTCMilliseconds()` return the components of the time in UTC.

▶ `setUTCDate()`, `setUTCFullYear()`, `setUTCMonth()`, `setUTCHours()`, `setUTCMinutes()`, `setUTCSeconds()`, and `setUTCMilliseconds()` set the time in UTC.

Converting Between Date Formats

Two special methods of the `Date` object allow you to convert between date formats. Instead of using these methods with a `Date` object you created, you use them with the built-in object `Date` itself. These include the following:

▶ `Date.parse()` converts a date string, such as `June 20, 1996`, to a `Date` object (number of milliseconds since 1/1/1970).

▶ `Date.UTC()` does the opposite. It converts a `Date` object value (number of milliseconds) to a UTC (GMT) time.

Using Third-Party Libraries

When you use JavaScript's built-in `Math` and `Date` functions, JavaScript does most of the work—you don't have to figure out how to convert dates between formats or calculate a cosine. Third-party libraries are not included with JavaScript, but they serve a similar purpose—enabling you to do complicated things with only a small amount of code.

Using one of these libraries is usually as simple as copying one or more files to your site and including a `<script>` tag in your document to load the library. Several popular JavaScript libraries are discussed in the following sections.

JavaScript libraries are a relatively new phenomenon, and new libraries are appearing regularly. See this book's website for an updated list of libraries.

Did you Know?

Prototype

Prototype, created by Sam Stephenson, is a JavaScript library that simplifies tasks such as working with DOM objects, dealing with data in forms, and remote scripting (AJAX). By including a single `prototype.js` file in your document, you have access to many improvements to basic JavaScript.

For example, you've used the `document.getElementById` method to obtain the DOM object for an element within a web page. Prototype includes an improved version of this in the `$()` function. Not only is it easier to type, but it is also more sophisticated than the built-in function and supports multiple objects.

Adding Prototype to your pages requires only one file, `prototype.js`, and one `<script>` tag:

```
<script type="text/javascript" src="prototype.js"> </script>
```

Prototype is free, open-source software. You can download it from its official website at http://prototype.conio.net. Prototype is also built into the Ruby on Rails framework for the server-side language Ruby—see http://www.rubyonrails.com/ for more information.

By the Way

Script.aculo.us

By the end of this book, you'll learn to do some impressive things with JavaScript—for example, animating an object within a page. The code for a task like this is complex, but you can also include effects in your pages using a prebuilt library. This enables you to use impressive effects with only a few lines of code.

Script.aculo.us by Thomas Fuchs is one such library. It includes functions to simplify drag-and-drop tasks, such as rearranging lists of items. It also includes a number of Combination Effects, which enable you to use highlighting and animated transitions within your pages. For example, a new section of the page can be briefly highlighted in yellow to get the user's attention, or a portion of the page can fade out or slide off the screen.

After you've included the appropriate files, using effects is as easy as using any of JavaScript's built-in methods. For example, the following statements use Script.aculo.us to fade out an element of the page with the `id` value `test`:

```
obj = document.getElementById("test");
new Effect.Fade(obj);
```

Script.aculo.us is built on the Prototype framework described in the previous section, and includes all of the functions of Prototype, so you could also simplify this further by using the $ function:

```
new Effect.Fade($("test"));
```

You will create a script that demonstrates several Script.aculo.us effects in the Try It Yourself section later this hour.

AJAX Frameworks

AJAX (Asynchronous JavaScript and XML), also known as *remote scripting*, enables JavaScript to communicate with a program running on the web server. This enables JavaScript to do things that were traditionally not possible, such as dynamically loading information from a database or storing data on a server without refreshing a page.

Unfortunately, AJAX requires some complex scripting, particularly because the methods you use to communicate with the server vary depending on the browser in use. Fortunately, many libraries have been created to fill the need for a simple way to use AJAX.

The Prototype library, described previously, includes AJAX features. There are also many dedicated AJAX libraries. One of the most popular is SAJAX (Simple AJAX), an open-source toolkit that makes it easy to use AJAX to communicate with PHP, Perl, and other languages from JavaScript. Visit the SAJAX website for details at http://www.modernmethod.com/sajax.

See Hour 17, "AJAX: Remote Scripting," for examples of remote scripting, with and without using third-party libraries.

Other Libraries

There are many more JavaScript libraries out there, and more are appearing all of the time as JavaScript is taken more seriously as an application language. Here are some more libraries you might want to explore:

▶ Dojo (http://www.dojotoolkit.org/) is an open-source toolkit that adds power to JavaScript to simplify building applications and user interfaces. It adds features ranging from extra string and math functions to animation and AJAX.

► The Yahoo! UI Library (http://developer.yahoo.net/yui/) was developed by
   Yahoo! and made available to everyone under an open-source license. It
   includes features for animation, DOM features, event management, and easy-
   to-use user interface elements such as calendars and sliders.

► MochiKit (http://mochikit.com/) is a lightweight library that adds features for
   working with the DOM, CSS colors, string formatting, and AJAX. It also supports a nice logging mechanism for debugging your scripts.

Try It Yourself   ▼

Adding Effects with a Library

To see how simple it is to use an external library, you will now create an example
script that includes the Script.aculo.us library and use event handlers to demonstrate several of the available effects.

> This example was created using version 1.5.1 of the Script.aculo.us library. It   **_Watch_**
> should work with later versions, but the library might have changed since this was   _Out!_
> written. If you have trouble, you might need to use this specific version.

Downloading the Library

To use the library, you will need to download it and copy the files you need to the
same folder where you will store your script. You can download the library from the
Script.aculo.us website at http://script.aculo.us/downloads.

The download is available as a Zip file. Inside the Zip file you will find a folder
called `scriptaculous-js-x.x.x`. You will need the following files from the folders
under this folder:

► `prototype.js` (the Prototype library) from the `lib` folder

► `effects.js` (the effects functions) from the `src` folder

Copy both of these files to a folder on your computer, and be sure to create your
demonstration script in the same folder.

> The Script.aculo.us download includes many other files, and you can include the   **_By the_**
> entire library if you intend to use all of its features. For this example, you only   _Way_
> need the two files described here.

Including the Files

To add the library to your HTML document, simply use `<script>` tags to include the two JavaScript files you copied from the download:

```
<script type="text/javascript" src="prototype.js"> </script>
<script type="text/javascript" src="effects.js"> </script>
```

If you include these statements as the first things in the `<head>` section of your document, the library functions will be available to other scripts or event handlers anywhere in the page.

Using Effects

After you have included the library, you simply need to include a bit of JavaScript to trigger the effects. We will use a section of the page wrapped in a `<div>` tag with the id value `test` to demonstrate the effects. Each effect is triggered by a simple event handler on a button. For example, this code defines the Fade Out button:

```
<input type="button" value="Fade Out"
    onClick="new Effect.Fade($('test'))">
```

This uses the $ function built into Prototype to obtain the object for the element with the id value `test`, and then passes it to the `Effect.Fade()` function built into Script.aculo.us.

Did you Know?

> This example will demonstrate six effects: `Fade`, `Appear`, `SlideUp`, `SlideDown`, `Highlight`, and `Shake`. There are more than 16 effects in the library, plus methods for supporting Drag and Drop and other features. See http://script.aculo.us for details.

Building the Script

After you have included the libraries, you can combine them with event handlers and some example text to create a complete demonstration of Script.aculo.us effects. The complete HTML document for this example is shown in Listing 8.2.

LISTING 8.2   The Complete Library Effects Example

```
<html>
<head>
<title>Testing script.aculo.us effects</title>
<script type="text/javascript" src="prototype.js"> </script>
<script type="text/javascript" src="effects.js"> </script>
</head>
<body">
<h1>Testing script.aculo.us Effects</h1>
<form name="form1">
```

LISTING 8.2   Continued

```
<input type="button" value="Fade Out"
    onClick="new Effect.Fade($('test'))">
<input type="button" value="Fade In"
    onClick="new Effect.Appear($('test'))">
<input type="button" value="Slide Up"
    onClick="new Effect.SlideUp($('test'))">
<input type="button" value="Slide Down"
    onClick="new Effect.SlideDown($('test'))">
<input type="button" value="Highlight"
    onClick="new Effect.Highlight($('test'))">
<input type="button" value="Shake"
    onClick="new Effect.Shake($('test'))">
</form>
<div id="test"
    style="background-color:#CCC; margin:20px; padding:10px;">
<h2>Testing Effects</h2>
<hr>
<p>This section of the document is within a &lt;div&gt; element
with the <b>id</b> value <b>test</b>. The event handlers on the
buttons above send this object to the
<a href="http://script.aculo.us/">script.aculo.us</a> library
to perform effects. Click the buttons to see the effects.
</p>
</div>
</body>
</html>
```

This document starts with two <script> tags to include the library's files. The effects are triggered by the event handlers defined for each of the six buttons. The <div> section at the end defines the test element that will be used to demonstrate the effects.

To try this example, make sure the prototype.js and effects.js files from Script.aculo.us are stored in the same folder as your script, and then load the HTML file into a browser. The display should look like Figure 8.2, and you can use the six buttons at the top of the page to trigger effects.

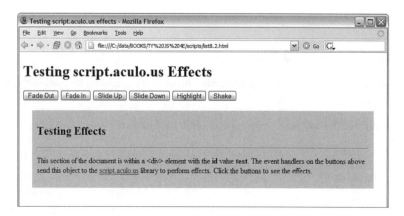

FIGURE 8.2
The library effects example as displayed by Firefox.

Summary

In this hour, you learned some specifics about the Math and Date objects built into JavaScript, and learned more than you ever wanted to know about random numbers. You also learned how third-party libraries can simplify your scripting, and you used a library to create special effects in a web page.

You've reached the end of Part II, which covered some basic building blocks of JavaScript programs. In Part III, you'll learn more about the Document Object Model, which contains objects that refer to various parts of the browser window and HTML document. This begins in Hour 9, "Responding to Events."

Q&A

Q. *The random numbers are generated so quickly I can't be sure it's happening at all. Is there a way to slow this process down?*

A. Yes. If you add one or more form fields to the example and use them to display the data as it is generated, you'll see a much slower result. It will still be done within a couple of seconds on a fast computer, though.

Q. *Can I use more than one third-party library in the same script?*

A. Yes, in theory: If the libraries are well written and designed not to interfere with each other, there should be no problem combining them. In practice, this will depend on the libraries you need and how they were written.

Q. *Can I build my own library to simplify scripting?*

A. Yes, as you deal with more complicated scripts, you'll find yourself using the same functions over and over. You can combine them into a library for your own use. This is as simple as creating a .js file.

Quiz Questions

Test your knowledge of JavaScript libraries and built-in functions by answering the following questions.

1. Which of the following objects *cannot* be used with the new keyword?

    a. Date

    b. Math

    c. String

2. How does JavaScript store dates in a `Date` object?

    a. The number of milliseconds since January 1, 1970

    b. The number of days since January 1, 1900

    c. The number of seconds since Netscape's public stock offering

3. What is the range of random numbers generated by the `Math.random` function?

    a. Between 1 and `100`

    b. Between 1 and the number of milliseconds since January 1, 1970

    c. Between `0` and 1

Quiz Answers

1. b. The `Math` object is static; you can't create a `Math` object.

2. a. Dates are stored as the number of milliseconds since January 1, 1970.

3. c. JavaScript's random numbers are between `0` and 1.

Exercises

To further explore the JavaScript features you learned about in this hour, you can perform the following exercises:

▶ Modify the random number script in Listing 8.1 to run three times, calculating a total of 15,000 random numbers, and display separate totals for each set of 5,000. (You'll need to use another `for` loop that encloses most of the script.)

▶ Visit the Script.aculo.us page at http://script.aculo.us/ to find the complete list of effects. Modify Listing 8.2 to add buttons for one or more additional effects.

PART III:

Learning More About the DOM

HOUR 9

Responding to Events

What You'll Learn in This Hour:

▶ How event handlers work

▶ How event handlers relate to objects

▶ Creating an event handler

▶ Testing an event handler

▶ Detecting mouse actions

▶ Detecting keyboard actions

▶ Intercepting events with a special handler

▶ Adding friendly link descriptions to a web page

In your experience with JavaScript so far, most of the scripts you've written have executed in a calm, orderly fashion, moving from the first statement to the last.

In this hour, you'll learn to use the wide variety of event handlers supported by JavaScript. Rather than executing in order, scripts using event handlers can interact directly with the user. You'll use event handlers in just about every script you write in the rest of this book.

Understanding Event Handlers

As you learned in Hour 3, "Getting Started with JavaScript Programming," JavaScript programs don't have to execute in order. You also learned they can detect *events* and react to them. Events are things that happen to the browser—the user clicking a button, the mouse pointer moving, or a web page or image loading from the server.

A wide variety of events enable your scripts to respond to the mouse, the keyboard, and other circumstances. Events are the key method JavaScript uses to make web documents interactive.

The script that you use to detect and respond to an event is called an *event handler.* Event handlers are among the most powerful features of JavaScript. Luckily, they're also among the easiest features to learn and use—often, a useful event handler requires only a single statement.

Objects and Events

As you learned in Hour 4, "Working with the Document Object Model (DOM)," JavaScript uses a set of objects to store information about the various parts of a web page—buttons, links, images, windows, and so on. An event can often happen in more than one place (for example, the user could click any one of the links on the page), so each event is associated with an object.

Each event has a name. For example, the onMouseOver event occurs when the mouse pointer moves over an object on the page. When the pointer moves over a particular link, the onMouseOver event is sent to that link's event handler, if it has one.

By the Way

> Notice the strange capitalization on the onMouseOver keyword. This is the standard notation for event handlers. The on is always lowercase, and each word in the event name is capitalized.

Creating an Event Handler

You don't need the <script> tag to define an event handler. Instead, you can add an event handler attribute to an individual HTML tag. For example, here is a link that includes an onMouseOver event handler:

```
<a href="http://www.jsworkshop.com/"
   onMouseOver="window.alert('You moved over the link.');">
Click here</a>
```

Note that this is all one <a> tag, although it's split into multiple lines. This specifies a statement to be used as the onMouseOver event handler for the link. This statement displays an alert message when the mouse moves over the link.

By the Way

> The previous example uses single quotation marks to surround the text. This is necessary in an event handler because double quotation marks are used to surround the event handler itself. (You can also use single quotation marks to surround the event handler and double quotes within the script statements.)

You can use JavaScript statements like the previous one in an event handler, but if you need more than one statement, it's a good idea to use a function instead. Just define the function in the header of the document, and then call the function as the event handler like this:

```
<a href="#bottom" onMouseOver="DoIt();">Move the mouse over this link.</a>
```

This example calls a function called DoIt() when the user moves the mouse over the link. Using a function is convenient because you can use longer, more readable JavaScript routines as event handlers. You'll use a longer function to handle events in the "Try It Yourself: Adding Link Descriptions to a Web Page" section of this hour.

> For simple event handlers, you can use two statements if you separate them with a semicolon. However, in most cases it's easier to use a function to perform the statements.

Defining Event Handlers with JavaScript

Rather than specifying an event handler in an HTML document, you can use JavaScript to assign a function as an event handler. This allows you to set event handlers conditionally, turn them on and off, and change the function that handles an event dynamically.

> Setting up event handlers this way is also a good practice in general: It allows you to use an external JavaScript file to define the function and set up the event, keeping the JavaScript code completely separate from the HTML file.

To define an event handler in this way, you first define a function, and then assign the function as an event handler. Event handlers are stored as properties of the document object or another object that can receive an event. For example, these statements define a function called mousealert(), and then assign it as the onMouseDown event handler for the document:

```
function mousealert() {
    alert ("You clicked the mouse!");
}
document.onmousedown = mousealert;
```

You can use this technique to set up an event handler for any HTML element, but an additional step is required: You must first find the object corresponding to the element. To do this, use the document.getElementById() function. First, define an element in the HTML document and specify an id attribute:

```
<a href="http://www.google.com/" id="link1">
```

Next, in the JavaScript code, find the object and apply the event handler:

```
obj = document.getElementById("link1");
obj.onclick = MyFunction;
```

You can do this for any object as long as you've defined it with a unique id attribute in the HTML file. Using this technique, you can easily assign the same function to handle events for multiple objects without adding clutter to your HTML code. See the "Try It Yourself" section in this hour for an example of this technique.

Supporting Multiple Event Handlers

What if you want more than one thing to happen when you click on an element? For example, suppose you want two functions called update and display to both execute when a button is clicked. You can't assign two functions to the onclick property. One solution is to define a function that calls both functions:

```
function UpdateDisplay() {
    update();
    display();
}
```

This isn't always the ideal way to do things. For example, if you're using two third-party scripts and both of them want to add an onLoad event to the page, there should be a way to add both. The W3C DOM standard defines a function, addEventListener, for this purpose. This function defines a *listener* for a particular event and object, and you can add as many listener functions as you need.

Unfortunately, addEventListener is not supported by Internet Explorer (as of versions 6 and 7), so you have to use a different function, attachEvent, in that browser. See Hour 15, "Unobtrusive Scripting," for a function that combines these two for a cross-browser event-adding script.

Using the event Object

When an event occurs, you might need to know more about the event—for example, for a keyboard event, you need to know which key was pressed. The DOM includes an event object that provides this information.

To use the event object, you can pass it on to your event handler function. For example, this statement defines an onKeyPress event that passes the event object to a function:

```
<body onKeyPress="getkey(event);">
```

You can then define your function to accept the event as a parameter:

```
function getkey(e) {
...
}
```

In Mozilla-based browsers (Firefox and Netscape), an event object is automatically passed to the event handler function, so this will work even if you use JavaScript rather than HTML to define an event handler. In Internet Explorer, the most recent event is stored in the window.event object. The previous HTML example passes this object to the event handler function. If you define the event handler with JavaScript, this is not possible, so you need to use some code to find the correct object:

```
Function getkey(e) {
    if (!e) e=window.event;
...
}
```

This checks whether the e variable is already defined. If not, it gets the window.event object and stores it in e. This ensures that you have a valid event object in any browser.

Unfortunately, while both Internet Explorer and Mozilla-based browsers support event objects, they support different properties. One property that is the same in both browsers is event.type, the type of event. This is simply the name of the event, such as mouseover for an onMouseOver event, and keypress for an onKeyPress event. The following sections list some additional useful properties for each browser.

Internet Explorer event Properties

The following are some of the commonly used properties of the event object for Internet Explorer 4.0 and later:

▶ **event.button**—The mouse button that was pressed. This value is 1 for the left button and usually 2 for the right button.

▶ **event.clientX**—The x-coordinate (column, in pixels) where the event occurred.

▶ **event.clientY**—The y-coordinate (row, in pixels) where the event occurred.

▶ **event.altkey**—A flag that indicates whether the Alt key was pressed during the event.

▶ **event.ctrlkey**—Indicates whether the Ctrl key was pressed.

▶ **event.shiftkey**—Indicates whether the Shift key was pressed.

▶ **event.keyCode**—The key code (in Unicode) for the key that was pressed.

▶ **event.srcElement**—The object where the element occurred.

See the Try it Yourself section of this hour for an example that uses the srcElement property and Mozilla's `target` property for a cross-browser method of determining the object for an event.

Netscape and Firefox event Properties

The following are some of the commonly used properties of the event object for Netscape 4.0 and later:

▶ **event.modifiers**—Indicates which modifier keys (Shift, Ctrl, Alt, and so on) were held down during the event. This value is an integer that combines binary values representing the different keys.

▶ **event.pageX**—The x-coordinate of the event within the web page.

▶ **event.pageY**—The y-coordinate of the event within the web page.

▶ **event.which**—The keycode for keyboard events (in Unicode), or the button that was pressed for mouse events (It's best to use the cross-browser button property instead.)

▶ **event.button**—The mouse button that was pressed. This works just like Internet Explorer except that the left button's value is 0 and the right button's value is 2.

▶ **event.target**—The object where the element occurred.

The event.pageX and event.pageY properties are based on the top-left corner of the element where the event occurred, not always the exact position of the mouse pointer.

Using Mouse Events

The DOM includes a number of event handlers for detecting mouse actions. Your script can detect the movement of the mouse pointer and when a button is clicked, released, or both.

Over and Out

You've already seen the first and most common event handler, onMouseOver. This handler is called when the mouse pointer moves over a link or other object.

The onMouseOut handler is the opposite—it is called when the mouse pointer moves out of the object's border. Unless something strange happens, this always happens sometime after the onMouseOver event is called.

This handler is particularly useful if your script has made a change when the pointer moved over the object—for example, displaying a message in the status line or changing an image. You can use an onMouseOut handler to undo the action when the pointer moves away.

You'll use both onMouseOver and onMouseOut handlers in the "Try it Yourself: Adding Link Descriptions to a Web Page" section at the end of this hour.

> One of the most common uses for the onMouseOver and onMouseOut event handlers is to create *rollovers*—images that change when the mouse moves over them. You'll learn how to create these in Hour 19, "Using Graphics and Animation."

Did you Know?

Using the onMouseMove Event

The onMouseMove event occurs any time the mouse pointer moves. As you might imagine, this happens quite often—the event can trigger hundreds of times as the mouse pointer moves across a page.

Because of the large number of generated events, browsers don't support the onMouseMove event by default. To enable it for a page, you need to use *event capturing*. This is similar to the dynamic events technique you learned earlier in this hour, but requires an extra step for some older browsers.

The basic syntax to support this event, for both browsers, is to set a function as the onMouseMove handler for the document or another object. For example, this statement sets the onMouseMove handler for the document to a function called MoveHere, which must be defined in the same page:

```
document.onMouseMove=MoveHere;
```

Additionally, older versions of Netscape require that you specifically enable the event using the document.captureEvents method:

```
document.captureEvents(Event.MOUSEMOVE);
```

Ups and Downs (and Clicks)

You can also use events to detect when the mouse button is clicked. The basic event handler for this is onClick. This event handler is called when the mouse button is clicked while positioned over the appropriate object.

> The object in this case can be a link. It can also be a form element. You'll learn more about forms in Hour 11, "Getting Data with Forms."

For example, you can use the following event handler to display an alert when a link is clicked:

```
<a href="http://www.jsworkshop.com/"
onClick="alert('You are about to leave this site.');">Click Here</a>
```

In this case, the onClick event handler runs before the linked page is loaded into the browser. This is useful for making links conditional or displaying a disclaimer before launching the linked page.

If your onClick event handler returns the false value, the link will not be followed. For example, the following is a link that displays a confirmation dialog. If you click Cancel, the link is not followed; if you click OK, the new page is loaded:

```
<a href="http://www.jsworkshop.com/"
onClick="return(window.confirm('Are you sure?'));">
Click Here</a>
```

This example uses the return statement to enclose the event handler. This ensures that the false value that is returned when the user clicks Cancel is returned from the event handler, which prevents the link from being followed.

The onDblClick event handler is similar, but is only used if the user double-clicks on an object. Because links usually require only a single click, you could use this to make a link do two different things depending on the number of clicks. (Needless to say, this could be confusing.) You can also detect double-clicks on images and other objects.

To give you even more control of what happens when the mouse button is pressed, two more events are included:

- onMouseDown is used when the user presses the mouse button.
- onMouseUp is used when the user releases the mouse button.

These two events are the two halves of a mouse click. If you want to detect an entire click, use onClick. Use onMouseUp and onMouseDown to detect just one or the other.

To detect which mouse button is pressed, you can use the button property of the event object. This property is assigned the value 0 or 1 for the left button, and 2 for the right button. This property is assigned for onClick, onDblClick, onMouseUp, and onMouseDown events.

> Browsers don't normally detect onClick or onDblClick events for the right mouse button. If you want to detect the right button, onMouseDown is the most reliable way.

Watch Out!

As an example of these event handlers, you can create a script that displays information about mouse button events and determines which button is pressed. Listing 9.1 shows the mouse event script.

LISTING 9.1   The JavaScript file for the mouse click example.

```
function mousestatus(e) {
    if (!e) e = window.event;
    btn = e.button;
    whichone = (btn < 2) ? "Left" : "Right";
    message=e.type + " : " + whichone + "\n";
    document.form1.info.value += message;
}
obj=document.getElementById("testlink");
obj.onmousedown = mousestatus;
obj.onmouseup = mousestatus;
obj.onclick = mousestatus;
obj.ondblclick = mousestatus;
```

This script includes a function, mousestatus(), that detects mouse events. This function uses the button property of the event object to determine which button was pressed. It also uses the type property to display the type of event, since the function will be used to handle multiple event types.

After the function, the script finds the object for a link with the id attribute testlink and assigns its onmousedown, onmouseup, onclick, and ondblclick events to the mousestatus function.

Save this script as click.js. Next, you will need an HTML document to work with the script, shown in Listing 9.2.

LISTING 9.2   The HTML file for the mouse click example.

```
<html>
<head>
<title>Mouse click test</title>
</head>
<body>
<h1>Mouse Click Test</h1>
```

LISTING 9.2   Continued

```
<p>Click the mouse on the test link below. A message below
will indicate which button was clicked.</p>
<h2><a href="#" id="testlink">Test Link</a></h2>
<form name="form1">
<textarea rows="10" cols="70" name="info"></textarea>
</form>
<script language="javascript" type="text/javascript"
   src="click.js">
</script>
</body>
</html>
```

This file defines a test link with the `id` property `testlink`, which is used in the script to assign event handlers. It also defines a form and a textarea used by the script to display the events. To test this document, save it in the same folder as the JavaScript file you created previously and load the HTML document into a browser. The results are shown in Figure 9.1.

FIGURE 9.1
The mouse click example in action.

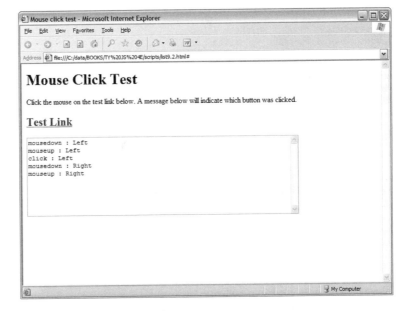

By the Way

Notice that a single click of the left mouse button triggers three events: onMouseDown, onMouseUp, and then onClick.

Using Keyboard Events

JavaScript can also detect keyboard actions. The main event handler for this purpose is onKeyPress, which occurs when a key is pressed and released, or held down. As with mouse buttons, you can detect the down and up parts of the keypress with the onKeyDown and onKeyUp event handlers.

Of course, you might find it useful to know which key the user pressed. You can find this out with the event object, which is sent to your event handler when the event occurs. In Netscape and Firefox, the event.which property stores the ASCII character code for the key that was pressed. In Internet Explorer, event.keyCode serves the same purpose.

ASCII (American Standard Code for Information Interchange) is the standard numeric code used by most computers to represent characters. It assigns the numbers 0–128 to various characters—for example, the capital letters A through Z are ASCII values 65 to 90.

Displaying Typed Characters

If you'd rather deal with actual characters than key codes, you can use the fromCharCode string method to convert them. This method converts a numeric ASCII code to its corresponding string character. For example, the following statement converts the event.which property to a character and stores it in the key variable:

```
Key = String.fromCharCode(event.which);
```

Because different browsers have different ways of returning the key code, displaying keys browser independently is a bit harder. However, you can create a script that displays keys for either browser. The following function will display each key as it is typed:

```
function DisplayKey(e) {
    // which key was pressed?
    if (e.keyCode) keycode=e.keyCode;
        else keycode=e.which;
    character=String.fromCharCode(keycode);
    // find the object for the destination paragraph
    k = document.getElementById("keys");
    // add the character to the paragraph
    k.innerHTML += character;
}
```

The DisplayKey() function receives the event object from the event handler and stores it in the variable e. It checks whether the e.keyCode property exists, and stores it in the keycode variable if present. Otherwise, it assumes the browser is Netscape or Firefox and assigns keycode to the e.which property.

The remaining lines of the function convert the key code to a character and add it to the paragraph in the document with the id attribute keys. Listing 9.3 shows a complete example using this function.

By the Way

The final lines in the DisplayKey() function use the getElementById() function and the innerHTML attribute to display the keys you type within a paragraph on the page. This technique is explained in Hour 13, "Using the W3C DOM."

LISTING 9.3 Displaying Typed Characters

```html
<html>
<head>
<title>Displaying Keypresses</title>
<script language="javascript" type="text/javascript">
    function DisplayKey(e) {
        // which key was pressed?
        if (e.keyCode) keycode=e.keyCode;
            else keycode=e.which;
        character=String.fromCharCode(keycode);
        // find the object for the destination paragraph
        k = document.getElementById("keys");
        // add the character to the paragraph
        k.innerHTML += character;
    }
</script>
</head>
<body onKeyPress="DisplayKey(event);">
<h1>Displaying Typed Characters</h1>
<p>This document includes a simple script that displays the keys
you type in the paragraph below. Type a few keys and try it. </p>
<p id="keys">
</p>
</body>
</html>
```

When you load this example into either Netscape or Internet Explorer, you can type and see the characters you've typed appear in a paragraph of the document. Figure 9.2 shows this example in action in Firefox.

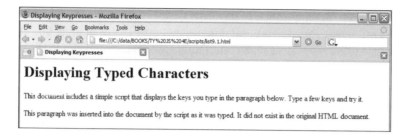

Using the onLoad and onUnload Events

Another event you'll use frequently is onLoad. This event occurs when the current page (including all of its images) finishes loading from the server.

The onLoad event is related to the window object, and to define it you use an event handler in the <body> tag. For example, the following is a <body> tag that uses a simple event handler to display an alert when the page finishes loading:

```
<body onLoad="alert('Loading complete.');">
```

> Because the onLoad event occurs after the HTML document has finished loading and displaying, you cannot use the document.write or document.open statements within an onLoad event handler. This would overwrite the current document.

Watch Out!

In JavaScript 1.1 and later, images can also have an onLoad event handler. When you define an onLoad event handler for an <img> tag, it is triggered as soon as the specified image has completely loaded.

To set an onLoad event using JavaScript, you assign a function to the onload property of the window object:

```
window.onload = MyFunction;
```

You can also specify an onUnload event for the <body> tag. This event will be triggered whenever the browser unloads the current document—this occurs when another page is loaded or when the browser window is closed.

Try It Yourself   ▼

Adding Link Descriptions to a Web Page

One of the most common uses for an event handler is to display descriptions of links when the user moves the mouse over them. For example, moving the mouse over the Order Form link might display a message such as "Order a product or check an order's status".

Link descriptions like these are typically displayed with the onMouseOver event handler. You will now create a script that displays messages in this manner and clears the message using the onMouseOut event handler. You'll use functions to simplify the process.

This example uses the innerHTML property to display the descriptions within a heading on the page. See Hour 13 for a complete description of this property.

This will also be an example of defining event handlers entirely with JavaScript. The HTML document, shown in Listing 9.4, does not include any <script> tags or event handlers—the only thing it requires is some id attributes on the objects we will be using in the script.

LISTING 9.4   The HTML Document for the Descriptive Links Example

```
<html>
<head>
<title>Descriptive Links</title>
</head>
<body>
<h1>Descriptive Links</h1>
<p>Move the mouse pointer over one of
these links to view a description:</p>
<ul>
<li><a href="order.html" id="order">Order Form</a>
<li><a href="email.html" id="email">Email</a>
<li><a href="complain.html" id="complain">Complaint Department</a>
</ul>
<h2 id="description"></h2>
<script language="JavaScript" type="text/javascript" src="linkdesc.js">
</script>
</body>
</html>
```

This document defines three links in a bulleted list. Each <a> tag is defined with an id attribute for the script to use to attach an event handler. The <h2> tag with the id value description, currently blank, will be used to display a description of each link.

Notice that the <script> tag is below the content of the HTML document. It would not work at the top of the document because the objects the script uses are not yet defined. You can also deal with this issue by using an onLoad event handler instead of a simple script to set up the event handlers.

The script will begin with a function to serve as the onMouseOver event handler for the links:

```
function hover(e) {
    if (!e) var e = window.event;
    // which link was the mouse over?
    whichlink = (e.target) ? e.target.id : e.srcElement.id;
    // choose the appropriate description
    if (whichlink=="order") desc = "Order a product";
    else if (whichlink=="email") desc = "Send us a message";
    else if (whichlink=="complain") desc = "Insult us, our products, or our
families";
    // display the description in the H2
    d = document.getElementById("description");
    d.innerHTML = desc;
}
```

The hover function uses the target or srcElement properties to find the target object for the link, and then finds its id attribute. Three if statements evaluate the id and choose an appropriate description. Finally, the script uses the getElementById() method to find the <h2> tag that will display the descriptions, and displays the description using the innerHTML property.

The conditional statement on the third line of the hover function checks whether the target property exists, and if not, it uses the srcElement property. This is called *feature sensing*—detecting whether the browser supports a feature—and is explained further in Hour 15, "Unobtrusive Scripting."

One more function will be required. The cleardesc() function will serve as the onMouseOut event handler and clear the description when the mouse is no longer over one of the links.

```
function cleardesc() {
    d = document.getElementById("description");
    d.innerHTML = "";
}
```

Now that the functions are defined, you need to set them as the event handlers for the links. Each link requires the following three lines of code:

```
orderlink = document.getElementById("order");
orderlink.onmouseover=hover;
orderlink.onmouseout=cleardesc;
```

After using getElementById() to find the object with the id attribute "order", this sets up the hover() and cleardesc() functions as its onMouseOver and onMouseOut event handlers. This will need to be repeated for the other two links. Putting all of this together, the complete JavaScript file for this example is shown in Listing 9.5.

LISTING 9.5   The JavaScript File for the Link Descriptions Example

```
function cleardesc() {
    d = document.getElementById("description");
    d.innerHTML = "";
}
function hover(e) {
    if (!e) var e = window.event;
    // which link was the mouse over?
    whichlink = (e.target) ? e.target.id : e.srcElement.id;
    // choose the appropriate description
    if (whichlink=="order") desc = "Order a product";
    else if (whichlink=="email") desc = "Send us a message";
    else if (whichlink=="complain") desc = "Insult us, our products, or our
families";
    // display the description in the H2
    d = document.getElementById("description");
    d.innerHTML = desc;
}
// Set up the event handlers
orderlink = document.getElementById("order");
orderlink.onmouseover=hover;
orderlink.onmouseout=cleardesc;
emaillink = document.getElementById("email");
emaillink.onmouseover=hover;
emaillink.onmouseout=cleardesc;
complainlink = document.getElementById("complain");
complainlink.onmouseover=hover;
complainlink.onmouseout=cleardesc;
```

To test the script, store it as linkdesc.js in the same folder as the HTML document, and load the HTML file into a browser; this script should work on any JavaScript-capable browser. Internet Explorer's display of the example is shown in Figure 9.3.

Did you Know?

> As usual, you can download the listings for this hour from this book's website.

FIGURE 9.3
Internet Explorer displays the descriptive links example.

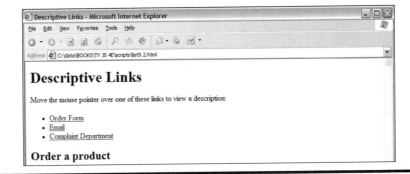

Summary

In this hour, you've learned to use events to detect mouse actions, keyboard actions, and other events, such as the loading of the page. You can use event handlers to perform a simple JavaScript statement when an event occurs, or to call a more complicated function.

JavaScript includes a variety of other events. Many of these are related to forms, which you'll learn more about in Hour 11. Another useful event is onError, which you can use to prevent error messages from displaying. This event is described in Hour 16, "Debugging JavaScript Applications."

In the next hour, you'll continue learning about the objects in the DOM. Specifically, Hour 10, "Using Windows and Frames," looks at the objects associated with windows, frames, and layers, and how they work with JavaScript.

Q&A

Q. *I noticed that the* `<img>` *tag in HTML can't have* `onMouseOver` *or* `onClick` *event handlers in some browsers. How can my scripts respond when the mouse moves over an image?*

A. The easiest way to do this is to make the image a link by surrounding it with an <a> tag. You can include the BORDER=0 attribute to prevent the blue link border from being displayed around the image.

Q. *My image rollovers using* `onMouseOver` *work perfectly in Internet Explorer, but not in Netscape. Why?*

A. Re-read the previous answer, and check whether you've used an onMouseOver event for an <img> tag. This is supported by Internet Explorer and Netscape 6, but not by earlier versions of Netscape.

Q. *What happens if I define both* `onKeyDown` *and* `onKeyPress` *event handlers? Will they both be called when a key is pressed?*

A. The onKeyDown event handler is called first. If it returns true, the onKeyPress event is called. Otherwise, no keypress event is generated.

Q. *When I use the* `onLoad` *event, my event handler sometimes executes before the page is done loading, or before some of the graphics. Is there a better way?*

A. This is a bug in some older browsers. One solution is to add a slight delay to your script using the setTimeout method. You'll learn how to use this method in Hour 10.

Quiz Questions

Test your knowledge of JavaScript events by answering the following questions.

1. Which of the following is the correct event handler to detect a mouse click on a link?

   a. `onMouseUp`

   b. `onLink`

   c. `onClick`

2. When does the `onLoad` event handler for the `<body>` tag execute?

   a. When an image is finished loading

   b. When the entire page is finished loading

   c. When the user attempts to load another page

3. Which of the following event object properties indicates which key was pressed for an `onKeyPress` event in Internet Explorer?

   a. `event.which`

   b. `event.keyCode`

   c. `event.onKeyPress`

Quiz Answers

1. c. The event handler for a mouse click is `onClick`.

2. b. The `<body>` tag's `onLoad` handler executes when the page and all its images are finished loading.

3. b. In Internet Explorer, the `event.keyCode` property stores the character code for each keypress.

Exercises

To gain more experience using event handlers in JavaScript, try the following exercises:

▶ Add one or more additional links to the document in Listing 9.4. Add event handlers to the script in Listing 9.5 to display a unique description for each link.

▶ Modify Listing 9.5 to display a default welcome message whenever a description isn't being displayed. (Hint: You'll need to include a statement to display the welcome message when the page loads. You'll also need to change the `cleardesc` function to restore the welcome message.)

HOUR 10

Using Windows and Frames

What You'll Learn in This Hour:

▶ The window object hierarchy
▶ Creating new windows with JavaScript
▶ Delaying your script's actions with timeouts
▶ Displaying alerts, confirmations, and prompts
▶ Using JavaScript to work with frames
▶ Creating a JavaScript-based navigation frame

You should now have a basic understanding of the objects in the level 0 DOM, and the events that can be used with each object.

In this hour, you'll learn more about some of the most useful objects in the level 0 DOM—browser windows and frames—and how JavaScript can work with them.

Controlling Windows with Objects

In Hour 4, "Working with the Document Object Model (DOM)," you learned that you can use DOM objects to represent various parts of the browser window and the current HTML document. You also learned that the history, document, and location objects are all children of the window object.

In this hour, you'll take a closer look at the window object itself. As you've probably guessed by now, this means you'll be dealing with browser windows. A variation of the window object also enables you to work with frames, as you'll see later in this hour.

The window object always refers to the current window (the one containing the script). The self keyword is also a synonym for the current window. As you'll learn in the next sections, you can have more than one window on the screen at the same time, and can refer to them with different names.

Properties of the window Object

Although there is normally a single window object, there might be more than one if you are using pop-up windows or frames. As you learned in Hour 4, the document, history, and location objects are properties (or children) of the window object. In addition to these, each window object has the following properties:

▶ **window.closed**—Indicates whether the window has been closed. This only makes sense when working with multiple windows because the current window contains the script and cannot be closed without ending the script.

▶ **window.defaultstatus** and **window.status**—The default message for the status line, and a temporary message to display on the status line. Some recent browsers disable status line changes by default, so you might not be able to use these.

▶ **window.frames[]**—An array of objects for frames, if the window contains them.

▶ **window.name**—The name specified for a frame, or for a window opened by a script.

▶ **window.opener**—In a window opened by a script, this is a reference to the window containing the script that opened it.

▶ **window.parent**—For a frame, a reference to the parent window containing the frame.

▶ **window.screen**—A child object that stores information about the screen the window is in—its resolution, color depth, and so on.

▶ **window.self**—A synonym for the current window object.

▶ **window.top**—A reference to the top-level window when frames are in use.

> The properties of the window.screen object include height, width, availHeight, and availWidth (the available height and width rather than total), and colorDepth, which indicates the color support of the monitor: 8 for 8-bit color, 32 for 32-bit color, and so on.

Creating a New Window

One of the most convenient uses for the window object is to create a new window. You can do this to display a document—for example, a pop-up advertisement or the instructions for a game—without clearing the current window. You can also create windows for specific purposes, such as navigation windows.

You can create a new browser window with the window.open() method. A typical statement to open a new window looks like this:

```
WinObj=window.open("URL", "WindowName", "Feature List");
```

The following are the components of the window.open() statement:

► The WinObj variable is used to store the new window object. You can access methods and properties of the new object by using this name.

► The first parameter of the window.open() method is a URL, which will be loaded into the new window. If it's left blank, no web page will be loaded. In this case, you could use JavaScript to fill the window with content.

► The second parameter specifies a window name (here, WindowName). This is assigned to the window object's name property and is used to refer to the window.

► The third parameter is a list of optional features, separated by commas. You can customize the new window by choosing whether to include the toolbar, status line, and other features. This enables you to create a variety of "floating" windows, which might look nothing like a typical browser window.

The features available in the third parameter of the window.open() method include width and height, to set the size of the window in pixels, and several features that can be set to either yes (1) or no (0): toolbar, location, directories, status, menubar, scrollbars, and resizable. You can list only the features you want to change from the default. This example creates a small window with no toolbar or status line:

```
SmallWin = window.open("","small","width=100,height=120,toolbar=0,status=0");
```

Opening and Closing Windows

Of course, you can close windows as well. The window.close() method closes a window. Browsers don't normally allow you to close the main browser window without the user's permission; this method's main purpose is for closing windows you have created. For example, this statement closes a window called updatewindow:

```
updatewindow.close();
```

As another example, Listing 10.1 shows an HTML document that enables you to open a small new window by pressing a button. You can then press another button to close the new window. The third button attempts to close the current window. Depending on your browser and its settings, this might or might not work. If it does close the window, most browsers will ask for confirmation first.

LISTING 10.1   An HTML Document That Uses JavaScript to Enable You to Create and Close Windows

```
<html>
<head><title>Create a New Window</title>
</head>
<body>
<h1>Create a New Window</h1>
<hr>
<p>Use the buttons below to test opening and closing windows in JavaScript.</p>
<hr>
<form NAME="winform">
<input TYPE="button" VALUE="Open New Window"
onClick="NewWin=window.open('','NewWin',
'toolbar=no,status=no,width=200,height=100'); ">
<p><input TYPE="button" VALUE="Close New Window"
onClick="NewWin.close();" ></p>
<p><input TYPE="button" VALUE="Close Main Window"
onClick="window.close();"></p>
</form>
<br><p>Have fun!</p>
<hr>
</body>
</html>
```

This example uses simple event handlers to do its work, one for each of the buttons. Figure 10.1 shows Firefox's display of this page, with the small new window on top.

FIGURE 10.1
A new browser window opened with JavaScript.

Moving and Resizing Windows

The DOM also enables you to move or resize windows. Although earlier browsers placed some restrictions on this, most modern browsers allow you to move and resize any window freely. You can do this using the following methods for any window object:

▶ window.moveTo() moves the window to a new position. The parameters specify the x (column) and y (row) position.

▶ window.moveBy() moves the window relative to its current position. The x and y parameters can be positive or negative, and are added to the current values to reach the new position.

▶ window.resizeTo() resizes the window to the width and height specified as parameters.

▶ window.resizeBy() resizes the window relative to its current size. The parameters are used to modify the current width and height.

As an example, Listing 10.2 shows an HTML document with a simple script that enables you to resize or move the main window.

LISTING 10.2 Moving and Resizing the Current Window

```
<html>
<head>
<title>Moving and resizing windows</title>
<script language="javascript" type="text/javascript">
    function DoIt() {
        if (document.form1.w.value && document.form1.h.value)
            self.resizeTo(document.form1.w.value, document.form1.h.value);
        if (document.form1.x.value && document.form1.y.value)
            self.moveTo(document.form1.x.value, document.form1.y.value);
    }
</script>
</head>
<body>
<h1>Moving and Resizing Windows</h1>
<form name="form1">
<b>Width:</b> <input type="text" name="w"><br>
<b>Height:</b> <input type="text" name="h"><br>
<b>X-position:</b> <input type="text" name="x"><br>
<b>Y-position:</b> <input type="text" name="y"><br>
<input type="button" value="Change Window" onClick="DoIt();">
</form>
</body>
</html>
```

In this example, the DoIt() function is called as an event handler when you click the Change Window button. This function checks whether you have specified width and height values. If you have, it uses the self.resizeTo() method to resize the current window. Similarly, if you have specified x and y values, it uses self.moveTo() to move the window.

Depending on their settings, some browsers might not allow your script to resize or move the main window. In particular, Firefox can be configured to disallow it. You

can enable it by selecting Tools, Options from the menu. Select the Content tab, click the Advanced button next to the Enable JavaScript option, and enable the Move or Resize Existing Windows option.

> This is one of those JavaScript features you should think twice about before using. These methods are best used for resizing or moving pop-up windows your script has generated—not as a way to force the user to use your preferred window size, which most users will find very annoying. You should also be aware that browser settings may be configured to prevent resizing or moving windows, so make sure your script still works even without resizing.

Using Timeouts

Sometimes the hardest thing to get a script to do is to do nothing at all—for a specific amount of time. Fortunately, JavaScript includes a built-in function to do this. The `window.setTimeout` method enables you to specify a time delay and a command that will execute after the delay passes.

> Timeouts don't actually make the browser stop what it's doing. Although the statement you specify in the `setTimeout` method won't be executed until the delay passes, the browser will continue to do other things while it waits (for example, acting on event handlers).

You begin a timeout with a call to the `setTimeout()` method, which has two parameters. The first is a JavaScript statement, or group of statements, enclosed in quotes. The second parameter is the time to wait in milliseconds (thousandths of seconds). For example, the following statement displays an alert dialog box after 10 seconds:

```
ident=window.setTimeout("alert('Time's up!')",10000);
```

> Like event handlers, timeouts use a JavaScript statement within quotation marks. Make sure that you use a single quote (apostrophe) on each side of each string within the statement, as shown in the preceding example.

A variable (`ident` in this example) stores an identifier for the timeout. This enables you to set multiple timeouts, each with its own identifier. Before a timeout has elapsed, you can stop it with the `clearTimeout()` method, specifying the identifier of the timeout to stop:

```
window.clearTimeout(ident);
```

Updating a Page with Timeouts

Normally, a timeout only happens once because the statement you specify in the setTimeout() method statement is only executed once. But often, you'll want your statement to execute over and over. For example, your script might be updating a clock or a countdown and need to execute once per second.

You can make a timeout repeat by issuing the setTimeout() method call again in the function called by the timeout. Listing 10.3 shows an HTML document that demonstrates a repeating timeout.

LISTING 10.3 Using Timeouts to Update a Page Every Two Seconds

```
<html>
<head><title>Timeout Example</title>
<script language="javascript" type="text/javascript">
var counter = 0;
// call Update function in 2 seconds after first load
ID=window.setTimeout("Update();",2000);
function Update() {
   counter++;
   document.form1.input1.value="The counter is now at " + counter;
// set another timeout for the next count
   ID=window.setTimeout("Update();",2000);
}
</script>
</head>
<body>
<h1>Timeout Example</h1>
<hr><p>
The text value below is being updated every two seconds.
Press the RESET button to restart the count, or the STOP button to stop it.
</p><hr>
<form NAME="form1">
<input TYPE="text" NAME="input1" SIZE="40"><br>
<input TYPE="button" VALUE="RESET" onClick="counter = 0;"><br>
<input TYPE="button" VALUE="STOP" onClick="window.clearTimeout(ID);">
</form>
<hr>
</body>
</html>
```

This program displays a message in a text field every two seconds, including a counter that increments each time. You can use the Reset button to start the count over and the Stop button to stop the counting.

This script calls the setTimeout() method when the page loads, and again at each update. The Update() function performs the update, adding one to the counter and setting the next timeout. The Reset button sets the counter to zero, and the Stop button demonstrates the clearTimeout() method. Figure 10.2 shows Internet Explorer's display of the timeout example after the counter has been running for a while.

FIGURE 10.2
The output of
the timeout
example.

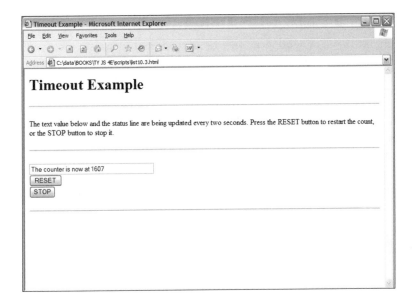

By the Way

This example and the next one use buttons, which are a simple example of what you can do with HTML forms and JavaScript. You'll learn much more about forms in Hour 11, "Getting Data with Forms."

Displaying Dialog Boxes

The window object includes three methods that are useful for displaying messages and interacting with the user. You've already used these in some of your scripts. Here's a summary:

▶ window.alert(message) displays an alert dialog box, shown in Figure 10.3. This dialog box simply gives the user a message.

▶ window.confirm(message) displays a confirmation dialog box. This displays a message and includes OK and Cancel buttons. This method returns true if OK is pressed and false if Cancel is pressed. A confirmation is displayed in Figure 10.4.

▶ window.prompt(message,default) displays a message and prompts the user for input. It returns the text entered by the user. If the user does not enter anything, the default value is used.

FIGURE 10.3
A JavaScript alert dialog box displays a message.

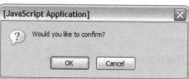

FIGURE 10.4
A JavaScript confirm dialog box asks for confirmation.

To use the confirm() and prompt() methods, use a variable to receive the user's response. For example, this statement displays a prompt and stores the text the user enters in the text variable:

```
text = window.prompt("Enter some text","Default value");
```

> You can usually omit the window object when referring to these methods because it is the default context of a script (for example, alert("text")).

Did you Know?

Creating a Script to Display Dialog Boxes

As a further illustration of these types of dialog boxes, Listing 10.4 shows an HTML document that uses buttons and event handlers to enable you to test dialog boxes.

LISTING 10.4   An HTML Document That Uses JavaScript to Display Alerts, Confirmations, and Prompts

```
<html>
<head><title>Alerts, Confirmations, and Prompts</title>
</head>
<body>
<h1>Alerts, Confirmations, and Prompts</h1>
<hr>
Use the buttons below to test dialogs in JavaScript.
<hr>
<form NAME="winform">
<p><input TYPE="button" VALUE="Display an Alert"
onClick="window.alert('This is a test alert.');  "></p>
<p><input TYPE="button" VALUE="Display a Confirmation"
onClick="window.confirm('Would you like to confirm?');"></p>
<p><input TYPE="button" VALUE="Display a Prompt"
onClick="window.prompt('Enter some Text:','This is the default value');">
</p>
</form>
<br>Have fun!
<hr>
</body>
</html>
```

This document displays three buttons, and each one uses an event handler to display one of the dialog boxes.

Figure 10.5 shows the script in Listing 10.4 in action. The prompt dialog box is currently displayed and shows the default value.

FIGURE 10.5
The dialog box example's output, including a prompt dialog box.

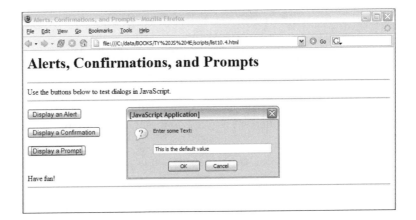

Working with Frames

Browsers also support *frames*, which enable you to divide the browser window into multiple panes. Each frame can contain a separate URL or the output of a script.

Using JavaScript Objects for Frames

When a window contains multiple frames, each frame is represented in JavaScript by a `frame` object. This object is equivalent to a `window` object, but it is used for dealing specifically with that frame. The `frame` object's name is the same as the `NAME` attribute you give it in the `<frame>` tag.

Remember the `window` and `self` keywords, which refer to the current window? When you are using frames, these keywords refer to the current frame instead. Another keyword, `parent`, enables you to refer to the main window.

Each frame object in a window is a child of the `parent` window object. Suppose you define a set of frames using the following HTML:

```
<frameset ROWS="*,*" COLS="*,*">
<frame NAME="topleft" SRC="topleft.htm">
<frame NAME="topright" SRC="topright.htm">
<frame NAME="bottomleft" SRC="botleft.htm">
<frame NAME="bottomright" SRC="botright.htm">
</frameset>
```

This simply divides the window into quarters. If you have a JavaScript program in the `topleft.htm` file, it would refer to the other windows as `parent.topright`, `parent.bottomleft`, and so on. The keywords `window` and `self` would refer to the `topleft` frame.

> If you use nested framesets, things are a bit more complicated. `window` still represents the current frame, `parent` represents the frameset containing the current frame, and `top` represents the main frameset that contains all the others.

By the Way

The `frames` **Array**

Rather than referring to frames in a document by name, you can use the `frames` array. This array stores information about each of the frames in the document. The frames are indexed starting with zero and beginning with the first `<frame>` tag in the frameset document.

For example, you could refer to the frames defined in the previous example using array references:

- ▶ `parent.frames[0]` is equivalent to the `topleft` frame.

- ▶ `parent.frames[1]` is equivalent to the `topright` frame.

- ▶ `parent.frames[2]` is equivalent to the `bottomleft` frame.

- ▶ `parent.frames[3]` is equivalent to the `bottomright` frame.

You can refer to a frame using either method interchangeably, and depending on your application, you should use the most convenient method. For example, a document with 10 frames would probably be easier to use by number, but a simple two-frame document is easier to use if the frames have meaningful names.

Try it Yourself ▼

Using Frames with JavaScript

As a simple example of addressing frames using JavaScript, you will now create an HTML document that divides the window into four frames, and a document with a script for the top-left corner frame. Buttons in the top-left frame will trigger JavaScript event handlers that display text in the other frames.

To begin, you will need a frameset document. Listing 10.5 shows a simple HTML document to divide the window into four frames.

LISTING 10.5   An HTML Document That Divides the Window into Four Frames

```
<frameset ROWS="*,*" COLS="*,*">
<frame NAME="top_left" SRC="topleft.html">
<frame NAME="top_right" SRC="">
<frame NAME="bottom_left" SRC="">
<frame NAME="bottom_right" SRC="">
</frameset>
```

The first frame defined here, top_left, to will contain an HTML document and a simple script. Listing 10.6 shows the HTML and JavaScript code for the top-left frame.

LISTING 10.6   The HTML and JavaScript for the Frame Example

```
<html>
<head>
<title>Frame Test</title>
<script language="javascript" type="text/javascript">
function FillFrame(framename) {
    // Find the object for the frame
    theframe=parent[framename];
    // Open and clear the frame's document
    theframe.document.open();
    // Create some output
    theframe.document.write("<h1>JavaScript Output</h1>");
    theframe.document.write("<p>This text is in the ");
    theframe.document.write(framename + " frame.</p>");
}
</script>
</head>
<body>
<h1>Frame Test</h1>
<form name="form1">
<input type="button" value="Top right"
onClick="FillFrame('top_right');">
<input type="button" value="Bottom left"
onClick="FillFrame('bottom_left');">
<input type="button" id="js" value="Bottom right"
onClick="FillFrame('bottom_right');">
</form>
</body>
</html>
```

This document defines three buttons with event handlers that call the FillFrame() function with a parameter for the frame name. The function finds the correct child of the parent window object for the specified frame, uses document.open to create a new document in the frame, and uses document.write to display text in the frame.

To try this example, save Listing 10.6 as topleft.html in the same folder as the frameset document from Listing 10.5, and load Listing 10.5 into a browser. Figure 10.6 shows the result of this example after all three buttons have been clicked.

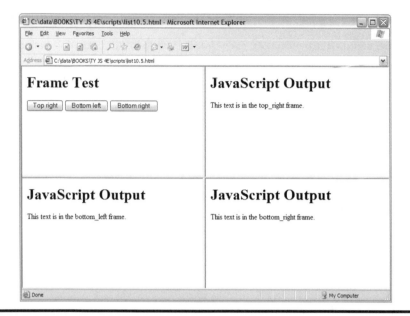

FIGURE 10.6
The frame example as displayed by Internet Explorer.

Summary

In this hour, you've learned how to use the window object to work with browser windows, and used its properties and methods to set timeouts and display dialog boxes. You've also learned how JavaScript can work with framed documents.

In the next hour, you'll move on to another unexplored area of the JavaScript object hierarchy—the form object. You'll learn how to use forms to create some of the most useful applications of JavaScript.

Q&A

Q. *When a script is running in a window created by another script, how can it refer back to the original window?*

A. JavaScript 1.1 and later include the window.opener property, which lets you refer to the window that opened the current window.

Q. *I've heard about layers, which are similar to frames, but more versatile, and are supported in the latest browsers. Can I use them with JavaScript?*

A Yes. You'll learn how to use layers with JavaScript in Hour 13, "Using the W3C DOM."

Q. *How can I update two frames at once when the user clicks on a single link?*

A. You can do this by using an event handler, as in Listing 10.6, and including two statements to load URLs into different frames.

Quiz Questions

Test your knowledge of the DOM's window features by answering the following questions.

1. Which of the following methods displays a dialog box with OK and Cancel buttons, and waits for a response?

   a. `window.alert`

   b. `window.confirm`

   c. `window.prompt`

2. What does the `window.setTimeout` method do?

   a. Executes a JavaScript statement after a delay

   b. Locks up the browser for the specified amount of time

   c. Sets the amount of time before the browser exits automatically

3. You're working with a document that contains three frames with the names `first`, `second`, and `third`. If a script in the second frame needs to refer to the first frame, what is the correct syntax?

   a. `window.first`

   b. `parent.first`

   c. `frames.first`

Quiz Answers

1. b. The `window.confirm` method displays a dialog box with OK and Cancel buttons.

2. a. The `window.setTimeout` method executes a JavaScript statement after a delay.

3. b. The script in the second frame would use `parent.first` to refer to the first frame.

Exercises

If you want to study the window object and its properties and methods further, perform these exercises:

▶ Return to the date/time script you created in Hour 2, "Creating Simple Scripts." This script only displays the date and time once when the page is loaded. Using timeouts, you can modify the script to reload automatically every second or two and display a "live" clock. (Use the location.reload() method, described in Hour 4.)

▶ Modify the examples in Listings 10.5 and 10.6 to use three horizontal frames instead of four frames in a grid. Change the buttons to make it clear which frame they will affect.

HOUR 11

Getting Data with Forms

What You'll Learn in This Hour:

▶ Understanding HTML forms

▶ Creating a form

▶ Using the form object to work with forms

▶ How form elements are represented by JavaScript

▶ Getting data from a form

▶ Sending form results by email

▶ Validating a form with JavaScript

In this hour, you'll explore one of the most powerful uses for JavaScript: working with HTML forms. You can use JavaScript to make a form more interactive, validate data the user enters, and enter data based on other data.

The Basics of HTML Forms

Forms are among the most useful features of the HTML language. As you'll learn during this hour, adding JavaScript to forms can make them more interactive and provide a number of useful features. The first step in creating an interactive form is to create the HTML form itself.

Defining a Form

An HTML form begins with the <form> tag. This tag indicates that a form is beginning, and it enables form elements to be used. The <form> tag includes several attributes:

▶ name is simply a name for the form. You can use forms without giving them names, but you'll need to assign a name to a form in order to easily use it with JavaScript.

▶ method is either GET or POST; these are the two ways the data can be sent to the server.

▶ action is the CGI script that the form data will be sent to when submitted. You can also use the mailto: action to send the form's results to an email address, as described later in this hour.

▶ enctype is the MIME type the form's data will be encoded with. This is usually not necessary; see the "Sending Form Results by Email" section of this hour for an example that requires it.

For example, here is a <form> tag for a form named Order. This form uses the GET method and sends its data to a CGI script called order.cgi in the same directory as the web page itself:

```
<form name="Order" method="GET" action="order.cgi">
```

For a form that will be processed entirely by JavaScript (such as a calculator or an interactive game), the method and action attributes are not needed. You can use a simple <form> tag that names the form:

```
<form name="calcform">
```

The <form> tag is followed by one or more form elements. These are the data fields in the form, such as text fields, buttons, and check boxes. In the next section, you'll learn how JavaScript assigns objects to each of the form elements.

Using the form Object with JavaScript

Each form in your HTML page is represented in JavaScript by a form object, which has the same name as the NAME attribute in the <form> tag you used to define it.

Alternatively, you can use the forms array to refer to forms. This array includes an item for each form element, indexed starting with 0. For example, if the first form in a document has the name form1, you can refer to it in one of two ways:

```
document.form1
document.forms[0]
```

The form Object's Properties

Along with the elements, each form object also has a list of properties, most of which are defined by the corresponding <form> tag. You can also set these from within JavaScript. They include the following:

▶ `action` is the form's `action` attribute, or the program to which the form data will be submitted.

▶ `encoding` is the `MIME` type of the form, specified with the `enctype` attribute. In most cases, this is not needed. See the "Sending Form Results by Email" section of this hour for an example of its use.

▶ `length` is the number of elements in the form. You cannot change this property.

▶ `method` is the method used to submit the form, either `GET` or `POST`. This determines the data format used to send the form result to a CGI script, and does not affect JavaScript.

▶ `target` specifies the window in which the result of the form (from the CGI script) will be displayed. Normally, this is done in the main window, replacing the form itself, but you can use this attribute to work with pop-up windows or frames.

Submitting and Resetting Forms

The `form` object has two methods, `submit()` and `reset()`. You can use these methods to submit the data or reset the form yourself, without requiring the user to press a button. One reason for this is to submit the form when the user clicks an image or performs another action that would not usually submit the form.

> If you use the `submit()` method to send data to a server or by email, most browsers will prompt the user to verify that he or she wants to submit the information. There's no way to do this behind the user's back.

Watch Out!

Detecting Form Events

The `form` object has two event handlers, `onSubmit` and `onReset`. You can specify a group of JavaScript statements or a function call for these events within the `<form>` tag that defines the form.

If you specify a statement or a function for the `onSubmit` event, the statement is called before the data is submitted to the CGI script. You can prevent the submission from happening by returning a value of `false` from the `onSubmit` event handler. If the statement returns `true`, the data will be submitted. In the same fashion, you can prevent a Reset button from working with an `onReset` event handler.

Scripting Form Elements

The most important property of the form object is the elements array, which contains an object for each of the form elements. You can refer to an element by its own name or by its index in the array. For example, the following two expressions both refer to the first element in the order form, the name1 text field:

```
document.order.elements[0]
document.order.name1
```

Both forms and elements can be referred to by their own names or as indices in the forms and elements arrays. For clarity, the examples in this hour use individual form and element names rather than array references. You'll also find it easier to use names in your own scripts.

If you do refer to forms and elements as arrays, you can use the length property to determine the number of objects in the array: document.forms.length is the number of forms in a document, and document.form1.elements.length is the number of elements in the form1 form.

You can also access form elements using the W3C DOM. In this case, you use an id attribute on the form element in the HTML document, and use the document.getElementById() method to find the object for the form. For example, this statement finds the object for the text field called firstname and stores it in the fn variable:

```
fn = document.getElementById("firstname");
```

This allows you to quickly access a form element without first finding the form object. You can assign an id to the <form> tag and find the corresponding object if you need to work with the form's properties and methods.

See Hour 13, "Using the W3C DOM," for details on the document.getElementById() method.

Text Fields

Probably the most commonly used form elements are text fields. You can use them to prompt for a name, an address, or any information. With JavaScript, you can display text in the field automatically. The following is an example of a simple text field:

```
<input type="TEXT" name="text1" value="hello" SIZE="30">
```

This defines a text field called `text1`. The field is given a default value of `"hello"` and allows up to 30 characters to be entered. JavaScript treats this field as a `text` object with the name `text1`.

Text fields are the simplest to work with in JavaScript. Each `text` object has the following properties:

▶ `name` is the name given to the field. This is also used as the object name.

▶ `defaultValue` is the default value and corresponds to the VALUE attribute. This is a read-only property.

▶ `value` is the current value. This starts out the same as the default value, but can be changed, either by the user or by JavaScript functions.

When you work with text fields, most of the time you will use the `value` attribute to read the value the user has entered or to change the value. For example, the following statement changes the value of a text field called `username` in the `order` form to `"John Q. User"`:

```
document.order.username.value = "John Q. User"
```

Text Areas

Text areas are defined with their own tag, `<textarea>`, and are represented by the `textarea` object. There is one major difference between a text area and a text field: Text areas enable the user to enter more than just one line of information. Here is an example of a text area definition:

```
<textarea name="text1" rows="2" cols="70">
This is the content of the TEXTAREA tag.
</textarea>
```

This HTML defines a text area called `text1`, with two rows and 70 columns available for text. In JavaScript, this would be represented by a text area object called `text1` under the `form` object.

The text between the opening and closing `<textarea>` tags is used as the initial value for the text area. You can include line breaks within the default value with the special character `\n`.

Working with Text in Forms

The `text` and `textarea` objects also have a few methods you can use:

▶ `focus()` sets the focus to the field. This positions the cursor in the field and makes it the current field.

▶ blur() is the opposite; it removes the focus from the field.

▶ select() selects the text in the field, just as a user can do with the mouse. All of the text is selected; there is no way to select part of the text.

You can also use event handlers to detect when the value of a text field changes. The text and textarea objects support the following event handlers:

▶ The onFocus event happens when the text field gains focus.

▶ The onBlur event happens when the text field loses focus.

▶ The onChange event happens when the user changes the text in the field and then moves out of it.

▶ The onSelect event happens when the user selects some or all of the text in the field. Unfortunately, there's no way to tell exactly which part of the text was selected. (If the text is selected with the select() method described previously, this event is not triggered.)

If used, these event handlers should be included in the <input> tag declaration. For example, the following is a text field including an onChange event that displays an alert:

```
<input type="TEXT" name="text1" onChange="window.alert('Changed.');">
```

Buttons

One of the most useful types of form element is a button. Buttons use the <input> tag and can use one of three different types:

▶ type=SUBMIT is a Submit button. This button causes the data in the form fields to be sent to the CGI script.

▶ type=RESET is a Reset button. This button sets all the form fields back to their default value, or blank.

▶ type=BUTTON is a generic button. This button performs no action on its own, but you can assign it one using a JavaScript event handler.

All three types of buttons include a name attribute to identify the button and a value attribute that indicates the text to display on the button's face. A few buttons were used in the examples in Hour 10, "Using Windows and Frames." As another example, the following defines a Submit button with the name sub1 and the value "Click Here":

```
<input type="SUBMIT" name="sub1" value="Click Here">
```

If the user presses a Submit or a Reset button, you can detect it with the onSubmit or onReset event handlers, described earlier in this hour. For generic buttons, you can use an onClick event handler.

Check Boxes

A check box is a form element that looks like a small box. Clicking on the check box switches between the checked and unchecked states, which is useful for indicating Yes or No choices in your forms. You can use the <input> tag to define a check box. Here is a simple example:

```
<input type="CHECKBOX" name="check1" value="Yes" checked>
```

Again, this gives a name to the form element. The value attribute assigns a meaning to the check box; this is a value that is returned to the server if the box is checked. The default value is "on." The checked attribute can be included to make the box checked by default.

A check box is simple: It has only two states. Nevertheless, the checkbox object in JavaScript has four different properties:

- ▶ name is the name of the check box, and also the object name.

- ▶ value is the "true" value for the check box—usually on. This value is used by server-side programs to indicate whether the check box was checked. In JavaScript, you should use the checked property instead.

- ▶ defaultChecked is the default status of the check box, assigned by the checked attribute in HTML.

- ▶ checked is the current value. This is a Boolean value: true for checked and false for unchecked.

To manipulate the check box or use its value, you use the checked property. For example, this statement turns on a check box called same in the order form:

```
document.order.same.checked = true;
```

The check box has a single method, click(). This method simulates a click on the box. It also has a single event, onClick, which occurs whenever the check box is clicked. This happens whether the box was turned on or off, so you'll need to examine the checked property to see what happened.

Radio Buttons

Another element for decisions is the radio button, using the `<input>` tag's `RADIO` type. Radio buttons are also known as option buttons. These are similar to check boxes, but they exist in groups and only one button can be checked in each group. They are used for a multiple-choice or "one of many" input. Here's an example of a group of radio buttons:

```
<input type="RADIO" name="radio1" value="Option1" checked> Option 1
<input type="RADIO" name="radio1" value="Option2"> Option 2
<input type="RADIO" name="radio1" value="Option3"> Option 3
```

These statements define a group of three radio buttons. The `name` attribute is the same for all three (which is what makes them a group). The `value` attribute is the value passed to a script or a CGI program to indicate which button is selected—be sure you assign a different value to each button.

By the Way

Radio buttons are named for their similarity to the buttons on old pushbutton radios. Those buttons used a mechanical arrangement so that when you pushed one button in, the others popped out.

As for scripting, radio buttons are similar to check boxes, except that an entire group of them shares a single name and a single object. You can refer to the following properties of the `radio` object:

- ▶ `name` is the name common to the radio buttons.

- ▶ `length` is the number of radio buttons in the group.

To access the individual buttons, you treat the `radio` object as an array. The buttons are indexed, starting with 0. Each individual button has the following properties:

- ▶ `value` is the value assigned to the button. (This is used by the server.)

- ▶ `defaultChecked` indicates the value of the `checked` attribute and the default state of the button.

- ▶ `checked` is the current state.

For example, you can check the first radio button in the `radio1` group on the `form1` form with this statement:

```
document.form1.radio1[0].checked = true;
```

However, if you do this, be sure you set the other values to `false` as needed. This is not done automatically. You can use the `click()` method to do both of these in one step.

Like a check box, radio buttons have a click() method and an onClick event handler. Each radio button can have a separate statement for this event.

You can have more than one group of radio buttons on a page, and they will act independently. Assign a separate name attribute value to each group.

Drop-Down Lists

A final form element is also useful for multiple-choice selections. The <select> HTML tag is used to define a *selection list*, or a drop-down list of text items. The following is an example of a selection list:

```
<select name="select1" SIZE=40>
<option value="choice1" SELECTED>This is the first choice.
<option value="choice2">This is the second choice.
<option value="choice3">This is the third choice.
</select>
```

Each of the <option> tags defines one of the possible choices. The value attribute is the name that is returned to the program, and the text outside the <option> tag is displayed as the text of the option.

An optional attribute to the <select> tag, multiple, can be specified to allow multiple items to be selected. Browsers usually display a single-selection <select> as a drop-down list and a multiple-selection list as a scrollable list.

The object for selection lists is the select object. The object itself has the following properties:

▶ name is the name of the selection list.

▶ length is the number of options in the list.

▶ options is the array of options. Each selectable option has an entry in this array.

▶ selectedIndex returns the index value of the currently selected item. You can use this to check the value easily. In a multiple-selection list, this indicates the first selected item.

The options array has a single property of its own, length, which indicates the number of selections. In addition, each item in the options array has the following properties:

▶ index is the index into the array.

▶ defaultSelected indicates the state of the selected attribute.

▶ selected is the current state of the option. Setting this property to true selects the option. The user can select multiple options if the multiple attribute is included in the <select> tag.

▶ name is the value of the name attribute. This is used by the server.

▶ text is the text that is displayed in the option.

The select object has two methods—blur() and focus()—which perform the same purposes as the corresponding methods for text objects. The event handlers are onBlur, onFocus, and onChange, also similar to other objects.

> You can change selection lists dynamically—for example, choosing a product in one list could control which options are available in another list. You can also add and delete options from the list.

Reading the value of a selected item is a two-step process. You first use the selectedIndex property, and then use the value property to find the value of the selected choice. Here's an example:

```
ind = document.navform.choice.selectedIndex;
val = document.navform.choice.options[ind].value;
```

This uses the ind variable to store the selected index, and then assigns the val variable to the value of the selected choice. Things are a bit more complicated with a multiple selection: You have to test each option's selected attribute separately.

Displaying Data from a Form

As a simple example of using forms, Listing 11.1 shows a form with name, address, and phone number fields, as well as a JavaScript function that displays the data from the form in a pop-up window.

LISTING 11.1   **A Form That Displays Data in a Pop-up Window**

```
<html>
<head>
<title>Form Example</title>
<script language="JavaScript" type="text/javascript">
function display() {
    DispWin = window.open('','NewWin',
```

LISTING 11.1 Continued

```
'toolbar=no,status=no,width=300,height=200')
    message = "<ul><li><b>NAME: </b>" + document.form1.yourname.value;
    message += "<li><b>ADDRESS: </b>" + document.form1.address.value;
    message += "<li><b>PHONE: </b>" + document.form1.phone.value + "</ul>";
    DispWin.document.write(message);
}
</script>
</head>
<body>
<h1>Form Example</h1>
Enter the following information. When you press the Display button,
the data you entered will be displayed in a pop-up window.
<form name="form1">
<p><b>Name:</b> <input type="TEXT" size="20" name="yourname">
</p>
<p><b>Address:</b> <input type="TEXT" size="30" name="address">
</p>
<p><b>Phone: </b> <input type="TEXT" size="15" name="phone">
</p>
<p><input type="BUTTON" value="Display" onClick="display();"></p>
</form>
</body>
</html>
```

Here is a breakdown of how this HTML document and script work:

▶ The <script> section in the document's header defines a function called dis-
  play() that opens a new window (as described in Hour 10) and displays the
  information from the form.

▶ The <form> tag begins the form. Because this form is handled entirely by
  JavaScript, no form action or method is needed.

▶ The <input> tags define the form's three fields: yourname, address, and
  phone. The last <input> tag defines the Display button, which is set to run the
  display() function.

As usual, you can download the listings for this hour from this book's website.

Did you Know?

Figure 11.1 shows this form in action. The Display button has been pressed, and the
pop-up window shows the results.

FIGURE 11.1
Displaying data
from a form in a
pop-up window.

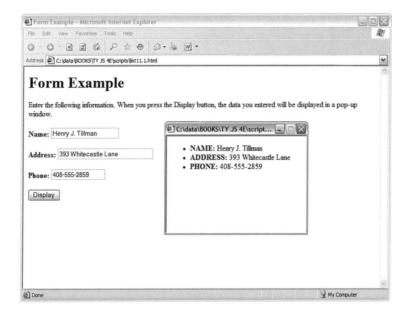

Sending Form Results by Email

One easy way to use a form is to send the results by email. You can do this without
using any JavaScript, although you could use JavaScript to validate the information
entered (as you'll learn later in this hour).

To send a form's results by email, you use the `mailto:` action in the form's `action`
attribute. Listing 11.2 is a modified version of the name and address form from
Listing 11.1 that sends the results by email.

LISTING 11.2   Sending a Form's Results by Email

```
<html>
<head>
<title>Email Form Example</title>
</head>
<body>
<h1>Email Form Example</h1>
Enter the following information. When you press the Submit button,
the data you entered will be sent by email.
<form name="form1" action="mailto:user@host.com"
  enctype="text/plain" method="POST">
<p><b>Name:</b> <input type="TEXT" size="20" name="yourname">
</p>
<p><b>Address:</b> <input type="TEXT" size="30" name="address">
</p>
<p><b>Phone: </b> <input type="TEXT" size="15" name="phone">
</p>
<p><input type="submit" value="Submit"></p>
</form>
</body>
</html>
```

To use this form, change user@host.com in the action attribute of the <form> tag to your email address. Notice the enctype=text/plain attribute in the <form> tag. This ensures that the information in the email message will be in a readable plaintext format rather than encoded.

Although this provides a quick and dirty way of retrieving data from a form, the disadvantage of this technique is that it is highly browser dependent. Whether it will work for each user of your page depends on the configuration of his or her browser and email client.

Because this technique does not consistently work on all browsers, I don't recommend you use it. For a more reliable way of sending form results, you can use a CGI form-to-email gateway. Several free CGI scripts and services are available. You'll find links to them on this book's website.

Watch Out!

Try It Yourself ▼

Validating a Form

One of JavaScript's most useful purposes is validating forms. This means using a script to verify that the information entered is valid—for example, that no fields are blank and that the data is in the right format.

You can use JavaScript to validate a form whether it's submitted by email or to a CGI script, or is simply used by a script. Listing 11.3 is a version of the name and address form that includes validation.

LISTING 11.3   A Form with a Validation Script

```
<html>
<head>
<title>Form Example</title>
<script language="JavaScript" type="text/javascript">
function validate() {
    if (document.form1.yourname.value.length < 1) {
        alert("Please enter your full name.");
        return false;
    }
    if (document.form1.address.value.length < 3) {
        alert("Please enter your address.");
        return false;
    }
    if (document.form1.phone.value.length < 3) {
        alert("Please enter your phone number.");
        return false;
    }
    return true;
}
```

LISTING 11.3   Continued

```
</script>
</head>
<body>
<h1>Form Example</h1>
<p>Enter the following information. When you press the Submit button,
the data you entered will be validated, then sent by email.</p>
<form name="form1" action="mailto:user@host.com" enctype="text/plain"
 method="POST" onSubmit="return validate();">
<p><b>Name:</b> <input type="TEXT" size="20" name="yourname">
</p>
<p><b>Address:</b> <input type="TEXT" size="30" name="address">
</p>
<p><b>Phone: </b> <input type="TEXT" size="15" name="phone">
</p>
<p><input type="SUBMIT" value="Submit"></p>
</form>
</body>
</html>
```

This form uses a function called `validate()` to check the data in each of the form fields. Each `if` statement in this function checks a field's length. If the field is long enough to be valid, the form can be submitted; otherwise, the submission is stopped and an alert message is displayed.

By the Way

> The validation in this script is basic—you could go further and ensure that the phone field contains only numbers, and the right amount of digits, by using JavaScript's string features described in Hour 5, "Using Variables, Strings, and Arrays."

This form is set up to send its results by email, as in Listing 11.2. If you wish to use this feature, be sure to read the information about email forms earlier in this hour and change `user@host.com` to your desired email address.

The `<form>` tag uses an `onSubmit` event handler to call the `validate()` function. The `return` keyword ensures that the value returned by `validate()` will determine whether the form is submitted.

Did you Know?

> You can also use the `onChange` event handler in each form field to call a validation routine. This allows the field to be validated before the Submit button is pressed.

Figure 11.2 shows this script in action, as displayed by Firefox. The form has been filled out except for the name, and a dialog box indicates that the name needs to be entered.

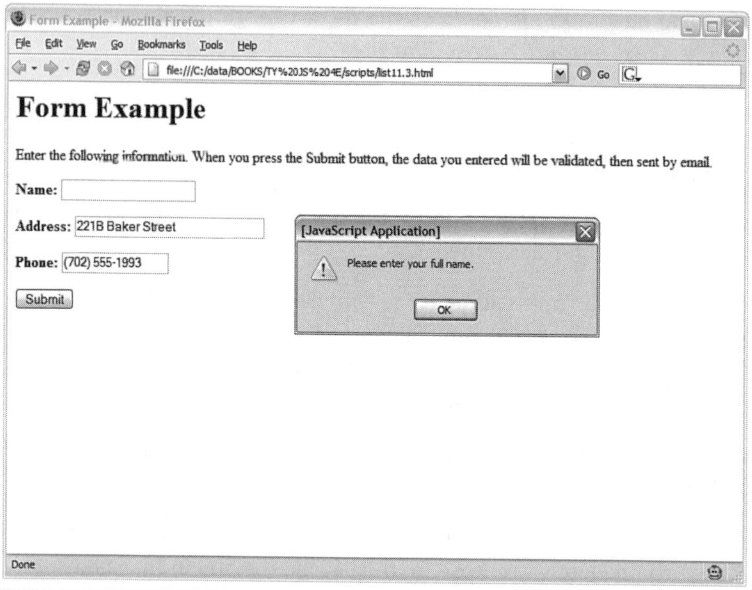

FIGURE 11.2
The form valida-
tion example in
action.

Summary

During this hour, you've learned all about HTML forms and how they can be used with JavaScript. You learned about the form object and the objects for the various form elements, and used them in several example scripts.

You also learned how to submit a form by email, and how to use JavaScript to validate a form before it is submitted.

In the next hour, you'll look at CSS (Cascading Style Sheets)—a standards-compliant way to achieve just about any visual effect on a page, and the foundation for using JavaScript to change a page's appearance.

Q&A

Q. *If I use JavaScript to add validation and other features to my form, can users with non-JavaScript browsers still use the form?*

A. Yes, if you're careful. Be sure to use a Submit button rather than the submit action. Also, the CGI script might receive nonvalidated data, so be sure to include the same validation in the CGI script. Non-JavaScript users will be able to use the form, but won't receive instant feedback about their errors.

Q. *Can I add new form elements on the fly or change them—for example, change a text box into a password field?*

A. Not in the traditional way described in this hour. However, you can change any aspect of a page, including adding, removing, or changing form elements, using the W3C DOM. See Hour 13 for details.

Q. *Is there any way to create a large number of text fields without dealing with different names for all of them?*

A. Yes. If you use the same name for several elements in the form, their objects will form an array. For example, if you defined 20 text fields with the name `member`, you could refer to them as `member[0]` through `member[19]`. This also works with other types of form elements.

Q. *Is there a way to place the cursor on a particular field when the form is loaded, or after my validation routine displays an error message?*

A. Yes. You can use the field's `focus()` method to send the cursor there. To do this when the page loads, you can use the `onLoad` method in the `<body>` tag. However, there is no way to place the cursor in a particular position within the field.

Quiz Questions

Test your knowledge of JavaScript and forms by answering the following questions.

1. Which of these attributes of a `<form>` tag determines where the data will be sent?

    a. `action`

    b. `method`

    c. `name`

2. Where do you place the `onSubmit` event handler to validate a form?

    a. In the `<body>` tag

    b. In the `<form>` tag

    c. In the `<input>` tag for the Submit button

3. What can JavaScript do with forms that a CGI script can't?

    a. Cause all sorts of problems

    b. Give the user instant feedback about errors

    c. Submit the data to a server

Quiz Answers

1. a. The `action` attribute determines where the data is sent.

2. b. You place the `onSubmit` event handler in the `<form>` tag.

3. b. JavaScript can validate a form and let the user know about errors immediately, without waiting for a response from a server.

Exercises

To further explore the JavaScript features you learned about in this hour, you can perform the following exercises:

▶ Change the `validate` function in Listing 11.3 so that after a message is displayed indicating that a field is wrong, the cursor is moved to that field. (Use the `focus()` method for the appropriate form element.)

▶ Add a text field to the form in Listing 11.3 for an email address. Add a feature to the `validate` function that verifies that the email address is at least five characters and that it contains the @ symbol.

HOUR 12

Working with Style Sheets

What You'll Learn in This Hour:

▶ Why style sheets are needed
▶ How to define Cascading Style Sheets (CSS)
▶ How to use a style sheet in a document
▶ Using an external style sheet file
▶ Using JavaScript to change styles dynamically

This hour begins with an introduction to style sheets, which you can use to take more control over how the browser displays your document. You can also use JavaScript with style sheets to change the appearance of a page dynamically.

Style and Substance

If you've ever tried to make a really good-looking web page, you've probably encountered some problems. First of all, HTML doesn't give you very much control over a page's appearance. For example, you can't change the amount of space between words—in fact, you can't even use two spaces between words because they'll be converted to a single space.

Second, even when you do your best to make a perfect-looking document using HTML, you will find that it doesn't necessarily display the same way on all browsers—or even on different computers running the same browser.

The reason for these problems is simple: HTML was never meant to handle such things as layout, justification, and spacing. HTML deals with a document's *structure*—in other words, how the document is divided into paragraphs, headings, lists, and other elements.

This isn't a bad thing. In fact, it's one of the most powerful features of HTML. You only define the structure of the document, so it can be displayed in all sorts of different ways

without changing its meaning. For example, a well-written HTML document can be displayed in Netscape, Firefox, or Internet Explorer, which generally treat elements the same way—there is a space between paragraphs, headings are in big, bold text, and so on.

Because HTML only defines the structure, the same document can be displayed in a text-based browser, such as Lynx. In this case, the different elements will be displayed differently, but you can still tell which text is a heading, which is a list, and so on.

> Text-based browsers aren't the only alternative way of displaying HTML. Browsers designed for the blind can read a web page using a speech synthesizer, with different voices or sounds that indicate the different elements.

As you should now understand, HTML is very good at its job—defining a document's structure. Not surprisingly, using this language to try to control the document's *presentation* will only drive you crazy.

Fortunately, the World Wide Web Consortium (W3C) realized that web authors need to control the layout and presentation of documents. This resulted in the *Cascading Style Sheets (CSS)* standard.

CSS adds a number of features to standard HTML to control style and appearance. More importantly, it does this without affecting HTML's capability to describe document structures. Although style sheets still won't make your document look 100% identical on all browsers and all platforms, it is certainly a step in the right direction.

Let's look at a real-world example. If you're browsing the Web with a CSS-supported browser and come across a page that uses CSS, you'll see the document exactly as it was intended. You can also turn off your browser's support for style sheets if you'd rather view all the pages in the same consistent way.

> Using CSS and simplifying HTML markup is also helpful in making pages compatible with the various tiny browsers used on mobile phones.

Defining and Using CSS Styles

You can define a CSS style sheet within an HTML document using the `<style>` tag. The opening `<style>` tag specifies the type of style sheet—CSS is currently the only valid type—and begins a list of styles to apply to the document. The `</style>` tag ends the style sheet. Here's a simple example:

```
<style type="text/css">
   H1 {color: blue;}
</style>
```

Because the style sheet definition itself doesn't create any output on the page, you should place the <style> tags in the <head> section of the HTML document.

> You can only use style sheet rules within the <style> tags. HTML tags are not valid within a style sheet.

Watch Out!

Creating Rules

Each element within the <style> tags is called a *rule*. To create a rule, you specify the HTML elements that it will affect, as well as a list of properties and values that control the appearance of those elements. We'll look at the properties in the next section.

As a simple example, the following style sheet contains a single rule. All Level 1 headings are blue:

```
<style type="text/css">
   H1 {color: blue;}
</style>
```

Each rule includes three components:

▶ A *selector* (H1 in the example) describing which HTML tags will be affected

▶ One or more *property names* (color in the example)

▶ A *value* for each property name (blue in the example)

Each rule uses braces to surround the list of properties and values, and a semicolon after each value. The semicolon is optional if you are only specifying one property and value.

You can specify multiple HTML tags for the selector, as well as multiple properties and values. For example, the following style sheet specifies that all headings are blue, italic, and centered:

```
<style type="text/css">
H1,H2,H3,H4,H5,H6 {color: blue;
                   font-style: italic;
                   text-align: center; }
</style>
```

> If you make a rule that sets the style of the <body> tag, it will affect the entire document. This becomes the default rule for the document, but you can override it with the styles of elements within the body of the page.

Setting Styles for Specific Elements

Rather than setting the style for all elements of a certain type, you can specify a style for an individual element only. For example, the following HTML tag represents a Level 1 heading colored red:

```
<h1 style="color: red; text-align: center;">This is a red heading.</h1>
```

This is called an *inline style* because it's specified in the HTML tag itself. You don't need to use <style> tags with this type of style. If you have used both, inline style rules override rules in a style sheet—for example, if the preceding tag appeared in a document that sets H1 headings to be blue in a style sheet, the heading would still be red.

Using id Attributes

You can also create a rule within a style sheet that will only apply to a certain element. The id attribute of an HTML tag enables you to assign a unique identifier to that element. For example, this tag defines a paragraph with the id attribute intro:

```
<p id="intro">This is a paragraph</p>
```

After you've assigned this attribute to the tag, you can include rules for it as part of a style sheet. CSS uses the pound sign (#) to indicate that a rule applies to a specific id. For example, the following style sheet sets the intro paragraph to be red in color:

```
<style type="text/css">
    #intro {color: red;}
</style>
```

> An id value should define a single element in a page. Most browsers will enable you to define more than one element with the same id value, but this is not valid and will not work consistently. It's best to use classes, as described in the next section, when you need to apply the same styles to multiple elements.

Using Classes

Although the id attribute is useful, you can only use each unique id value with a single HTML tag. If you need to apply the same style to several tags, you can use the class attribute instead. For example, this HTML tag defines a paragraph in a class called smallprint:

```
<p class="smallprint">This is the small print</p>
```

To refer to a class within a style sheet, you use a period followed by the class name.
Here is a style sheet that defines styles for the `smallprint` class:

```
<style type="text/css">
    .smallprint {color: black;
                 font-size: 10px; }
</style>
```

Using CSS Properties

CSS supports a wide variety of properties, such as `color` and `text-align`, in the previous example. The following sections list some of the most useful CSS properties for aligning text, changing colors, working with fonts, and setting margins and borders.

Aligning Text

One of the most useful features of style sheets is the capability to change the spacing and alignment of text. Most of these features aren't available using standard HTML. You can use the following properties to change the alignment and spacing of text:

▶ **letter-spacing**—Specifies the spacing between letters.

▶ **text-decoration**—Enables you to create lines over, under, or through the text, or to choose blinking text. The value can be none (default), underline, overline, line-through, or blink. Blinking text is, thankfully, unsupported by most browsers.

▶ **vertical-align**—Enables you to move the element up or down to align with other elements on the same line. The value can be baseline, sub, super, top, text-top, middle, text-bottom, and bottom.

▶ `text-align`—Specifies the justification of text. This can be `left`, `right`, `center`, or `justify`.

▶ `text-transform`—Changes the capitalization of text. `capitalize` makes the first letter of each word uppercase; `uppercase` makes *all* letters uppercase; and `lowercase` makes all letters lowercase.

▶ `text-indent`—Enables you to specify the amount of indentation for paragraphs and other elements.

▶ `line-height`—Enables you to specify the distance between the top of one line of text and the top of the next.

Changing Colors and Background Images

You can also use style sheets to gain more control over the colors and background images used on your web page. CSS includes the following properties for this purpose:

▶ `color`—Specifies the color of the text within an element. This is useful for emphasizing text or for using a specific color scheme for the document. You can specify a named color (for example, `red`) or red, green, and blue values to define a specific color (for example, `#0522A5`).

▶ `background-color`—Specifies the background color of an element. By setting this value, you can make paragraphs, table cells, and other elements with unique background colors. As with `color`, you can specify a color name or numeric color.

▶ `background-image`—Specifies the URL for an image to be used as the background for the element. This is specified with the keyword `url` and a URL in parentheses, as in `url(/back.gif)`.

▶ `background-repeat`—Specifies whether the background image is repeated (tiled). The image can be repeated horizontally, vertically, or both.

▶ `background-attachment`—Controls whether the background image scrolls when you scroll through the document. `fixed` means that the background image stays still while the document scrolls; `scroll` means the image scrolls with the document (like background images on normal web documents).

▶ `background-position`—Enables you to offset the position of the background image.

▶ `background`—Provides a quick way to set all of the background elements in this list. You can specify all of the attributes in a single background rule.

The basic list of colors supported by most browsers for the `color` and `background-color` properties includes `aqua`, `black`, `blue`, `fuchsia`, `gray`, `green`, `lime`, `maroon`, `navy`, `olive`, `orange`, `purple`, `red`, `silver`, `teal`, `white`, and `yellow`.

Did you Know?

Working with Fonts

Style sheets also enable you to control the fonts used on the web document and how they are displayed. You can use the following properties to control fonts:

▶ `font-family`—Specifies the name of a font, such as `arial` or `helvetica`, to use with the element. Because not all users have the same fonts installed, you can list several fonts. The CSS specification also supports several generic font families that are guaranteed to be available: `serif`, `sans-serif`, `cursive`, `fantasy`, and `monospace`.

▶ `font-style`—Specifies the style of a font, such as `normal`, `italic`, or `oblique`.

▶ `font-variant`—This value is `normal` for normal text, and `small-caps` to display lowercase letters as small capitals.

▶ `font-weight`—Enables you to specify the weight of text: `normal` or `bold`. You can also specify a numeric font weight for a specific amount of boldness.

▶ `font-size`—The point size of the font.

▶ `font`—This is a quick way to set all the font properties in this list. You can list all the values in a single `font` rule.

Margins and Borders

Last but not least, you can use style sheets to control the general layout of the page. The following properties affect margins, borders, and the width and height of elements on the web page:

▶ `margin-top`, `margin-bottom`, `margin-left`, `margin-right`—Specify the margins of the element. You can specify the margins as an exact number or as a percentage of the page's width.

▶ `margin`—Allows you to specify a single value for all four of the margins.

▶ `width`—Specifies the width of an element, such as an image.

▶ `height`—Specifies the height of an element.

▶ `float`—Enables the text to flow around an element. This is particularly useful with images or tables.

▶ `clear`—Specifies that the text should stop flowing around a floating image.

Along with these features, CSS style sheets enable you to create sections of the document that can be positioned independently. This feature is described in Hour 13, "Using the W3C DOM."

Units for Style Sheets

Style sheet properties support a wide variety of *units*, or types of values you can specify. Most properties that accept a numeric value support the following types of units:

▶ px—Pixels (for example, 15px). Pixels are the smallest addressable units on a computer screen or other device. In some devices with non-typical resolutions (for example, handheld computers) the browser might rescale this value to fit the device.

▶ pt—Points (for example, 10pt). Points are a standard unit for font size. The size of text of a specified point size varies depending on the monitor resolution. Points are equal to 1/72 of an inch.

▶ ex— Approximate height of the letter x in the current font (for example, 1.2ex).

▶ em—Approximate width of the letter m in the current font (for example, 1.5em). This is usually equal to the font-size property for the current element.

▶ %—Percentage of the containing object's value (for example, 150%).

Which unit you choose to use is generally a matter of convenience. Point sizes are commonly used for fonts, pixel units for the size and position of layers or other objects, and so on.

Creating a Simple Style Sheet

As an example of CSS, you can now create a web page that uses a wide variety of styles:

▶ For the entire body, the text is blue.

▶ Paragraphs are centered and have a wide margin on either side.

▶ Level 1, 2, and 3 headings are red.

▶ Bullet lists are boldface and green by default.

The following is the CSS style sheet to define these properties, using the `<style>` tags:

```
<style type="text/css">
BODY {color: blue}
P {text-align: center;
   margin-left:20%;
   margin-right:20%}
H1, H2, H3 {color: red}
UL {color: green;
    font-weight: bold}
</style>
```

Here's a rundown of how this style sheet works:

- ▶ The `<style>` tags enclose the style sheet.

- ▶ The BODY section sets the page body's default text color to blue.

- ▶ The P section defines the style for paragraphs.

- ▶ The H1, H2, H3 section defines the style for heading tags.

- ▶ The UL section defines a style for bullet lists.

To show how this style sheet works, Listing 12.1 shows a document that includes this style sheet and a few examples of overriding styles for particular elements. Figure 12.1 shows Internet Explorer's display of this example.

LISTING 12.1   An Example of a Document Using CSS Style Sheets

```
<html>
<head><title>Style Sheet Example</title>
<style type="text/css">
BODY {color: blue}
P {text-align: center;
   margin-left:20%;
   margin-right:20%}
H1, H2, H3 {color: red}
UL {color: green;
   font-weight: bold}
</style>
</head>
<body>
<h1>Welcome to this page</h1>
<p>The above heading is red, since we specified that H1-H3 headings
are red. This paragraph is blue, which is the default color for
the entire body. It's also centered and has 20% margins, which we
specified as the default for paragraphs.
</p>
<p style="color:black">This paragraph has black text, because it overrides
the default color in the paragraph tag. We didn't override the centering,
so this paragraph is also centered.</p>
<ul>
```

LISTING 12.1   Continued

```
<li>This is a bullet list.
<li>It's green and bold, because we specified those defaults for bullet lists.
<li style="color:red">This item is red, overriding the default.
<li>This item is back to normal.
</ul>
<p>This is another paragraph with the default paragraph style.</p>
</body>
</html>
```

Did you Know?

Remember that you can download the code for this listing from this book's website.

FIGURE 12.1
The style sheet example as displayed by Internet Explorer.

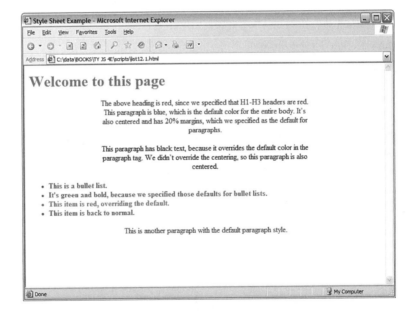

Using External Style Sheets

The preceding example only changes a few aspects of the HTML document's appearance, but it adds about 10 lines to its length. If you were trying to make a very stylish page and had defined new styles for all of the attributes, you would end up with a very long and complicated document.

For this reason, you can use a CSS style sheet from a separate file in your document. This makes your document short and to the point. More importantly, it enables you to define a single style sheet and use it to control the appearance of all of the pages on your site.

Linking to External Style Sheets

You can refer to an external CSS file by using the `<link>` tag in the `<head>` section of one or more HTML documents:

```
<link rel="stylesheet" type="text/css" href="style.css">
```

This tag refers to an external CSS style sheet stored in the `style.css` file.

> **By the Way**
>
> Using external style sheets is a good practice because it separates content (HTML), presentation (CSS), and behavior (JavaScript). See Hour 15, "Unobtrusive Scripting," for more information on best practices.

Creating External `.css` Files

After you've linked to an external `.css` file, you need to create the file itself. The external style sheet is a simple text file that you can create with the same editor you use for HTML documents.

The `.css` file should contain a list of CSS rules, in the same format you would use between `<style>` tags. However, the file should not include `<style>` tags or any other HTML tags. Here is what the styles from the previous example would look like as an external style sheet:

```
BODY {color: blue}
P {text-align: center;
   margin-left:20%;
   margin-right:20%}
H1, H2, H3 {color: red}
UL {color: green;
   font-weight: bold}
```

Controlling Styles with JavaScript

The new W3C DOM (Document Object Model) makes it easy for JavaScript applications to control the styles on a page. Whether or not you use style sheets, you can use JavaScript to modify the style of any element on a page.

As you learned in Hour 4, "Working with the Document Object Model (DOM)," the DOM enables you to access the entire HTML document and all of its elements as scriptable objects. You can change any object's style by modifying its `style` object properties.

The names and values of objects under the `style` object are the same as you've learned in this hour. For example, you can change an element's color by modifying its `style.color` attribute:

```
element.style.color="blue";
```

Here, element represents the object for an element. There are many ways of finding an element's corresponding object, which you will learn about in detail in Hour 13.

In the meantime, an easy way to find an element's object is to assign an identifier to it with the id attribute. The following statement creates an <h1> element with the identifier "head1":

```
<h1 id = "head1">This is a heading</h1>
```

Now that you've assigned an identifier, you can use the getElementById() method to find the DOM object for the element:

```
element = document.getElementById("head1");
```

You can also use a shortcut to set styles and avoid the use of a variable by directly working with the getElementbyId() method:

```
document.getElementById("head1").style.color="blue";
```

This statement combines the preceding examples by directly assigning the blue color style to the head1 element of the page. You'll use this technique to create a dynamic page in the following Try It Yourself section.

▼ **Try It Yourself**

Creating Dynamic Styles

Using the DOM style objects, you can create a page that enables you to directly control the colors used in the page's text. To begin with, you will need a form with which to select colors. You can use <select> tags to allow a color choice:

```
<select name="heading" onChange="changehead();">
    <option value="black">Black</option>
    <option value="red">Red</option>
    <option value="blue">Blue</option>
    <option value="green">Green</option>
    <option value="yellow">Yellow</option>
</select>
```

By the Way

> If you are unsure of the syntax used in forms, you might want to review Hour 11, "Getting Data with Forms."

Notice that this <select> definition uses onChange attributes in the <select> tags to call two functions, changehead() and changebody(), when their respective selection changes.

Combining two of these selections with some basic HTML results in the complete HTML document shown in Listing 12.2.

LISTING 12.2   The HTML File for the Dynamic Styles Example

```
<html>
<head>
<title>Controlling Styles with JavaScript</title>
<script language="Javascript" type="text/javascript"
    src="styles.js">
</script>
</head>
<body>
<h1 id="head1">
Controlling Styles with JavaScript</h1>
<hr>
<p id="p1">
Select the color for paragraphs and headings using the form below.
The colors you specified will be dynamically changed in this document.
The change occurs as soon as you change the value of either of the
drop-down lists in the form.
</p>
<form name="form1">
<b>Heading color: </b>
<select name="heading" onChange="changehead();">
    <option value="black">Black</option>
    <option value="red">Red</option>
    <option value="blue">Blue</option>
    <option value="green">Green</option>
    <option value="yellow">Yellow</option>
</select>
<br>
<b>Body text color: </b>
<select name="body" onChange="changebody();">
    <option value="black">Black</option>
    <option value="red">Red</option>
    <option value="blue">Blue</option>
    <option value="green">Green</option>
    <option value="yellow">Yellow</option>
</select>
</form>
</body>
</html>
```

Notice that the <h1> tag has an id attribute of "head1", and the <p> tag has an id of "p1". These are the values the script will use in the getElementById() function. The <script> tag in the <head> section links the document to the styles.js script, which you will create next.

Save your HTML file as styles.html. You can test it in a browser now, but the dynamic features will not work until you create the JavaScript file containing the script functions. Listing 12.3 shows the JavaScript code for this example.

LISTING 12.3   The JavaScript File for the Dynamic Styles Example

```
function changehead() {
  i = document.form1.heading.selectedIndex;
  headcolor = document.form1.heading.options[i].value;
  document.getElementById("head1").style.color = headcolor;
}
function changebody() {
  i = document.form1.body.selectedIndex;
  doccolor = document.form1.body.options[i].value;
  document.getElementById("p1").style.color = doccolor;
}
```

This script first defines the `changehead()` function. This reads the index for the currently selected heading color, and then reads the color value for the index. This function uses the `getElementById()` method described in the previous section to change the color. The `changebody()` function uses the same syntax to change the body color.

Store your JavaScript file as `styles.js`, and be sure it is in the same folder as the HTML document you saved from Listing 12.2.

To test the dynamic styles script, load Listing 12.2 (`styles.html`) into the browser. Select the colors, and notice the immediate change in the heading or body of the page. Figure 12.2 shows a typical display of this document after the colors have been changed.

FIGURE 12.2
The dynamic styles example in action.

Summary

In this hour, you've used style sheets to control the appearance of web documents. You've learned the CSS syntax for creating style sheets, and used JavaScript to control the styles of a document.

In the next hour, you will move on to Dynamic HTML (DHTML) using layers and other features of the W3C DOM.

Q&A

Q. *What's the difference between changing the appearance of text with traditional tags, such as <b> and <i>, and using a style sheet?*

A. Functionally, there is no difference. In principle, though, the HTML should define the structure of the document, and CSS should define the presentation.

Q. *What happens if two style sheets affect the same text?*

A. The CSS specification is designed to allow style sheets to overlap, or cascade. Thus, you can specify a style for the body of the document and override it for specific elements, such as headings and paragraphs. You can even go one step further and override the style for one particular instance of an element. CSS has a set of rules governing which styles have precedence over others, although you might find that different browsers interpret CSS differently when you have many overlapping styles.

Q. *With CSS in one separate file and JavaScript in another, doesn't web development get confusing?*

A. Yes, this can make a simple page unnecessarily complex. However, as you build more complex pages, you'll find it very helpful to have three separate files. This lets you deal with the content and structure (HTML), presentation (CSS), and behavior (JavaScript) separately.

Q. *What if users don't like the styles I use in my pages?*

A. This is another distinct advantage style sheets have over browser-specific tags. With the latest browsers, users can choose a default style sheet of their own and override any properties they want.

Quiz Questions

Test your knowledge of style sheets and JavaScript by answering the following questions.

1. Which of the following tags is the correct way to begin a CSS style sheet?

    a. `<style>`

    b. `<style type="text/css">`

    c. `<style rel="css">`

2. Why isn't the normal HTML language very good at defining layout and presentation?

    a. Because it was designed by programmers.

    b. Because magazines feared the competition.

    c. Because its main purpose is to define document structure.

3. Which feature of new browsers allows you to use JavaScript statements to change styles?

    a. HTML 4.0

    b. The DOM

    c. CSS 2.0

Quiz Answers

1. b. You begin a CSS style sheet with the tag `<style type="text/css">`.

2. c. HTML is primarily intended to describe the structure of documents.

3. b. The DOM (Document Object Model) enables you to change styles using JavaScript.

Exercises

If you want to gain more experience using CSS style sheets, try the following exercise:

▶ Modify Listing 12.2 to include an `<h2>` tag with a subheading. Add a form element to select this tag's color, and a corresponding `changeh2` function in the script.

▶ Now that Listing 12.2 has three different changeable elements, there is quite a bit of repetition in the script. Create a single `ChangeColor` function that takes a parameter for the element to change, and modify the `onChange` event handlers to send the appropriate element `id` value as a parameter to this function.

HOUR 13

Using the W3C DOM

What You'll Learn in This Hour:

▶ How the W3C DOM standard makes dynamic pages easier
▶ How the DOM's objects are structured
▶ Understanding nodes, parents, children, and siblings
▶ Creating positionable layers
▶ Using CSS's positioning properties
▶ Controlling positioning with JavaScript

Throughout this book, you've learned about the DOM (Document Object Model), JavaScript's way of referencing objects within web documents. In the last hour, you learned to modify style sheet properties on the fly using JavaScript.

During this hour, you'll learn more about how the DOM represents the objects that make up a web document, and how to use DOM objects to move objects within a page.

The DOM and Dynamic HTML

Due to the basic DOM of older browsers, JavaScript could only have a limited effect on a page. There were certain elements, such as forms and images, that you could control with JavaScript, but if you wanted to do something more complex—such as adding or removing several paragraphs, making a form appear out of nowhere, or displaying data dynamically within text—you were out of luck.

To escape this limitation, browser manufacturers created *Dynamic HTML*, or DHTML—an extended DOM that allowed JavaScript to manipulate more of a page. Unfortunately, this was still limiting—you had to work with certain defined parts of the page called *layers* rather than having complete control over the page.

Worse yet, Microsoft and Netscape created completely different and incompatible versions of DHTML, which led to some complicated and unreliable scripting.

Fortunately, you won't have to learn about those incompatible versions of DHTML because the W3C DOM   has made them unnecessary. Although browsers still aren't perfectly interchangeable, today's browsers support enough of the standard DOM to enable you to fully control the content of pages without much concern over browser issues. In this hour and the next hour, you'll create several examples of DOM scripts that will work fine in all modern browsers.

By the Way

> There are still browser issues, of course. Hour 15, "Unobtrusive Scripting," will show you how to deal with browser differences and how to minimize your chances of running into problems with new browsers.

Understanding DOM Structure

In Hour 4, "Working with the Document Object Model (DOM)," you learned about how some of the most important DOM objects are organized: The window object contains the document object, and so on. Although these objects were the only ones available in older browsers, the new DOM adds objects under the document object for every element of a page.

To better understand this concept, let's look at the simple HTML document in Listing 13.1. This document has the usual <head> and <body> sections, a heading, and a single paragraph of text.

LISTING 13.1   A Simple HTML Document

```
<html>
<head>
<title>A simple HTML Document</title>
</head>
<body>
<h1>This is a Heading</h1>
<p>This is a paragraph</p>
</body>
</html>
```

Like all HTML documents, this one is composed of various *containers* and their contents. The <html> tags form a container that includes the entire document, the <body> tags contain the body of the page, and so on.

In the DOM, each container within the page and its contents are represented by an object. The objects are organized into a tree-like structure, with the document object

itself at the root of the tree, and individual elements such as the heading and paragraph of text at the leaves of the tree. Figure 13.1 shows a diagram of these relationships.

In the following sections, you will examine the structure of the DOM more closely.

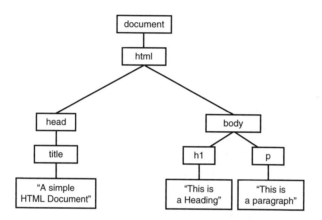

FIGURE 13.1
How the DOM represents an HTML document.

> Don't worry if this tree structure confuses you; you can do almost anything by simply assigning IDs to elements and referring to them. This is the method used in earlier hours of this book, as well as in the Try It Yourself section of this hour. In Hour 14, "Using Advanced DOM Features," you will look at more complicated examples that require you to understand the way objects are organized in the DOM.

By the Way

Nodes

Each container or element in the document is called a *node* in the DOM. In the example in Figure 13.1, each of the objects in boxes is a node, and the lines represent the relationships between the nodes.

You will often need to refer to individual nodes in scripts. You can do this by assigning an ID, or by navigating the tree using the relationships between the nodes.

Parents and Children

As you learned earlier in this book, each JavaScript object can have a *parent*—an object that contains it—and can also have *children*—objects that it contains. The DOM uses the same terminology.

In Figure 13.1, the document object is the parent object for the remaining objects, and does not have a parent itself. The html object is the parent of the head and body objects, and the h1 and p objects are children of the body object.

Text nodes work a bit differently. The actual text in the paragraph is a node in itself, and is a child of the p object. Similarly, the text within the <h1> tags is a child of the h1 object.

By the
~~Way~~

In Hour 14, you will learn methods of referring to objects by their parent and child relationships, as well as ways of adding and removing nodes from the document.

Siblings

The DOM also uses another term for organization of objects: *siblings*. As you might expect, this refers to objects that have the same parent—in other words, objects at the same level in the DOM object tree.

In Figure 13.1, the h1 and p objects are siblings: Both are children of the body object. Similarly, the head and body objects are siblings under the html object.

Creating Positionable Elements (Layers)

Using the W3C DOM, you can control any element in a web page, such as a paragraph or an image. You can change an element's style, as you learned in the previous hour. You can also use the DOM to change the position, visibility, and other attributes of the element.

Before the W3C DOM and CSS2 standards, you could only reposition *layers*, special groups of elements defined with a proprietary tag. Although you can now position any element, it's still useful to work with groups of elements in many cases.

You can effectively create a layer, or a group of HTML objects that can be controlled as a group, using the <div> or <span> tags.

By the
~~Way~~

The <div> and <span> tags are part of the HTML 3.0 standard. <span> defines an arbitrary section of the HTML document, and does not specify any formatting for the text it contains. <div> is similar, but includes a line break before and after its contents.

To create a layer with <div>, enclose the content of the layer between the two division tags and specify the layer's properties in the style attribute of the <div> tag. Here's a simple example:

```
<div id="layer1" style="position:absolute; left:100; top:100">
<p>This is the content of the layer.</p>
</div>
```

This code defines a layer with the name layer1. This is a moveable layer positioned 100 pixels down and 100 pixels to the right of the upper-left corner of the browser window. You'll learn more details about the positioning properties in the next section.

As with all CSS properties, you can specify the position property and other layer properties in a `<style>` block, in an external style sheet, or in the style attribute of an HTML tag. You can also control these properties using JavaScript, as described later in this hour.

Did you Know?

Setting Object Position and Size

You can use various properties in the style attribute of the `<div>` tag when you define a layer to set its position, visibility, and other features. The following properties control the object's position and size:

▶ position is the main positioning attribute and can affect the following properties. The position property can have one of three values:

  ▶ static defines items that are laid out in normal HTML fashion, and cannot be moved. This is the default.

  ▶ absolute specifies that an item will be positioned using coordinates you specify.

  ▶ relative defines an item that is offset a certain amount from the static position, where the element would normally have been laid out within the HTML page.

▶ left and top specify offsets for the position of the item. For absolute positioning, this is relative to the main browser window or a containing item. For relative positioning, it's relative to the usual static position.

▶ right and bottom are an alternative way to specify the position of the item. You can use these when you need to align the object's right or bottom edge.

▶ width and height are similar to the standard HTML width and height attributes and specify a width and height for the item.

▶ z-index specifies how items overlap. Normally indexes start with 1 and go up with each layer added "on top" of the page. By changing this value, you can specify which item is on top.

> Properties such as `left` and `top` work in pixels by default. You can also use any of the units described in the previous hour: px, pt, ex, em, or percentages.

Setting Overflow Properties

Sometimes the content inside a layer is larger than the size the layer can display. Two properties affect how the layer is displayed in this case:

▶ `overflow` indicates whether the content of an element is cut off at the edges of the element, or whether a scroll bar allows viewing the rest of the item. Values include `visible` to display content outside the element; `hidden` to hide the clipped content; `scroll` to display scroll bars; `auto` to let the browser decide whether to display scroll bars; or `inherit` to use a parent object's setting.

▶ `clip` specifies the clipping rectangle for an item. Only the portion of the item inside this rectangle is displayed. Normally this is the same as the element's dimensions, but you can define an offset inside the element here.

Using Visibility Properties

Along with positioning objects, you can use CSS positioning to control whether the objects are visible at all, and how the document is formatted around them. These properties control how objects are displayed:

▶ `display` specifies whether an item is displayed in the browser. A value of "none" hides the object. Other values include `block` to display the object preceded and followed by line breaks, `inline` to display it without line breaks, and `list-item` to display it as part of a list.

▶ `visibility` specifies whether an item is visible. Values include `visible` (default), `hidden`, and `inherit`. A value of `inherit` means the item inherits the visibility of any item it appears within (such as a table or a paragraph).

The difference between `display` and `visibility` is that objects set to `display: none` will not be displayed at all, and the page will be laid out as if the element wasn't there. Objects set to `visibility: hidden` will still be included in the layout of the page, but as empty space.

Setting Background and Border Properties

You can use the following properties to set the color and background image for a layer or other object and control whether borders are displayed:

- ▶ background-color specifies the color for the background of any text in the layer.

- ▶ background-image specifies a background image for any text in the layer.

- ▶ border-width sets the width of the border for all four sides. This can be a numeric value or the keywords thin, medium, or thick.

- ▶ border-style sets the style of border. Values include none (default), dotted, dashed, solid, double, groove, ridge, inset, or outset.

- ▶ border-color sets the color of the border. As with other color properties, this can be a named color such as blue or an RGB color such as #FF03A5.

Controlling Positioning with JavaScript

As you learned in the previous hour, you can control the style attributes for an object with the attributes of the object's style property. You can control the positioning attributes listed in the previous section the same way.

Suppose you have created a layer with the following <div> tags:

```
<div id="layer1" style="position:absolute; left:100; top:100">
<p>This is the content of the layer.</p>
</div>
```

To move this layer up or down within the page using JavaScript, you can change its style.top attribute. For example, the following statements move the layer 100 pixels down from its original position:

```
var obj = document.getElementById("layer1");
obj.style.top=200;
```

The document.getElementById() method returns the object corresponding to the layer's <div> tag, and the second statement sets the object's top positioning property to 200. As you learned in the previous hour, you can also combine these two statements:

```
document.getElementById("layer1").style.top = 200;
```

This simply sets the style.top property for the layer without assigning a variable to the layer's object. You will use this technique in this hour's Try It Yourself section.

Some CSS properties, such as text-indent and border-color, have hyphens in their names. When you use these properties in JavaScript, you combine the hyphenated sections and use a capital letter: textIndent and borderColor.

By the Way

▼ **Try It Yourself**

Creating a Movable Layer

As an example of positioning an element with JavaScript, you can now create an HTML document that defines a layer, and combine it with a script to allow the layer to be moved, hidden, or shown using buttons. Listing 13.2 shows the HTML document that defines the buttons and the layer.

LISTING 13.2   The HTML Document for the Movable Layer Example

```html
<html>
<head>
<title>Positioning Elements with JavaScript</title>
<script language="javascript" type="text/javascript"
    src="position.js">
</script>
<style>
#square {
    position:absolute;
    top: 150;
    left: 100;
    width: 200;
    height: 200;
    border: 2px solid black;
    padding: 10px;
    background-color: #E0E0E0;
}
</style>
</head>
<body>
<h1>Positioning Elements</h1>
<hr>
<form name="form1">
<input type="button" name="left" value="<- Left"
    onClick="pos(-1,0);">
<input type="button" name="right" value="Right ->"
    onClick="pos(1,0);">
<input type="button" name="up" value="Up"
    onClick="pos(0,-1);">
<input type="button" name="down" value="Down"
    onClick="pos(0,1);">
<input type="button" name="hide" value="Hide"
    onClick="hideSquare();">
<input type="button" name="show" value="Show"
    onClick="showSquare();">
</form>
<hr>
<div id="square">
<p>This square is an absolutely positioned
layer that you can move using the buttons above.</p>
</div>
</body>
</html>
```

In addition to some basic HTML, this document consists of the following:

▶ The <script> tag in the header reads a script called position.js, which you will create later in this section.

▶ The <style> section is a brief style sheet that defines the properties for the movable layer. It sets the position property to absolute to indicate that it can be positioned at an exact location, sets the initial position in the top and left properties, and sets border and background-color properties to make the layer clearly visible.

▶ The <input> tags within the <form> section define six buttons: four to move the layer left, right, up, or down, and two to control whether it is visible or hidden.

▶ The <div> section defines the layer itself. The id attribute is set to the value "square". This id is used in the style sheet to refer to the layer, and will also be used in your script.

Type this document (or download it from this book's website) and save it. If you load it into a browser, you should see the buttons and the "square" layer, but the buttons won't do anything yet. The script in Listing 13.3 adds the action to the HTML.

LISTING 13.3   The Script for the Movable Layer Example

```
var x=100,y=150;
function pos(dx,dy) {
    if (!document.getElementById) return;
    x += 10*dx;
    y += 10*dy;
    obj = document.getElementById("square");
    obj.style.top=y;
    obj.style.left=x;
}
function hideSquare() {
    if (!document.getElementById) return;
    obj = document.getElementById("square");
    obj.style.display="none";
}
function showSquare() {
    if (!document.getElementById) return;
    obj = document.getElementById("square");
    obj.style.display="block";
}
```

The var statement at the beginning of the script defines two variables, x and y, that will store the current position of the layer. The pos function is called by the event handlers for all four of the movement buttons.

The parameters of the pos() function, dx and dy, tell the script how the layer should move: If dx is negative, a number will be subtracted from x, moving the layer to the left. If dx is positive, a number will be added to x, moving the layer to the right. Similarly, dy indicates whether to move up or down.

The pos() function begins by making sure the getElementById() function is supported, so it won't attempt to run in older browsers. It then multiplies dx and dy by 10 (to make the movement more obvious) and applies them to x and y. Finally, it sets the top and left properties to the new position, moving the layer.

Two more functions, hideSquare() and showsquare(), hide or show the layer by setting its display property to "none" (hidden) or "block" (shown).

To use this script, save it as position.js and then load the HTML document, Listing 13.2, into your browser. Figure 13.2 shows this script in action.

FIGURE 13.2
The movable layer example in Internet Explorer.

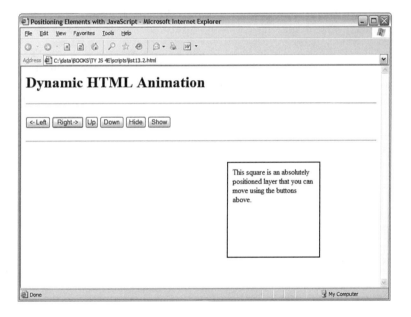

Summary

In this hour, you've learned a bit more about the structure of DOM objects that make up a page, how to use HTML and CSS to define a positionable layer, and how you can use positioning properties dynamically with JavaScript.

Layers are only a simple aspect of what you can do to a page with the W3C DOM. In the next hour, you'll learn how to manipulate the DOM tree to add elements, remove elements, and dynamically change the text within a page.

Q&A

Q. *What happens when my web page includes multiple HTML documents, such as when frames are used?*

A. In this case, each window or frame has its own document object that stores the elements of the HTML document it contains.

Q. *If the DOM allows any object to be dynamically changed, why does the positioning example need to use `<div>` tags to define a layer?*

A. The example could just as easily move a heading, or a paragraph. The layer is just a convenient way to group objects and to create a square object with a border.

Q. *Exactly which browsers support positioning elements with the DOM?*

A. Support for the W3C DOM first appeared in Internet Explorer 5.0 and Netscape 5.0, although it was buggy. Current browsers, such as Internet Explorer 6 and 7, Firefox 1.x, and Opera 7 and 8, have solid and consistent DOM support.

Quiz Questions

Test your knowledge of the W3C DOM by answering the following questions.

1. Which of the following tags is used to create a layer?

   a.   `<layer>`

   b.   `<div>`

   c.   `<style>`

2. Which property controls an element's left-to-right position?

    a. `left`

    b. `width`

    c. `lrpos`

3. Which of the following CSS rules would create a heading that is not currently visible in the page?

    a. `h1 {visibility: invisible;}`

    b. `h1 {display: none;}`

    c. h1 {style: invisible;}

Quiz Answers

1. b. The `<div>` tag can be used to create positionable layers.

2. a. The `left` property controls an element's left-to-right position.

3. b. The `none` value for the `display` property makes it invisible. The `visibili-ty` property could also be used, but its possible `values` are visible or hidden.

Exercises

If you want to gain more experience using the W3C DOM, try the following exercises:

▶ Modify the positioning example in Listings 13.2 and 13.3 to move the square one pixel at a time rather than ten at a time.

▶ Modify the positioning example to eliminate the `<div>` layer and move a paragraph element instead. You will need to move the `id` attribute to the paragraph.

Using Advanced DOM Features

What You'll Learn in This Hour:

▶ Using the properties of DOM nodes
▶ Understanding DOM node methods
▶ Hiding and showing objects within a page
▶ Modifying text within a page
▶ Adding text to a page
▶ Creating a dynamic navigation tree

During this hour, you will take a closer look at the objects in the DOM, and the properties and methods you can use to control them. You will also explore several examples of dynamic HTML pages using these DOM features.

Working with DOM Nodes

As you learned in Hour 13, "Using the W3C DOM," the DOM organizes objects within a web page into a tree-like structure. Each node (object) in this tree can be accessed in JavaScript. In the next sections you will learn how you can use the properties and methods of nodes to manage them.

> The following sections only describe the most important properties and methods of nodes, and those that are supported by current browsers. For a complete list of available properties, see the W3C's DOM specification at http://www.w3.org/TR/DOM-Level-2/.
>
> **By the Way**

Basic Node Properties

You have already used the `style` property of nodes to change their style sheet values. Each node also has a number of basic properties that you can examine or set. These include the following:

▶ `nodeName` is the name of the node (not the ID). For nodes based on HTML tags, such as `<p>` or `<body>`, the name is the tag name: `P` or `BODY`. For the document node, the name is a special code: `#document`. Similarly, text nodes have the name `#text`.

▶ `nodeType` is an integer describing the node's type: 1 for normal HTML tags, 3 for text nodes, and 9 for the document node.

▶ `nodeValue` is the actual text contained within a text node. This property is not valid for other types of nodes.

▶ `innerHTML` is the HTML content of any node. You can assign a value including HTML tags to this property and change the DOM child objects for a node dynamically.

The `innerHTML` property is not a part of the W3C DOM specification. However, it is supported by the major browsers, and is often the easiest way to change content in a page. You can also accomplish this in a more standard way by deleting and creating nodes, as described later in this hour.

Node Relationship Properties

In addition to the basic properties described previously, each node has a number of properties that describe its relation to other nodes. These include the following:

▶ `firstChild` is the first child object for a node. For nodes that contain text, such as h1 or p, the text node containing the actual text is the first child.

▶ `lastChild` is the node's last child object.

▶ `childNodes` is an array that includes all of a node's child nodes. You can use a loop with this array to work with all the nodes under a given node.

▶ `previousSibling` is the sibling (node at the same level) previous to the current node.

▶ `nextSibling` is the sibling after the current node.

> Remember that, like all JavaScript objects and properties, the node properties and functions described here are case sensitive. Be sure you type them exactly as shown.

Document Methods

The document node itself has several methods you might find useful. You have already used one of these, getElementById(), to refer to DOM objects by their ID properties. The document node's methods include the following:

▶ getElementById(*id*) returns the element with the specified *id* attribute.

▶ getElementsByTagName(*tag*) returns an array of all of the elements with a specified tag name. You can use the wildcard * to return an array containing all the nodes in the document.

▶ createTextNode(*text*) creates a new text node containing the specified text, which you can then add to the document.

▶ createElement(*tag*) creates a new HTML element for the specified tag. As with createTextNode, you need to add the element to the document after creating it. You can assign content within the element by changing its child objects or the innerHTML property.

Node Methods

Each node within a page has a number of methods available. Which of these are valid depends on the node's position in the page, and whether it has parent or child nodes. These include the following:

▶ appendChild(new) appends the specified new node after all of the object's existing nodes.

▶ insertBefore(new, old) inserts the specified new child node before the specified old child node, which must already exist.

▶ replaceChild(new, old) replaces the specified old child node with a new node.

▶ removeChild(node) removes a child node from the object's set of children.

▶ hasChildNodes() returns a Boolean value of true if the object has one or more child nodes, or false if it has none.

▶ cloneNode() creates a copy of an existing node. If a parameter of true is supplied, the copy will also include any child nodes of the original node.

Hiding and Showing Objects

We will now move on to a number of real-world examples using the DOM objects to manipulate web pages. As a simple example, you can create a script that hides or shows objects within a page.

As you learned in Hour 13, objects have a `visibility` style property that specifies whether they are currently visible within the page:

```
Object.style.visibility="hidden"; // hides an object
Object.style.visibility="visible"; // shows an object
```

Using this property, you can create a script that hides or shows objects in either browser. Listing 14.1 shows the HTML document for a script that allows two headings to be shown or hidden.

LISTING 14.1   Hiding and Showing Objects

```
<html>
<head>
<title>Hiding and Showing Objects</title>
<script language="Javascript" type="text/javascript">
function ShowHide() {
   if (!document.getElementById) return;
   var head1 = document.getElementById("head1");
   var head2 = document.getElementById("head2");
   var showhead1 = document.form1.head1.checked;
   var showhead2 = document.form1.head2.checked;
   head1.style.visibility=(showhead1) ? "visible" : "hidden";
   head2.style.visibility=(showhead2) ? "visible" : "hidden";
}
</script>
</head>
<body>
<h1 ID="head1">This is the first heading</h1>
<h1 ID="head2">This is the second heading</h1>
<p>Using the W3C DOM, you can choose
whether to show or hide the headings on
this page using the checkboxes below.</p>
<form name="form1">
<input type="checkbox" name="head1"
   checked onClick="ShowHide();">
<b>Show first heading</b><br>
<input type="checkbox" name="head2"
   checked onClick="ShowHide();">
<b>Show second heading</b><br>
</form>
</body>
</html>
```

The `<h1>` tags in this document define headings with the identifiers `head1` and `head2`. The `<form>` section defines a form with two check boxes, one for each of the

headings. When a check box is modified, the onClick method is used to call the ShowHide() function.

This function is defined within the <script> statements in the header. The function assigns the head1 and head2 variables to the objects for the headings, using the getElementById() method. Next, it assigns the showhead1 and showhead2 variables to the contents of the check boxes. Finally, the function uses the style.visibility attributes to set the visibility of the headings.

Figure 14.1 shows this example in action in Internet Explorer. In the figure, the second heading's check box has been unchecked, so only the first heading is visible.

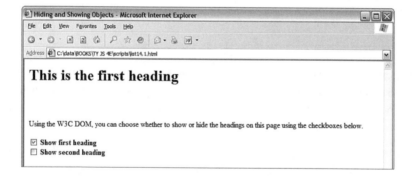

FIGURE 14.1
The text hiding/showing example in Internet Explorer.

Modifying Text Within a Page

Next, you can create a simple script to modify the contents of a heading within a web page. As you learned earlier this hour, the nodeValue property of a text node contains its actual text, and the text node for a heading is a child of that heading. Thus, the syntax to change the text of a heading with the identifier head1 would be

```
Var head1 = document.getElementById("head1");
Head1.firstChild.nodeValue = "New Text Here";
```

This assigns the variable head1 to the heading's object. The firstChild property returns the text node that is the only child of the heading, and its nodeValue property contains the heading text.

Using this technique, it's easy to create a page that allows the heading to be changed dynamically. Listing 14.2 shows the complete HTML document for this script.

LISTING 14.2   The Complete Text-Modifying Example

```html
<html>
<head>
<title>Dynamic Text in JavaScript</title>
<script language="Javascript" type="text/javascript">
function ChangeTitle() {
   if (!document.getElementById) return;
   var newtitle = document.form1.newtitle.value;
   var head1 = document.getElementById("head1");
   head1.firstChild.nodeValue=newtitle;
}
</script>
</head>
<body>
<h1 ID="head1">Dynamic Text in JavaScript</h1>
<p>Using the W3C DOM, you can dynamically
change the heading at the top of this
page. Enter a new title and click the
Change button.</p>
<form name="form1">
<input type="text" name="newtitle" size="25">
<input type="button" value="Change!"
  onClick="ChangeTitle();">
</form>
</body>
</html>
```

This example defines a form that allows the user to enter a new heading for the page. Pressing the button calls the ChangeTitle() function, defined in the header. This function gets the value the user entered in the form, and changes the heading's value to the new text.

Figure 14.2 shows this page in action in Internet Explorer after a new title has been entered and the Change button has been clicked.

FIGURE 14.2
The heading-changing example in action.

Adding Text to a Page

Next, you can create a script that actually adds text to a page. To do this, you must first create a new text node. This statement creates a new text node with the text "this is a test":

```
var node=document.createTextNode("this is a test");
```

Next, you can add this node to the document. To do this, you use the appendChild method. The text can be added to any element that can contain text, but we will use a paragraph. The following statement adds the text node defined previously to the paragraph with the identifier p1:

```
document.getElementById("p1").appendChild(node);
```

Listing 14.3 shows the HTML document for a complete example that uses this technique, using a form to allow the user to specify text to add to the page.

LISTING 14.3   Adding Text to a Page

```
<html>
<head>
<title>Adding to a page</title>
<script language="Javascript" type="text/javascript">
function AddText() {
   if (!document.getElementById) return;
   var sentence=document.form1.sentence.value;
   var node=document.createTextNode(" " + sentence);
   document.getElementById("p1").appendChild(node);
   document.form1.sentence.value="";
}
</script>
</head>
<body>
<h1>Create Your Own Content</h1>
<p id="p1">Using the W3C DOM, you can dynamically
add sentences to this paragraph. Type a sentence
and click the Add button.</p>
<form name="form1">
<input type="text" name="sentence" size="65">
<input type="button" value="Add" onClick="AddText();">
</form>
</body>
</html>
```

In this example, the <p> section defines the paragraph that will hold the added text. The <form> section defines a form with a text field called sentence, and an Add button, which calls the AddText() function. This function is defined in the header.

The `AddText()` function first assigns the `sentence` variable to the text typed in the text field. Next, it creates a new text node containing the sentence, and appends the new text node to the paragraph.

Load this document into a browser to test it, and try adding several sentences by typing them and clicking the Add button. Figure 14.3 shows Firefox's display of this document after several sentences have been added to the paragraph.

FIGURE 14.3
Firefox shows
the text-adding
example.

Try It Yourself

Creating a Navigation Tree

One common use of JavaScript and the DOM is to create a dynamic tree-like navigation system for a site, with sections that can be expanded and collapsed. Although this is unnecessary for small sites, it's a good way to organize what may be hundreds of links for a larger site. To further experiment with the techniques you learned about in this hour, you can create a simple navigation tree using the DOM.

To begin, you will need an HTML document that defines the content of the navigation tree, shown in Listing 14.4.

LISTING 14.4   The HTML for the Navigation Tree Example

```
<html>
<head><title>Creating a Navigation Tree</title>
<style>
   A {text-decoration: none;}
   #productsmenu,#supportmenu,#contactmenu {
     display: none;
     margin-left: 2em;
   }
</style>
</head>
<body>
<h1>Navigation Tree Example</h1>
<p>The navigation tree below allows you to expand and
collapse items.</p>
<ul>
 <li><a id="products" href="#">[+] Products</a>
```

LISTING 14.4   Continued

```
  <ul ID="productsmenu">
    <li><a href="prodlist.html">Product List</a></li>
    <li><a href="order.html">Order Form</a></li>
    <li><a href="pricelist.html">Price List</a></li>
  </ul>
</li>
<li><a id="support" href="#">[+] Support</a>
  <ul id="supportmenu">
    <li><a href="sforum.html">Support Forum</a></li>
    <li><a href="scontact.html">Contact Support</a></li>
  </ul>
</li>
<li><a ID="contact" href="#">[+] Contact Us</a>
  <ul id="contactmenu">
    <li><a href="contact1.html">Service Department</a></li>
    <li><a href="contact2.html">Sales Department</a></li>
  </ul>
</li>
</ul>
<script language="javascript" type="text/javascript"
  src="tree.js">
</script>
</body>
</html>
```

In this document, the links are laid out as a nested list using <ul> and <li> tags. Using a standard list like this rather than <div> tags has two benefits: First, the browser formats the tree as a list with bullets automatically. Second, it supports older browsers—even a browser that does not support CSS or JavaScript will load and display the list correctly. It won't have the dynamic features, but the links will still work.

The tree has three main nodes: Products, Support, and Contact Us. Each one has a link you can click to display or hide the links in that section. The id attribute has been used on each <a> tag so the script can attach an event handler to it. Each node also has a submenu defined with <ul> and <li> tags. An id attribute is also used on the <ul> tag so the script can hide or display the list.

The <script> tag at the end of the document includes the script you will create next. The tag is placed after the body of the page so that the script can add event handlers to elements in the page.

The <style> block at the beginning of the document adds some formatting to the links, and uses the display: none attribute to initially hide the submenus. They will be revealed by the script when the link is clicked.

The script for this example is shown in Listing 14.5.

LISTING 14.5   The JavaScript File for the Navigation Tree Example

```
function Toggle(e) {
  // Don't try this in old browsers
  if (!document.getElementById) return;
  // Get the event object
  if (!e) var e = window.event;
  // Which link was clicked?
  whichlink = (e.target) ? e.target.id : e.srcElement.id;
  // get the menu object
  obj=document.getElementById(whichlink+"menu");
  // Is the menu visible?
  visible=(obj.style.display=="block")
  // Get the key object (the link itself)
  key=document.getElementById(whichlink);
  // Get the name (Products, Contact, etc.)
  keyname = key.firstChild.nodeValue.substring(3);
  if (visible) {
    // hide the menu
    obj.style.display="none";
    key.firstChild.nodeValue = "[+]" + keyname;
  } else {
    // show the menu
    obj.style.display="block";
    key.firstChild.nodeValue = "[-]" + keyname;
  }
}
document.getElementById("products").onclick=Toggle;
document.getElementById("support").onclick=Toggle;
document.getElementById("contact").onclick=Toggle;
```

The Toggle() function shows or hides a menu. It first determines which of the links triggered the event, and then uses the link's id attribute to find the objects for the menu and for the link itself. If the menu is currently visible, it is hidden, and if it is currently hidden, it is revealed. The appropriate symbol [+] or [-] is added to the link name and displayed by modifying the text node's nodeValue attribute.

The last three lines of the script assign the Toggle() function as the onClick event handler for the three top-level links of the tree.

To use this script, save it as tree.js in the same folder as the HTML document you created previously, and load the HTML file into a browser. Figure 14.4 shows the example in action after all three nodes of the tree have been expanded.

Did you Know?

> To add items to the navigation tree, add links to the HTML file. If you add a new submenu, you need to assign an id attribute to the link, use the same word plus menu as the id of the menu, and assign its onclick event to the Toggle() function at the end of the script.

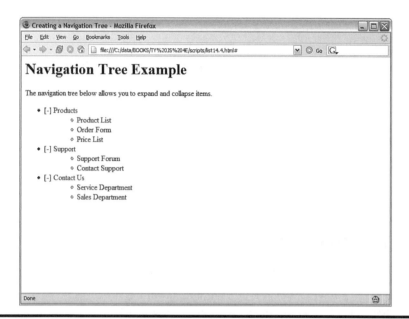

FIGURE 14.4
The navigation tree example as displayed by Firefox.

Summary

In this hour, you learned some of the advanced features of the new W3C DOM (Document Object Model). You learned the functions and properties you can use to manage DOM objects, and used example scripts to hide and show elements within a page, modify text, and add text. Finally, you created a dynamic navigation tree using DOM features.

Congratulations—you've reached the end of Part III! Now that you've learned all about the DOM, you will move on to some advanced aspects of JavaScript. In the next hour, you will learn how to create scripts that unobtrusively handle multiple browsers, and some best practices for more involved scripting.

Q&A

Q. *Can I avoid assigning an* **id** *attribute to every DOM object I want to handle with a script?*

A. Yes. Although the scripts in this hour typically use the id attribute for convenience, you can actually locate any object in the page by using combinations of node properties such as firstChild and nextSibling. However, keep in mind that any change you make to the HTML can change an element's place in the DOM hierarchy, so the id attribute is a reliable way to handle this.

Q. *Can I include HTML tags, such as <b>, in the new text I assign to a text node?*

A. Text nodes are limited to text if you use the `nodeValue` attribute. However, the `innerHTML` property does not have this limitation and can be used to insert any HTML.

Q. *Is there a reference that specifies which DOM properties and methods work in which browser versions?*

A. Yes, several websites are available that keep up-to-date lists of browser features. Some of these are listed in Appendix A, "Other JavaScript Resources."

Quiz Questions

Test your knowledge of the DOM by answering the following questions.

1. If para1 is the DOM object for a paragraph, what is the correct syntax to change the text within the paragraph to "New Text"?

   a. `para1.value="New Text";`

   b. `para1.firstChild.nodeValue="New Text";`

   c. `para1.nodeValue="New Text";`

2. Which of the following DOM objects never has a parent node?

   a. `body`

   b. `div`

   c. `document`

3. Which of the following is the correct syntax to get the DOM object for a heading with the identifier head1?

   a. `document.getElementById("head1")`

   b. `document.GetElementByID("head1")`

   c. `document.getElementsById("head1")`

Quiz Answers

1. b. The actual text is the `nodeValue` attribute of the text node, which is a child of the paragraph node.

2. c. The `document` object is the root of the DOM object tree, and has no parent object.

3. a. `getElementById` has a lowercase *g* at the beginning, and a lowercase *d* at the end, contrary to what you might know about normal English grammar.

Exercises

If you want to gain more experience using the advanced DOM features you learned in this hour, try the following exercise:

▶ Add a third check box to Listing 14.1 to allow the paragraph of text to be shown or hidden. You will need to add an id attribute to the <p> tag, add a check box to the form, and add the appropriate lines to the script.

▶ Add a fourth node to the navigation tree in Listing 14.4, and make the appropriate changes to the script in Listing 14.5 to make the new section of the tree expand and collapse correctly.

PART IV:

Working with Advanced JavaScript Features

HOUR 15

Unobtrusive Scripting

What You'll Learn in This Hour:

▶ Best practices for creating unobtrusive scripts
▶ Separating content, presentation, and behavior
▶ Following web standards to create cross-browser scripts
▶ Reading and displaying browser information
▶ Using feature sensing to avoid errors
▶ Supporting non-JavaScript browsers

You have now learned enough JavaScript to create some complex effects—and potentially to create some complex problems. In Part IV, you will learn about some of JavaScript's more advanced features, and learn how to avoid problems as you progress to longer and more complicated scripts.

In this hour, you'll learn some guidelines for creating scripts and pages that are easy to maintain, easy to use, and follow web standards. This is known as *unobtrusive scripting*: Scripts add features without getting in the way of the user, the developer maintaining the code, or the designer building the layout of the site. You'll also learn how to make sure your scripts will work in multiple browsers, and won't stop working when a new browser comes along.

Scripting Best Practices

As you start to develop more complex scripts, it's important to know some scripting *best practices*. These are guidelines for using JavaScript that more experienced programmers have learned the hard way. Here are a few of the benefits of following these best practices:

▶ Your code will be readable and easy to maintain, whether you're turning the page over to someone else or just trying to remember what you did a year ago.

▶ You'll create code that follows standards, and won't be crippled by a new version of a particular browser.

▶ You'll create pages that work even without JavaScript.

▶ It will be easy to adapt code you create for one site to another site or project.

▶ Your users will thank you for creating a site that is easy to use, and easy to fix when things go wrong.

Whether you're writing an entire AJAX web application or simply enhancing a page with a three-line script, it's useful to know some of the concepts that are regularly considered by those who write complex scripts for a living. The following sections introduce some of these best practices.

Content, Presentation, and Behavior

When you create a web page, or especially an entire site or application, you're dealing with three key areas: *content*, *presentation*, and *behavior*.

▶ *Content* consists of the words that a visitor can read on your pages. You create the content as text, and mark it up with HTML to define different classes of content—headings, paragraphs, links, and so on.

▶ *Presentation* is the appearance and layout of the words on each page—text formatting, fonts, colors, and graphics. Although it was common in the early days of the Web to create the presentation using HTML only, you can now use Cascading Style Sheets (CSS) to define the presentation.

▶ *Behavior* is what happens when you interact with a page—items that highlight when you move over them, forms you can submit, and so on. This is where JavaScript comes in, along with server-side languages such as PHP.

It's a good idea to keep these three areas in mind, especially as you create larger sites. Ideally, you want to keep content, presentation, and behavior separated as much as possible. One good way to do this is to create an external CSS file for the presentation and an external JavaScript file for the behavior, and link them to the HTML document.

Keeping things separated like this makes it easier to maintain a large site—if you need to change the color of the headings, for example, you can make a quick edit to the CSS file without having to look through all of the HTML markup to find the right place to edit. It also makes it easy for you to reuse the same CSS and JavaScript on multiple pages of a site. Last, but not least, this will encourage you to use each language where its strengths lie, making your job easier.

Progressive Enhancement

One of the old buzzwords of web design was *graceful degradation*. The idea was that you could build a site that used all of the bells and whistles of the latest browsers, as long as it would "gracefully degrade" to work on older browsers. This mostly meant testing on a few older browsers and hoping it worked, and there was always the possibility of problems in browsers that didn't support the latest features.

Ironically, you might expect browsers that lack the latest features to be older, less popular ones, but some of the biggest problems are with brand-new browsers—those included with mobile phones and other new devices, all of which are primitive compared to the latest browsers running on computers.

One new approach to web design that addresses this problem is known as *progressive enhancement*. The idea is to keep the HTML documents as simple as possible, so they'll definitely work in even the most primitive browsers. After you've tested that and made sure the basic functionality is there, you can add features that make the site easier to use or better looking for those with new browsers.

If you add these features unobtrusively, they have little chance of preventing the site from working in its primitive HTML form. Here are some guidelines for progressive enhancement:

- ▶ Enhance the presentation by adding rules to a separate CSS file. Try to avoid using HTML markup strictly for presentation, such as <b> for boldface or <blockquote> for an indented section.

- ▶ Enhance behavior by adding scripts to an external JavaScript file.

- ▶ Add events without using inline event handlers, as described in Hour 9, "Responding to Events," and later in this hour.

- ▶ Use feature sensing, described later this hour, to ensure that JavaScript code only executes on browsers that support the features it requires.

> The term *progressive enhancement* first appeared in a presentation and article on this topic by Steve Champeon. The original article, along with many more web design articles, is available on his company's website at http://hesketh.com/.

By the Way

Adding Event Handlers

In Hour 9, you learned that there is more than one way to set up an event handler. The simplest way is to add them directly to an HTML tag. For example, this <body> tag has an event handler that calls a function called Startup.

```
<body onLoad="Startup();">
```

This method still works, but it does mean putting JavaScript code in the HTML page, which means you haven't fully separated content and behavior. To keep things entirely separate, you can set up the event handler in the JavaScript file instead, using syntax like this:

```
window.onload=Startup;
```

Right now, this is usually the best way to set up events: It keeps JavaScript out of the HTML file, and it works in all browsers since Netscape 4 and Internet Explorer 4. However, it does have one problem: You can't attach more than one event to the same element of a page. For example, you can't have two different onLoad event handlers that both execute when the page loads.

When you're the only one writing scripts, this is no big deal—you can combine the two into one function. But when you're trying to use two or three third-party scripts on a page, and all of them want to add an onLoad event handler to the body, you have a problem.

The W3C Event Model

To solve this problem and standardize event handling, the W3C created an event model as part of the DOM level 2 standard. This uses a method, addEventListener(), to attach a handler to any event on any element. For example, the following uses the W3C model to set up the same onLoad event handler as the previous examples:

```
window.addEventListener('load', Startup, false);
```

The first parameter of addEventListener() is the event name without the on prefix—load, click, mouseover, and so on. The second parameter specifies the function to handle the event, and the third is an advanced flag that indicates how multiple events should be handled. (false works for most purposes.)

Any number of functions can be attached to an event in this way. Because one event handler doesn't replace another, you use a separate function, removeEventListener(), which uses the same parameters:

```
window.removeEventListener('load', Startup, false);
```

The problem with the W3C model is that Internet Explorer (as of versions 6 and 7) doesn't support it. Instead, it supports a proprietary method, attachEvent(), which does much the same thing. Here's the Startup event handler defined Microsoft-style:

```
window.attachEvent('onload', Startup);
```

The attachEvent() method has two parameters. The first is the event, with the on prefix—onload, onclick, onmouseover, and so on. The second is the function that

will handle the event. Internet Explorer also supports a detachEvent() method with the same parameters for removing an event handler.

Attaching Events the Cross-Browser Way

As you can see, attaching events in this new way is complex and will require different code for different browsers. In most cases, you're better off using the traditional method to attach events, and that method is used in most of this book's examples. However, if you really need to support multiple event handlers, you can use some if statements to use either the W3C method or Microsoft's method. For example, the following code adds the ClickMe() function as an event for the element with the id attribute btn:

```
obj = document.getElementById("btn");
if (obj.addEventListener) {
   obj.addEventListener('click',ClickMe,false);
} else if (obj.attachEvent) {
   obj.attachEvent('onclick',ClickMe);
} else {
   obj.onclick=ClickMe;
}
```

This checks for the addEventListener() method, and uses it if it's found. Otherwise, it checks for the attachEvent() method, and uses that. If neither is found, it uses the traditional method to attach the event handler. This technique is called *feature sensing* and is explained in detail later this hour.

Many universal functions are available to compensate for the lack of a consistent way to attach events. If you are using a third-party library, there's a good chance it includes an event function that can simplify this process for you.

> The Yahoo! UI Library includes an event-handling function that can attach events in any browser, attach the same event handler to many objects at once, and other nice features. See http://developer.yahoo.net/yui/ for details, and see Hour 8, "Using Built-in Functions and Libraries," for information about using third-party libraries.

Did you Know?

Web Standards: Avoid Being Browser Specific

The Web was built on standards, such as the HTML standard developed by the W3C. Now there are a lot of standards involved with JavaScript—CSS, the W3C DOM, and the ECMAScript standard that defines JavaScript's syntax.

Right now, both Microsoft and the Mozilla Project are improving their browsers' support for web standards, but there are always going to be some browser-specific, nonstandard features, and some parts of the newest standards won't be consistently supported between browsers.

Although it's perfectly fine to test your code in multiple browsers and do whatever it takes to get it working, it's a good idea to follow the standards rather than browser-specific techniques when you can. This ensures that your code will work on future browsers that improve their standards support, whereas browser-specific features might disappear in new versions.

> One reason to make sure you follow standards is that your pages can be better interpreted by search engines, which often helps your site get search traffic. Separating content, presentation, and behavior is also good for search engines because they can focus on the HTML content of your site without having to skip over JavaScript or CSS.

Documenting Your Code

As you create more complex scripts, don't forget to include comments in your code to document what it does, especially when some of the code seems confusing or is difficult to get working. It's also a good idea to document all of the data structures and variables, and function arguments used in a larger script.

Comments are a good way to organize code, and will help you work on the script in the future. If you're doing this for a living, you'll definitely need to use comments so that others can work on your code as easily as you can.

Usability

While you're adding cool features to your site, don't forget about *usability*—making things as easy, logical, and convenient as possible for users of your site. Although there are many books and websites devoted to usability information, a bit of common sense goes a long way.

For example, suppose you use a drop-down list as the only way to navigate between pages of your site. This is a common use for JavaScript, and it works well, but is it usable? Try comparing it to a simple set of links across the top of a page.

▶ The list of links lets you see at a glance what the site contains; the drop-down list requires you to click to see the same list.

▶ Users expect links and can spot them quickly—a drop-down list is more likely to be part of a form than a navigation tool, and thus won't be the first thing they look for when they want to navigate your site.

▶ Navigating with a link takes a single click—navigating with the drop-down list takes at least two clicks.

Remember to consider the user's point of view whenever you add JavaScript to a site, and be sure you're making the site easier to use—or at least not harder to use. Also make sure the site is easy to use even without JavaScript.

Design Patterns

If you learn more about usability, you'll undoubtedly see *design patterns* mentioned. This is a computer science term meaning "an optimal solution to a common problem." In web development, design patterns are ways of designing and implementing part of a site that webmasters run into over and over.

For example, if you have a site that displays multiple pages of data, you'll have "Next Page" and "Previous Page" links, and perhaps numeric links for each page. This is a common design pattern—a problem many web designers have had to solve, and one with a generally agreed-upon solution. Other common web design patterns include a login form, a search engine, or a list of navigation links for a site.

Of course, you can be completely original and make a search engine, a shopping cart, or a login form that looks nothing like any other, but unless you have a way of making them even easier to use, you're better off following the pattern, and giving your users an experience that matches their expectations.

Although you can find some common design patterns just by browsing sites similar to yours and noticing how they solved particular problems, there are also sites that specialize in documenting these patterns, and they're a good place to start if you need ideas on how to make your site work.

The Yahoo! Developer Network documents a variety of design patterns used on their network of sites, many of which are implemented using JavaScript: http://developer.yahoo.net/ypatterns/.

Did you Know?

Accessibility

One final aspect of usability to consider is *accessibility*—making your site as accessible as possible for all users, including the disabled. For example, blind users might use a text-reading program to read your site, which will ignore images and most scripts. More than just good manners, accessibility is mandated by law in some countries.

The subject of accessibility is complex, but you can get most of the way there by following the philosophy of progressive enhancement: Keep the HTML as simple as possible, keep JavaScript and CSS separate, and make JavaScript an enhancement rather than a requirement for using your site.

Reading Browser Information

In Hour 4, "Working with the Document Object Model (DOM)," you learned about the various objects (such as window and document) that represent portions of the browser window and the current web document. JavaScript also includes an object called navigator that you can use to read information about the user's browser.

The navigator object isn't part of the DOM, so you can refer to it directly. It includes a number of properties, each of which tells you something about the browser. These include the following:

- navigator.appCodeName is the browser's internal code name, usually Mozilla.

- navigator.appName is the browser's name, usually Netscape or Microsoft Internet Explorer.

- navigator.appVersion is the version of the browser being used—for example, 4.0(Win95;I).

- navigator.userAgent is the user-agent header, a string that the browser sends to the web server when requesting a web page. It includes the entire version information—for example, Mozilla/4.0(Win95;I).

- navigator.language is the language (such as English or Spanish) of the browser. This is stored as a code, such as "en_US" for U.S. English. This property is supported only by Netscape and Firefox.

- navigator.platform is the computer platform of the current browser. This is a short string, such as Win16, Win32, or MacPPC. You can use this to enable any platform-specific features—for example, ActiveX components.

As you might have guessed, the navigator object is named after Netscape Navigator, the browser that originally supported JavaScript. Fortunately, this object is also supported by Internet Explorer and most other recent browsers.

Displaying Browser Information

As an example of how to read the navigator object's properties, Listing 15.1 shows a script that displays a list of the properties and their values for the current browser.

LISTING 15.1   A Script to Display Information About the Browser

```html
<html>
<head>
<title>Browser Information</title>
</head>
<body>
<h1>Browser Information</h1>
<hr>
<p>
The <b>navigator</b> object contains the following information
about the browser you are using.
</p>
<ul>
<script language="JavaScript" type="text/javascript">
document.write("<li><b>Code Name:</b> " + navigator.appCodeName);
document.write("<li><b>App Name:</b> " + navigator.appName);
document.write("<li><b>App Version:</b> " + navigator.appVersion);
document.write("<li><b>User Agent:</b> " + navigator.userAgent);
document.write("<li><b>Language:</b> " + navigator.language);
document.write("<li><b>Platform:</b> " + navigator.platform);
</script>
</ul>
<hr>
</body>
</html>
```

This script includes a basic HTML document. A script is used within the body of the document to display each of the properties of the `navigator` object using the `document.write()` statement.

To try this script, load it into the browser of your choice. If you have more than one browser or browser version handy, try it in each one. Firefox's display of the script is shown in Figure 15.1.

Dealing with Dishonest Browsers

If you tried the browser information script in Listing 15.1 using one of the latest versions of Internet Explorer, you probably got a surprise. Figure 15.2 shows how Internet Explorer 6.0 displays the script.

There are several unexpected things about this display. First of all, the `navigator.language` property is listed as undefined. This isn't much of a surprise because this property isn't yet supported by Internet Explorer.

More important, you'll notice that the word `Mozilla` appears in the Code Name and User Agent fields. The full user agent string reads as follows:

```
Mozilla/4.0 (compatible; MSIE 6.0; Windows NT 5.1)
```

FIGURE 15.1
Firefox displays
the browser
information
script.

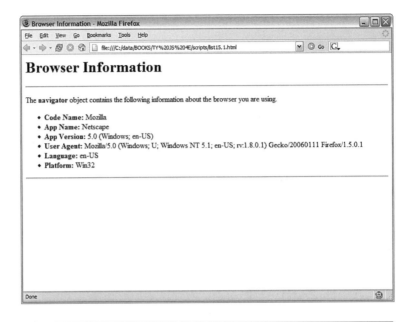

FIGURE 15.2
Internet Explorer
displays the
browser infor-
mation script.

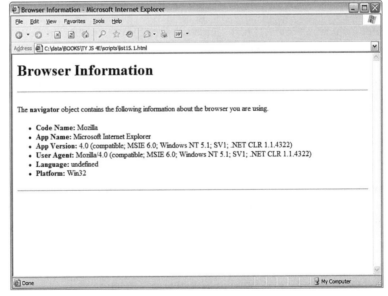

Believe it or not, Microsoft did have a good reason for this. At the height of the
browser wars, about the time Netscape 3.0 and IE 3.0 came out, it was becoming
common to see "Netscape only" pages. Some webmasters who used features such as
frames and JavaScript set their servers to turn away browsers without `Mozilla` in
their user agent string. The problem with this was that most of these features were
also supported by Internet Explorer.

Microsoft solved this problem in IE 4.0 by making IE's user agent read `Mozilla`, with the word `compatible` in parentheses. This allows IE users to view those pages, but still includes enough details to tell web servers which browser is in use.

You've probably already noticed the other problem with Internet Explorer 6.0's user agent string: the portion reading `Mozilla/4.0`. Not only is IE claiming to be Netscape, but it's also masquerading as version 4.0. Why?

As it turns out, this was another effort by Microsoft to stay one step ahead of the browser wars, although this one doesn't make quite as much sense. Because poorly written scripts were checking specifically for "Mozilla/4" for dynamic HTML pages, Microsoft was concerned that its 5.0 version would fail to run these pages. Since changing it now would only create more confusion, this tradition continues with IE 6.0.

> Microsoft isn't alone in confusing browser IDs. Netscape version 6 displays a user agent string beginning with `Mozilla/5`, and an app version of 5.0. (Netscape 5.0 was Netscape's open-source browser, code named Mozilla, which formed the foundation of Netscape 6 and Firefox.)

By the Way

Although these are two interesting episodes in the annals of the browser wars, what does all this mean to you? Well, you'll need to be careful when your scripts are trying to differentiate between IE and Netscape, and between different versions. You'll need to check for specific combinations instead of merely checking the `navigator.appVersion` value. Fortunately, there's a better way to handle this, as you'll learn in the next section.

Cross-Browser Scripting

If all of those details about detecting different browser versions seem confusing, here's some good news—in most cases, you can write cross-browser scripts without referring to the `navigator` object at all. This is not only easier, it's better, because browser-checking code is often confused by new browser versions, and has to be updated each time a new browser is released.

Feature Sensing

Checking browser versions is sometimes called *browser sensing*. The better way of dealing with multiple browsers is called *feature sensing*. In feature sensing, rather than checking for a specific browser, you check for a specific feature. For example, suppose your script needs to use the `document.getElementById()` function. You can begin a script with an `if` statement that checks for the existence of this function:

```
if (document.getElementById) {
   // do stuff
}
```

If the `getElementById` function exists, the block of code between the brackets will be executed. Another common way to use feature sensing is at the beginning of a function that will make use of a feature:

```
function changeText() {
   if (!document.getElementById) return;
   // the rest of the function executes if the feature is supported
}
```

If this looks familiar, it's because it's been used in several previous examples in this book. For example, most of the code listings in Hour 14, "Using Advanced DOM Features," make use of feature sensing to prevent errors in browsers that don't support the W3C DOM.

You don't need to check for *every* feature before you use it—for example, there's not much point in verifying that the `window` object exists in most cases. You can also assume that the existence of one feature means others are supported: If `getElementById()` is supported, chances are the rest of the W3C DOM functions are supported.

Feature sensing is a very reliable method of keeping your JavaScript unobtrusive—if a browser supports the feature, it works, and if the browser doesn't, your script stays out of the way. It's also much easier than trying to keep track of hundreds of different browser versions and what they support.

Feature sensing is also handy when working with third-party libraries, as discussed in Hour 8. You can check for the existence of an object or a function belonging to the library to verify that the library file has been loaded before your script uses its features.

Dealing with Browser Quirks

So, if feature sensing is better than browser sensing, why do you still need to know about the `navigator` object? There's one situation where it still comes in handy, although if you're lucky you won't find yourself in that situation.

As you develop a complex script and test it in multiple browsers, you might run across a situation where your perfectly standard code works as it should in one browser, and fails to work in another. Assuming you've eliminated the possibility of a problem with your script, you've probably run into a browser bug, or a difference in features between browsers at the very least. Here are some tips for this situation:

▶ Double-check for a bug in your own code. See Hour 16, "Debugging JavaScript Applications," for debugging tips.

▶ Search the Web to see if others have run into the same bug. Often you'll find that someone else has already found a workaround.

▶ Try a different approach to the code, and you might sidestep the bug.

▶ If the problem is that a feature is missing in one browser, use feature sensing to check for that feature.

▶ When all else fails, use the navigator object to detect a particular browser and substitute some code that works in that browser. This should be your last resort.

Peter-Paul Koch's QuirksMode, www.quirksmode.org, is a good place to start when you're looking for specific information about browser bugs.

Did you Know?

Supporting Non-JavaScript Browsers

Some visitors to your site will be using browsers that don't support JavaScript at all. These aren't just a few holdouts using ancient browsers—actually, there are more non-JavaScript browsers than you might think:

▶ Both Internet Explorer and Firefox include an option to turn off JavaScript, and some users do so. More often, the browser might have been set up by their ISP or employer with JavaScript turned off by default, usually in a misguided attempt to increase security.

▶ Some corporate firewalls and personal antivirus software block JavaScript.

▶ Some ad-blocking software mistakenly prevents scripts from working even if they aren't related to advertising.

▶ More and more mobile phones are coming with web browsers these days, and most of these support little to no JavaScript.

▶ Some disabled users use special-purpose browsers or text-only browsers that might not support JavaScript.

As you can see, it would be foolish to assume that all of your visitors will support JavaScript. Two techniques you can use to make sure these users can still use the site are discussed in the following sections.

Search engines are another "browser" that will visit your site frequently, and they usually don't pay any attention to JavaScript. If you want search engines to fully index your site, it's critical that you avoid making JavaScript a requirement to navigate the site.

Using the `<noscript>` Tag

One way to be friendly to non-JavaScript browsers is to use the `<noscript>` tag. Supported in most modern browsers, this tag displays a message to non-JavaScript browsers. Browsers that support JavaScript ignore the text between the `<noscript>` tags, whereas others display it. Here is a simple example:

```
<noscript>
This page requires JavaScript. You can either switch to a browser
that supports JavaScript, turn your browser's script support on,
or switch to the <a href="nojs.html">Non-JavaScript</a> version of
this page.
</noscript>
```

Although this works, the trouble is that `<noscript>` is not consistently supported by all browsers that support JavaScript. An alternative that avoids `<noscript>` is to send users with JavaScript support to another page. This can be accomplished with a single JavaScript statement:

```
<script language="JavaScript" type="text/javascript">
window.location="JavaScript.html";
</script>
```

This script redirects the user to a different page. If the browser doesn't support JavaScript, of course, the script won't be executed, and the rest of the page can display a warning message to explain the situation.

Keeping JavaScript Optional

Although you can detect JavaScript browsers and display a message to the rest, the best choice is to simply make your scripts unobtrusive. Use JavaScript to enhance rather than as an essential feature, keep JavaScript in separate files, assign event handlers in the JavaScript file rather than in the HTML, and browsers that don't support JavaScript will simply ignore your script.

In those rare cases where you absolutely need JavaScript—for example, an AJAX application or a JavaScript game—you can warn users that JavaScript is required. However, it's a good idea to offer an alternative JavaScript-free way to use your site, especially if it's an e-commerce or business site that your business relies on. Don't turn away customers with lazy programming.

One place you should definitely *not* require JavaScript is in the navigation of your site. Although you can create drop-down menus and other fancy navigation tools using JavaScript, they prevent users' non-JavaScript browsers from viewing all of your site's pages. They also prevent search engines from viewing the entire site, compromising your chances of getting search traffic.

Google's Gmail application (mail.google.com), one of the most well-known uses of AJAX, requires JavaScript for its elegant interface. However, Google offers a Basic HTML View that can be used without JavaScript. This allows them to support older browsers and mobile phones without compromising the user experience for those with modern browsers.

By the Way

Avoiding Errors

If you've made sure JavaScript is only an enhancement to your site, rather than a requirement, those with browsers that don't support JavaScript for whatever reason will still be able to navigate your site. One last thing to worry about: It's possible for JavaScript to cause an error, or confuse these browsers into displaying your page incorrectly.

This is a particular concern with browsers that partially support JavaScript, such as mobile phone browsers. They might interpret a `<script>` tag and start the script, but might not support the full JavaScript language or DOM. Here are some guidelines for avoiding errors:

▶ Use a separate JavaScript file for all scripts. This is the best way to guarantee that the browser will ignore your script completely if it does not have JavaScript support.

▶ Use feature sensing whenever your script tries to use the newer DOM features, such as `document.getElementById()`.

▶ Test your pages with your browser's JavaScript support turned off. Make sure nothing looks strange, and make sure you can still navigate the site.

The developer's toolbars for Firefox and Internet Explorer include a convenient way to turn off JavaScript for testing. See Hour 16 for details.

Did you Know?

▼ Try It Yourself

Creating an Unobtrusive Script

As an example of unobtrusive scripting, you can create a script that adds functionality to a page with JavaScript without compromising its performance in older
browsers. In this example, you will create a script that creates graphic check boxes
as an alternative to regular check boxes.

> Note: See Hour 11, "Getting Data with Forms," for the basics of working with
> forms in JavaScript.

Let's start with the final result: Figure 15.3 shows this example as it appears in
Firefox. The first check box is an ordinary HTML one, and the second is a graphic
check box managed by JavaScript.

FIGURE 15.3
The graphic
check box
example in
action.

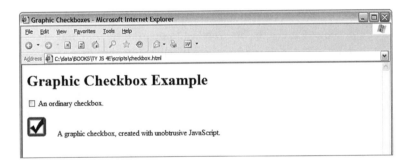

The graphic check box is just a larger graphic that you can click on to display the
checked or unchecked version of the graphic. Although this could just be a simple
JavaScript simulation that acts like a check box, it's a bit more sophisticated. Take a
look at the HTML for this example in Listing 15.2.

LISTING 15.2   The HTML File for the Graphic Check box Example

```
<html>
<head>
<title>Graphic Checkboxes</title>
</head>
<body>
<h1>Graphic Checkbox Example</h1>
<form name="form1">
<p>
<input type = "checkbox" name="check1" id="check1">
An ordinary checkbox.
</p><p>
<input type = "checkbox" name="check2" id="check2">
```

LISTING 15.2   Continued

```
A graphic checkbox, created with unobtrusive JavaScript.
</p>
</form>
<script language="JavaScript" type="text/javascript"
    src="checkbox.js">
</script>
</body>
</html>
```

If you look closely at the HTML, you'll see that the two check boxes are defined in exactly the same way with the standard <input> tag. Rather than substitute for a check box, this script actually replaces the regular check box with the graphic version. The script for this example is shown in Listing 15.3.

LISTING 15.3   The JavaScript File for the Graphic Check box Example

```
function graphicBox(box) {
    // be unobtrusive
    if (!document.getElementById) return;
    // find the object and its parent
    obj = document.getElementById(box);
    parentobj = obj.parentNode;
    // hide the regular checkbox
    obj.style.visibility = "hidden";
    // create the image element and set its onclick event
    img = document.createElement("IMG");
    img.onclick = Toggle;
    img.src = "unchecked.gif";
    // save the checkbox id within the image ID
    img.id = "img" + box;
    // display the graphic checkbox
    parentobj.insertBefore(img,obj);
}
function Toggle(e) {
    if (!e) var e=window.event;
    // find the image ID
    img = (e.target) ? e.target : e.srcElement;
    // find the checkbox by removing "img" from the image ID
    checkid = img.id.substring(3);
    checkbox = document.getElementById(checkid);
    // "click" the checkbox
    checkbox.click();
    // display the right image for the clicked or unclicked state
    if (checkbox.checked) file = "checked.gif";
        else file="unchecked.gif";
    img.src=file;
}
//replace the second checkbox with a graphic
graphicBox("check2");
```

This script has three main components:

▶ The `graphicBox()` function converts a regular check box to a graphic one. It starts by hiding the existing check box by changing its `style.visibility` property, and then creates a new image node containing the `unchecked.gif` graphic and inserts it into the DOM next to the original check box. (These DOM features were described in the previous hour.) It gives the image an `id` attribute containing the text `img` plus the check box's `id` attribute to make it easier to find the check box later.

▶ The `Toggle()` function is specified by `graphicBox()` as the event handler for the new image's `onClick` event. This function removes `img` from the image's `id` attribute to find the `id` of the real check box. It executes the `click()` method on the check box, toggling its value. Finally, it changes the image to `unchecked.gif` or `checked.gif` depending on the state of the real check box.

▶ The last line of the script file runs the `graphicBox()` function to replace the second check box with the `id` attribute `check2`.

Using this technique has three important advantages. First, it's an unobtrusive script. The HTML has been kept simple, and browsers that don't support JavaScript will display the ordinary check box. Second, because the real check box is still on the page but hidden, it will work correctly when the form is submitted to a server-side script. Last but not least, you can use it to create any number of graphic check boxes simply by defining regular ones in the HTML file and adding a call to `graphicBox()` to transform each one.

See Hour 19, "Using Graphics and Animation," for details on the image manipulation features used in this example.

To try this example, save the JavaScript file as `checkbox.js`, and be sure the HTML file is in the same folder. You'll also need two graphics the same size, `unchecked.gif` and `checked.gif`, in the same folder. You can download all of the files you need for this example from this book's website.

Summary

In this hour, you've learned many guidelines for creating scripts that work in as many browsers as possible, and learned how to avoid errors and headaches when working with different browsers. Most important, you learned how you can use JavaScript while keeping your pages small, efficient, and valid with web standards.

In the next hour, you'll learn about another thing you'll run into frequently when working with more advanced scripts: bugs. Hour 16 shows you how to avoid common JavaScript errors, and how to use debugging tools and techniques to find and fix errors when they happen.

Q&A

Q. *Is it possible to create 100% unobtrusive JavaScript that can enhance a page without causing any trouble for anyone?*

A. Not quite. For example, the unobtrusive script in the Try It Yourself section of this hour is close—it will work in the latest browsers, and the regular check box will display and work fine in even ancient browsers. However, it can still fail if someone with a modern browser has images turned off: The script will hide the check box because JavaScript is supported, but the image won't be there. This is a rare circumstance, but it's an example of how any feature you add can potentially cause a problem for some small percentage of your users.

Q. *Can I detect the user's email address using the* `navigator` *object or another technique?*

A. No, there is no reliable way to detect users' email addresses using JavaScript. (If there was, you would get hundreds of advertisements in your mailbox every day from companies that detected your address as you browsed their pages.) You can use a signed script to obtain the user's email address, but this requires the user's permission and only works in some versions of Netscape.

Q. *Are there browsers besides Firefox, Netscape, and Internet Explorer that support JavaScript?*

A. Yes. Opera is a multiplatform browser that supports JavaScript and the W3C DOM. Apple's Safari browser for Macintosh also supports JavaScript. It's always best to support all browsers if you can, and to focus on web standards rather than particular browsers.

Quiz Questions

Test your knowledge of unobtrusive scripting by answering the following questions.

1. Which of the following is the best place to put JavaScript code?

    a. Right in the HTML document

    b. In a separate JavaScript file

    c. In a CSS file

2. Which of the following is something you *can't* do with JavaScript?

    a. Send browsers that don't support a feature to a different page

    b. Send users of Internet Explorer to a different page

    c. Send users of non-JavaScript browsers to a different page

3. Which of the following is the best way to define an event handler that works in all modern browsers?

    a. `<body onLoad="MyFunction()">`

    b. `window.onload=MyFunction;`

    c. `window.attachEvent('load',MyFunction,false);`

Quiz Answers

1. b. The best place for JavaScript is in a separate JavaScript file.

2. c. You can't use JavaScript to send users of non-JavaScript browsers to a different page because the script won't be executed at all.

3. b. The code `window.onload=MyFunction;` defines an event handler in all modern browsers. This is better than using an inline event handler as in (a) because it keeps JavaScript out of the HTML document. Option (c) uses the W3C's standard method, but does not work in Internet Explorer.

Exercises

If you want to gain more experience creating cross-browser scripts, try the following exercises:

▶ Add several check boxes to the HTML document in Listing 15.2, and add the corresponding function calls to the script in Listing 15.3 to replace all of them with graphic check boxes.

▶ Modify the script in Listing 15.3 to convert all check boxes with a `class` value of `graphic` into graphic check boxes. You can use `getElementsByTagName()` and then check each item for the right `className` property.

HOUR 16

Debugging JavaScript Applications

What You'll Learn in This Hour:

- ▶ Using good programming practices to avoid bugs
- ▶ Tips for debugging with the JavaScript console
- ▶ Using alert messages and comments to debug scripts
- ▶ Creating custom error handlers
- ▶ Using advanced debugging tools
- ▶ Debugging an actual script

As you move on to more advanced JavaScript applications in the remaining hours of this book, it's important to know how to deal with problems in your scripts. In this hour, you'll learn a few pointers on keeping your scripts bug-free, and you'll look at the tools and techniques you can use to find and eliminate bugs when they occur.

Avoiding Bugs

A bug is an error in a program that prevents it from doing what it should do. If you've tried writing any scripts on your own, you've probably run into one or more bugs. If not, you will—no matter how careful you are.

Although you'll undoubtedly run into a few bugs if you write a complex script, you can avoid many others by carefully writing and double-checking your script.

Using Good Programming Practices

There's not a single programmer out there whose programs always work the first time, without any bugs. However, good programmers share a few habits that help them avoid some of the more common bugs. Here are a few good habits you can develop to improve your scripts:

▶ Format your scripts neatly and try to keep them readable. Use consistent spacing and variable names that mean something. It's hard to determine what's wrong with a script when you can't even remember what a particular line does.

▶ Similarly, use JavaScript comments liberally to document your script. This will help if you need to work on the script after you've forgotten the details of how it works—or if someone else inherits the job.

▶ End all JavaScript statements with semicolons. Although this is optional, it makes the script more readable. Additionally, it might help the browser to produce meaningful error messages.

▶ Declare all variables with the var keyword. This is optional in most cases, but it will help make sure you really mean to create a new variable and will avoid problems with variable scope.

▶ Divide complicated scripts logically into functions. This will make the script easier to read, and it will also make it easy to pinpoint the cause of a problem.

▶ Write a large script in several phases and test the script at each phase before adding more features. This way, you can avoid having several new errors appear at once.

Avoiding Common Mistakes

Along with following good scripting practices, you should also watch for common mistakes in your scripts. Different people make different mistakes in JavaScript programming, but the following sections explore some of the most common ones.

Syntax Errors

A syntax error is an incorrect keyword, operator, punctuation mark, or other item in a script. Most often, it's caused by a typing error.

Typical syntax errors include mistyped commands, missing parentheses, and functions with the wrong number of arguments. Syntax errors are usually obvious—both to you when you look at the script and to the browser's JavaScript interpreter when you load the script. These errors usually result in an error message and can easily be corrected.

Assignment and Equality

One of the most common syntax errors made by beginning JavaScript programmers is confusing the assignment operator (=) with the equality operator (==). This can be a hard error to spot because it might not result in an error message.

If you're confused about which operator to use, follow this simple rule: Use = to change the value of a variable, and use == to compare two values. Here's an example of a statement that confuses the two:

```
If (a = 5) alert("found a five.");
```

The statement looks logical enough, but a = 5 will actually assign the value 5 to the a variable rather than compare the two. The browser usually detects this type of error and displays an error message in the JavaScript console, but the opposite type of error (using == when you mean =) may not be detected.

Local and Global Variables

Another common mistake is confusing local and global variables, such as trying to use the value of a variable that was declared in a function outside the function. If you actually need to do this, you should either use a global variable or return a value from the function.

Hour 5, "Using Variables, Strings, and Arrays," describes the differences between local and global variables in detail.

By the Way

Using Objects Correctly

Another common error is to refer to JavaScript objects incorrectly. It's important to use the correct object names and to remember when to explicitly name the parent of an object.

For example, you can usually refer to the window.alert() method as simply alert(). However, there are some cases when you must use window.alert(), such as in some event handlers. If you find that alert() or another method or property is not recognized by the browser, try specifying the window object.

Another common mistake is to assume that you can omit the document object's name, such as using write() instead of document.write(). This won't work because most scripts have a window object as their scope.

HTML Errors

Last but not least, don't forget that JavaScript isn't the only language that can have errors. It's easy to accidentally create an error in an HTML document—for example, forgetting to include a closing </table> tag, or even a closing </script> tag.

Although writing proper HTML is beyond the scope of this book, you should be aware that sometimes improper HTML can cause errors in your JavaScript. When you experience bugs, be sure to double-check the HTML, especially the objects (such as forms or images) that your script manipulates.

Watch Out!

> Your script can also introduce HTML errors if it modifies the DOM, particularly if it uses the `innerHTML` property. Double-check HTML produced by a script to avoid these problems.

Basic Debugging Tools

If checking your script for common mistakes and obvious problems doesn't fix things, it's time to start debugging. This is the process of finding errors in a program and eliminating them. Some basic tools for debugging scripts are described in the following sections.

Firefox's JavaScript Console

The first thing you should do if your script doesn't work is check for error messages. In Firefox and other Mozilla-based browsers, the messages are not displayed by default, but are logged to the JavaScript console.

To access the console, type `javascript:` in the browser's Location field or select Tools, JavaScript Console from the menu. The console displays the last few error messages that have occurred, as shown in Figure 16.1.

Along with reading the error messages, you can use the console to type a JavaScript command or expression and see its results. This is useful if you need to make sure a line of your script uses the correct syntax.

FIGURE 16.1
The JavaScript console displays recent error messages.

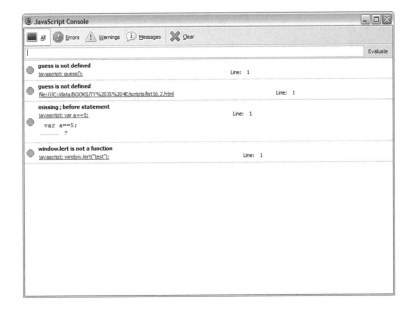

Displaying Error Messages in Internet Explorer

Microsoft Internet Explorer 4.0 and later do not display JavaScript error messages by default. This can make browsing poorly written pages a more pleasant experience, but it can be frustrating to JavaScript programmers.

To enable the display of error messages in Internet Explorer, select Internet Options from the Tools menu. Select the Advanced tab. In the list under Browsing, deselect the Disable Script Debugging option and enable the Display a Notification About Every Script Error option.

If you haven't enabled the display of error messages, Internet Explorer still displays an error icon on the status line when an error occurs. You can double-click this icon to display the error message.

Alert Messages

If you're lucky, the error messages in the console will tell you how to fix your script. However, your script might not generate any error messages at all—but still fail to work correctly. In this case, the real debugging process begins.

One useful debugging technique is to add temporary statements to your script to let you know what's going on. For example, you can use an `alert` statement to display the value of a variable. After you understand what's happening to the variable, you can figure out what's wrong with the script.

> **By the Way**
>
> You can also display debugging information in a separate browser window or frame. You can use `document.write` in some cases, but this only works when the document hasn't finished loading yet and thus isn't a reliable debugging tool.

Using Comments

When all else fails, you can use JavaScript comments to eliminate portions of your script until the error goes away. If you do this carefully, you can pinpoint the place where the error occurred.

You can use `//` to begin a single-line comment, or `/*` and `*/` around a section of any length. Using comments to temporarily turn off statements in a program or a script is called *commenting out* and is a common technique among programmers.

> **By the Way**
>
> JavaScript comments were introduced and described in more detail in Hour 3, "Getting Started with JavaScript Programming."

Other Debugging Tools

Although you can use alert messages and a little common sense to quickly find a bug in a simple script, larger scripts can be difficult to debug. Here are a few tools you might find useful as you develop and debug larger JavaScript applications:

▶ HTML validators can check your HTML documents to see if they meet the HTML standard. The validation process can also help you find errors in your HTML. The W3C has a validator online at http://validator.w3.org/.

▶ Mozilla's JavaScript debugger enables you to set breakpoints, display variable values, and perform other debugging tasks. You can download the debugger at http://www.mozilla.org/projects/venkman/.

▶ Microsoft Script Debugger is similar, but works with Internet Explorer. It is available at http://msdn.microsoft.com/library/en-us/sdbug/Html/sdbug_1.asp.

▶ Although text and HTML editors are good basic editing tools, they can also help with debugging by displaying line numbers and using color codes to indicate valid commands.

Appendix B, "Tools for JavaScript Developers," includes links to HTML validators, editors, and other debugging tools.

Creating Error Handlers

In some cases, there may be times when an error message is unavoidable and, in a large JavaScript application, errors are bound to happen. Your scripts can respond to errors in a friendlier way using error handlers.

Using the onerror Property

You can set up an error handler by assigning a function to the onerror property of the window object. When an error occurs in a script in the document, the browser calls the function you specify instead of the normal error dialog. For example, these statements set up a function that displays a simple message when an error occurs:

```
function errmsg(message,url,line) {
   alert("There wasn't an error. Nothing to see here.");
   return true;
}
window.onerror=errmsg;
```

These statements define a function, errmsg(), which handles errors by displaying a simple dialog. The last statement assigns the errmsg() function to the window.onerror property.

The return true; statement tells the browser that this function has handled the error, and prevents the standard error dialog from being displayed. If you use return false; instead, the standard error dialog will be displayed after your function exits.

> You can't define an onError event handler in HTML. You must define it using the window.onerror property as shown here.

By the Way

Displaying Information About the Error

When the browser calls your error-handling function, it passes three parameters: the error message, the URL of the document where the error happened, and the line number. The simple error handler in the previous example didn't use these values. You can create a more sophisticated handler that displays the information.

> As usual, you can download this hour's examples from this book's website.

Did you Know?

Listing 16.1 shows a complete example including an enhanced errmsg() function. This version displays the error message, URL, and line number in a dialog box.

LISTING 16.1 Handling Errors with a JavaScript Function

```
<html><head>
<title>Error handling test</title>
<script language="JavaScript" type="text/javascript">
function errmsg(message,url,line) {
   amsg = "A JavaScript error has occurred. Please let us know about it.\n";
   amsg += "Error Message: " + message + "\n";
   amsg += "URL: " + url + "\n";
   amsg += "Line #: " + line;
   alert(amsg);
   return true;
}
window.onerror=errmsg;
</script>
</head>
<body>
<h1> Error handling test</h1>
<p>This page includes a JavaScript function to handle errors.
Test it by clicking the button below.</p>
<form>
   <input type="button" value="ERROR" onClick="garble">
</form>
</body>
</html>
```

This example includes a button with a nonsensical event handler. To test the error handler, click the button to generate an error. Figure 16.2 shows the example in action in Internet Explorer with the alert message displayed.

FIGURE 16.2
The error-handler example in action.

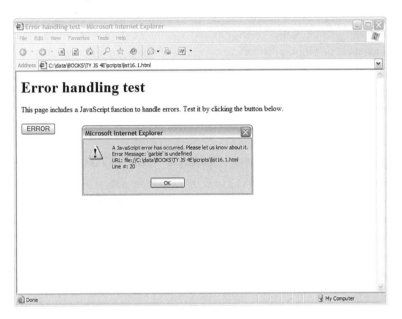

If you try to use an error handler and still get system error messages, make sure there isn't a syntax error in your error handler itself.

Using try **and** catch

A more modern way of handling errors, supported by the latest browsers, is the try and catch keywords. To use it, include the try keyword, then a block of code (within braces) that might cause an error, then the catch keyword, and a block of code to handle the error:

```
try {
  DoThis();
} catch(err) {
  alert(err.description);
}
```

The try block of code always executes. If it generates an error, the catch block is executed. If there is no error, the catch block does not execute.

The error-handling code is passed an argument (err in the example) indicating the type of error. This is an object with properties including name (the error name) and description (a description of the error).

Handling errors with `try` and `catch` is a good way to deal with browser-specific code that might cause errors when run in the wrong browser. See the next hour for an example that uses `try` and `catch` to create a cross-browser AJAX function.

Advanced Debugging Tools

Although it's possible to get a simple script working with an alert message or two, you might find some other tools useful as you build more complex scripts, and especially as you work with scripts that modify the DOM. The following are some useful debugging tools available for Firefox and Internet Explorer.

Web Developer Toolbar (Firefox)

The Web Developer Extension by Chris Pederick is an open-source extension for Firefox and other Mozilla-based browsers. This extension adds a toolbar to the browser with a variety of functions useful to developers. The following features are useful for JavaScript in particular:

▶ **Disable, JavaScript**—Disables JavaScript, useful for making sure pages function on non-JavaScript browsers.

▶ **Information, Display ID and Class Details**—Displays the values of `id` and `class` attributes for all of the elements in a page; useful for attaching event handlers or CSS styles.

▶ **Information, View JavaScript**—Displays all of the scripts that affect the current page, including those in external files.

▶ **View Source, View Generated Source**—Displays the HTML source of the current page. Unlike the browser's regular View Source function, this displays the source after any scripts have acted upon it; useful for debugging scripts that modify the DOM.

Along with these functions, the toolbar includes many useful tools for debugging HTML and CSS, working with forms, and validating pages. To install it or for more information, see its official site at http://chrispederick.com/work/webdeveloper/.

Developer Toolbar (Internet Explorer)

Inspired by the Web Developer Extension for Firefox, Microsoft created a Developer Toolbar for Internet Explorer. Currently in beta, the toolbar works with Internet Explorer 6.0 or later. Here are some of its features useful for JavaScript programmers:

▶ **View DOM**—Allows you to browse the DOM of the current page and view details of elements, similar to Firefox's DOM Inspector. This feature is shown in Figure 16.3.

▶ **Disable, Script**—Disables JavaScript, enabling you to test how your site works without it.

▶ **View, Class and ID Information**—Displays `id` and `class` attribute values; useful for attaching event handlers or CSS styles.

FIGURE 16.3
The Internet Explorer Developer Toolbar's view DOM feature.

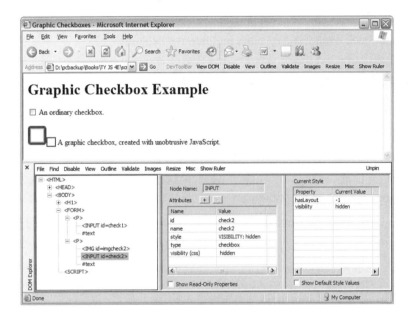

To download the IE Developer Toolbar, go to http://www.microsoft.com/downloads/ and search for "Developer Toolbar." The download is available for free and includes an easy installer.

DOM Inspector (Firefox)

The DOM Inspector is a tool built in to Firefox and other Mozilla-based browsers that enables you to browse the DOM of a web page and view the attributes of elements. You need to specifically select this feature at installation time, so you might need to reinstall Firefox to gain access to this feature. To see if your copy includes the DOM Inspector, open the Tools menu and check for a DOM Inspector menu item.

To use this tool, open the page you wish to inspect and then select Tools, DOM Inspector. You can then browse the DOM by clicking the [+] symbols for each section

of the hierarchy. Select an item within the DOM tree to view its details in the right section of the window. The DOM Inspector is shown in Figure 16.4.

FIGURE 16.4
The DOM Inspector opened within Firefox.

Viewing Generated Source

When your script modifies the DOM, the browser's View Source feature only gives you part of the picture—you see the source of the page when it was loaded, rather than the source created by your script as it modified the page. To test scripts that modify the DOM, you can view the *generated source* as modified by the script.

In Firefox, this feature is built in: If you select part of a page, right-click, and select View Selection Source, you'll see the generated source. You can also use the Tools menu of the Web Developer Toolbar, discussed previously, to view the generated source.

For Internet Explorer, you can use a *bookmarklet*—a short script stored as a browser bookmark—to view the generated source in a window. This bookmarklet is available at Jesse Ruderman's site at http://www.squarefree.com/bookmarklets/.

JavaScript Shell

Sometimes it's helpful to be able to simply type a few JavaScript commands to see what they do, either to narrow down a bug or simply to remember the syntax of a rarely used feature. The JavaScript Shell is a bookmarklet that opens a shell window that lets you type JavaScript commands and shows the results.

The shell opens in the context of the current document, so you can use it to explore the DOM of a page or to test scripts you're working on. This feature works only in Firefox, but an online version of the shell without the context feature works in Internet Explorer.

The JavaScript Shell is available from http://www.squarefree.com/bookmarklets/.

▼   **Try It Yourself**

Debugging a Script

You should now have a good understanding of what can go wrong with JavaScript programs and the tools you have available to diagnose these problems. You can now try your hand at debugging a script.

Listing 16.2 shows a script I wrote to play the classic "Guess a Number" game. The script picks a number between 1 and 100 and then allows the user 10 guesses. If a guess is incorrect, it provides a hint as to whether the target number is higher or lower.

This is a relatively simple script with a twist: It includes at least one bug and doesn't work at all in its present form.

LISTING 16.2   The Number-Guesser Script (Complete with Bugs)

```
1    <html>
2    <head>
3    <title>Guess a Number</title>
4    <script LANGUAGE="JavaScript" type="text/javascript">
5    var num = Math.random() * 100 + 1;
6    var tries = 0;
7    function Guess() {
8    var g = document.form1.guess1.value;
9    tries++;
10   status = "Tries: " + tries;
11   if (g < num)
12       document.form1.hint.value = "No, guess higher.";
13   if (g > num)
14       document.form1.hint.value = "No, guess lower.";
15   if (g == num) {
16       window.alert("Correct! You guessed it in " + tries + " tries.");
17       location.reload();
18       }
19   if (tries == 10) {
20       window.alert("Sorry, time's up. The number was: " + num);
21       location.reload();
22       }
23   }
24   </script>
25   </head>
26   <body>
```

LISTING 16.2 Continued

```
27   <h1>Guess a Number</h1>
28   <hr>
29   <p>I'm thinking of a number between 1 and 100. Try to guess
30   it in less than 10 tries.</p>
31   <form name="form1">
32   <input type="text" size="25" name="hint" value="Enter your Guess.">
33   <br>
34   <b>Guess:</b>
35   <input type="text" name="guess1" size="5">
36   <input type="button" value="Guess"  onClick="guess();">
37   </form>
38   </body>
39   </html>
```

Here's a summary of how this script should work:

▶ The first line within the <script> section picks a random number and stores it in the num variable.

▶ The Guess() function is defined in the header of the document. This function is called each time the user enters a guess.

▶ Within the Guess() function, several if statements test the user's guess. If it is incorrect, a hint is displayed in the text box. If the guess is correct, the script displays an alert message to congratulate the user.

Testing the Script

To test this program, load the HTML document into your browser. It appears to load correctly and does not immediately cause any errors. However, when you enter a guess and press the Guess button, a JavaScript error occurs.

According to the JavaScript console, the error message is this:

```
Line 36: guess is undefined
```

Internet Explorer's error message refers to the same line number:

```
Line 36, character 1: Object expected
```

Fixing the Error

As the error message indicates, there must be something wrong with the function call to the Guess() function in the event handler on line 36. The line in question looks like this:

```
<input type="button" value="Guess"  onClick="guess();">
```

Upon further examination, you'll notice that the first two lines of the function are as follows (lines 7 and 8 of Listing 16.2):

```
function Guess() {
var guess = document.form1.guess1.value;
```

Although this might look correct at first glance, there's a problem here: guess() is lowercase in the event handler, whereas the function definition uses a capitalized Guess(). This is easy to fix. Simply change the function call in the event handler from guess() to Guess(). The corrected line will look like this:

```
<input type="button" value="Guess"  onClick="Guess();">
```

Testing Again

Now that you've fixed the error, try the script again. This time it loads without an error, and you can enter a guess without an error. The hints about guessing higher or lower are even displayed correctly.

However, to truly test the script, you'll need to play the game all the way through. When you do, you'll discover that there's still another problem in the script: You can't win, no matter how hard you try.

After your 10 guesses are up, an alert message informs you that you've lost the game. Coincidentally, this alert message also tells you what's wrong with the script. Figure 16.5 shows how the browser window looks after a complete game, complete with this dialog box.

FIGURE 16.5
The number guesser script's display after a game is finished.

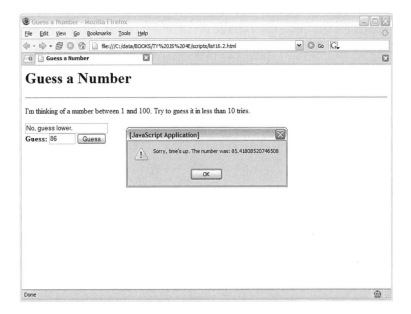

As you can see from the alert message, it's no wonder you didn't win: The random number the computer picked includes more than 10 decimal places, and you've been guessing integers. You could guess decimal numbers, but you'd need a whole lot more than 10 guesses, and the game would start to lose its simplicity and charm.

To fix this problem, look at the statement at the beginning of the script that generates the random number:

```
var num = Math.random() * 100 + 1;
```

This uses the Math.random() method, which results in a random number between 0 and 1. The number is then multiplied and incremented to result in a number between 1 and 100.

This statement does indeed produce a number between 1 and 100, but not an integer. To fix the problem, you can add the Math.floor() method to chop off the decimal portion of the number. Here's a corrected statement:

```
var num = Math.floor(Math.random() * 100) + 1;
```

To fix the script, make this change and then test it again. If you play a game or two, you'll find that it works just fine. Listing 16.3 shows the complete, debugged script.

LISTING 16.3   The Complete, Debugged Number-Guesser Script

```
<html>
<head>
<title>Guess a Number</title>
<script LANGUAGE="JavaScript" type="text/javascript">
var num = Math.floor(Math.random() * 100) + 1;
var tries = 0;
function Guess() {
var g = document.form1.guess1.value;
tries++;
status = "Tries: " + tries;
if (g < num)
    document.form1.hint.value = "No, guess higher.";
if (g > num)
    document.form1.hint.value = "No, guess lower.";
if (g == num) {
    window.alert("Correct! You guessed it in " + tries + " tries.");
    location.reload();
    }
if (tries == 10) {
    window.alert("Sorry, time's up. The number was: " + num);
    location.reload();
    }
}
</script>
</head>
<body>
<h1>Guess a Number</h1>
<hr>
<p>I'm thinking of a number between 1 and 100. Try to guess
```

LISTING 16.3   Continued

```
it in less than 10 tries.</p>
<form name="form1">
<input type="text" size="25" name="hint" value="Enter your Guess.">
<br>
<b>Guess:</b>
<input type="text" name="guess1" size="5">
<input type="button" value="Guess"  onClick="Guess();">
</form>
</body>
</html>
```

Figure 16.6 shows the debugged example in action in Firefox after a successful game.

FIGURE 16.6
The number-guesser example after a successful game.

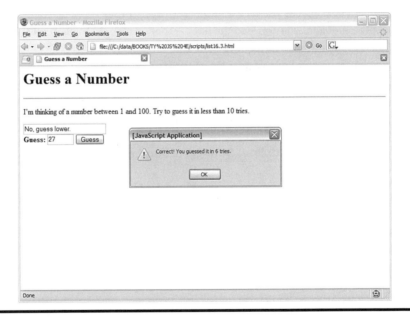

Summary

In this hour, you've learned how to debug JavaScript programs. You examined some techniques for producing scripts with a minimum of bugs and learned about some tools that will help you find bugs in scripts. Finally, you tried your hand at debugging a script.

In Hour 17, "AJAX: Remote Scripting," you'll continue your JavaScript education by learning about AJAX, a technique that lets JavaScript work with server-side files and programs without reloading pages.

Q&A

Q. *Why are some errors displayed after the script runs for a time, whereas others are displayed when the script loads?*

A. The JavaScript interpreter looks at scripts in the body or the heading of the document, such as function definitions, when the page loads. Event handlers aren't checked until the event happens. Additionally, a statement might look fine when the page loads, but will cause an error because of the value of a variable it uses later.

Q. *What is the purpose of the* `location.reload` *statements in the number-guesser script?*

A. This is an easy way to start a new game because reloading the page reinitializes the variables. This results in a new number being picked, and the default "Guess a Number" message is displayed in the hint field.

Q. *Which browser is best for developing and debugging scripts?*

A. You may or may not agree, but I find that Firefox offers the best tools for debugging scripts, such as the JavaScript console and the Web Developer Toolbar. Regardless of your preferred browser, be sure to test your scripts in multiple browsers to find any browser-specific issues they might have.

Quiz Questions

Test your knowledge of debugging JavaScript by answering the following questions.

1. If you mistype a JavaScript keyword, which type of error is the result?

    a. Syntax error

    b. Function error

    c. Pilot error

2. The process of dealing with errors in a script or a program is known as

    a. Error detection

    b. Frustration

    c. Debugging

3. Which of the following is a useful technique when a script is not working but does not generate an error message?

    a. Rewriting from scratch

    b. Removing `<script>` tags

    c. Adding `alert` statements

Quiz Answers

1. a. A syntax error can result from a mistyped JavaScript keyword.

2. c. Debugging is the process of finding and fixing errors in a program.

3. c. You can add `alert` statements to a script to display variables or the current status of the script and aid in debugging.

Exercises

If you want to gain more experience debugging scripts, try the following exercises:

▶ Although the number-guesser script in Listing 16.3 avoids JavaScript errors, it is still vulnerable to user errors. Add a statement to verify that the user's guess is between 1 and 100. If it isn't, display an alert message and make sure that the guess doesn't count toward the total of 10 guesses.

▶ Load Listing 16.2, the number-guesser script with bugs, into Mozilla's JavaScript Debugger or Microsoft's Script Debugger. Try using the watch and breakpoint features and see whether you find this to be an easier way to diagnose the problem.

AJAX: Remote Scripting

What You'll Learn in This Hour:

▶ How AJAX enables JavaScript to communicate with server-side programs and files

▶ Using the XMLHttpRequest object's properties and methods

▶ Creating your own AJAX library

▶ Using AJAX to read data from an XML file

▶ Debugging AJAX applications

▶ Using AJAX to communicate with a PHP program

Remote scripting, also known as AJAX, is a browser feature that enables JavaScript to escape its client-side boundaries and work with files on a web server, or with server-side programs. In this hour, you'll learn how AJAX works and create two working examples.

Introducing AJAX

Traditionally, one of the major limitations of JavaScript is that it couldn't communicate with a web server. For example, you could create a game in JavaScript, but keeping a list of high scores stored on a server would require submitting a page to a server-side form.

One of the limitations of web pages in general was that getting data from the user to the server, or from the server to the user, generally required a new page to be loaded and displayed.

AJAX (Asynchronous JavaScript and XML) is the answer to both of these problems. AJAX refers to JavaScript's capability to use a built-in object, XMLHttpRequest, to communicate with a web server without submitting a form or loading a page. Although not part of the DOM standard yet, this object is supported by Internet Explorer, Firefox, and other modern browsers.

Although the term *AJAX* was coined in 2005, XMLHttpRequest has been supported by browsers for years—it was developed by Microsoft and first appeared in Internet Explorer 5. Nonetheless, it has only recently become a popular way of developing applications because browsers that support it have become more common. Another name for this technique is *remote scripting.*

By the Way

The term *AJAX* first appeared in an online article by Jesse James Garrett of Adaptive Path on February 18, 2005. It still appears here: http://adaptivepath.com/publications/essays/archives/000385.php

The JavaScript Client (Front End)

JavaScript traditionally only has one way of communicating with a server—submitting a form. Remote scripting allows for much more versatile communication with the server. The *A* in AJAX stands for *asynchronous*, which means that the browser (and the user) isn't left hanging while waiting for the server to respond. Here's how a typical AJAX request works:

1. The script creates an XMLHttpRequest object and sends it to the web server. The script can continue after sending the request.

2. The server responds by sending the contents of a file, or the output of a server-side program.

3. When the response arrives from the server, a JavaScript function is triggered to act on the data.

4. Because the goal is a more responsive user interface, the script usually displays the data from the server using the DOM, eliminating the need for a page refresh.

In practice, this happens quickly, but even with a slow server, it can still work. Also, because the requests are asynchronous, more than one can be in progress at a time.

The Back End

The part of an application that resides on the web server is known as the *back end.* The simplest back end is a static file on the server—JavaScript can request the file with XMLHttpRequest, and then read and act on its contents. More commonly, the back end is a server-side program running in a language like PHP, Perl, or Ruby.

JavaScript can send data to a server-side program using GET or POST methods, the same two ways an HTML form works. In a GET request, the data is encoded in the URL that loads the program. In a POST request, it is sent separately, and can contain more data.

XML

The *X* in AJAX stands for *XML* (extensible markup language), the universal markup language upon which the latest versions of HTML are built. A server-side file or program can send data in XML format, and JavaScript can act on the data using its methods for working with XML. These are similar to the DOM methods you've already used—for example, you can use the getElementsByTagName() method to find elements with a particular tag in the data.

Keep in mind that XML is just one way to send data, and not always the easiest. The server could just as easily send plain text, which the script could display, or HTML, which the script could insert into the page using the innerHTML property. Some programmers have even used server-side scripts to return data in JavaScript format, which can be easily executed using the eval function.

> **By the Way**
>
> JSON (JavaScript Object Notation) takes the idea of encoding data in JavaScript and formalizes it. See http://www.json.org/ for details and code examples in many languages.

Popular Examples of AJAX

Although typical HTML and JavaScript is used to build web pages and sites, AJAX techniques often result in *web applications*—web-based services that perform work for the user. Here are a few well-known examples of AJAX:

▶ Google's Gmail mail client (http://mail.google.com/) uses AJAX to make a fast-responding email application. You can delete messages and perform other tasks without waiting for a new page to load.

▶ Amazon.com uses AJAX for some functions. For example, if you click on one of the Yes/No voting buttons for a product comment, it sends your vote to the server and a message appears next to the button thanking you, all without loading a page.

▶ Digg (http://www.digg.com) is a site where users can submit news stories and vote to determine which ones are displayed on the front page. The voting happens inside the page next to each story.

These are just a few examples. Subtle bits of remote scripting are appearing all over the Web, and you might not even notice them—you'll just be annoyed a little bit less often at waiting for a page to load.

Frameworks and Libraries

Because remote scripting can be complicated, especially considering the browser differences you'll learn about later this hour, several frameworks and libraries have been developed to simplify AJAX programming.

For starters, three of the libraries described earlier in this book, Dojo, Prototype, and script.aculo.us, include functions to simplify remote scripting. There are also some dedicated libraries for languages like PHP, Python, and Ruby.

Some libraries are designed to add server-side functions to JavaScript, whereas others are designed to add JavaScript interactivity to a language like PHP. You'll build a simple library later this hour that will be used to handle the remote scripting functions for this hour's examples.

Did you Know?

> See this book's website for an up-to-date list of AJAX libraries. See Hour 8, "Using Built-in Functions and Libraries," for information about using third-party libraries with JavaScript.

Limitations of AJAX

Remote scripting is a relatively new technology, so there are some things it can't do, and some things to watch out for. Here are some of the limitations and potential problems of AJAX:

- ▶ The script and the XML data or server-side program it requests data from must be on the same domain.

- ▶ Internet Explorer 5 and 6 use ActiveX to implement XMLHttpRequest. Although the security settings allow this by default, users with different settings might be unable to use AJAX. (Internet Explorer 7 does not have this problem.)

- ▶ Some older browsers and some less common browsers (such as mobile browsers) don't support XMLHttpRequest, so you can't count on its availability for all users.

- ▶ Requiring AJAX might compromise the accessibility of a site for disabled users.

- ▶ Users are accustomed to seeing a new page load each time they change something, so there might be a learning curve for them to understand an AJAX application.

As with other advanced uses of JavaScript, the best approach is to be unobtrusive—make sure there's still a way to use the site without AJAX support if possible, and use feature sensing to prevent errors on browsers that don't support it. See Hour 15, "Unobtrusive Scripting," for details.

Using XMLHttpRequest

You will now take a look at how to use XMLHttpRequest to communicate with a server. This might seem a bit complex, but the process is the same for any request. Later, you will create a reusable code library to simplify this process.

Creating a Request

The first step is to create an XMLHttpRequest object. To do this, you use the new keyword, as with other JavaScript objects. The following statement creates a request object in some browsers:

```
ajaxreq = new XMLHttpRequest();
```

The previous example works with Firefox, Mozilla, and Safari, and with Internet Explorer 7, but not Internet Explorer 5 or 6. For those browsers, you have to use ActiveX syntax:

```
ajaxreq = new ActiveXObject("Microsoft.XMLHTTP");
```

The library section later this hour demonstrates how to use the correct method depending on the browser in use. In either case, the variable you use (ajaxreq in the example) stores the XMLHttpRequest object. You'll use the methods of this object to open and send a request, as explained in the following sections.

Opening a URL

The open() method of the XMLHttpRequest object specifies the filename as well as the method in which data will be sent to the server: GET or POST. These are the same methods supported by web forms.

```
ajaxreq.open("GET","filename");
```

For the GET method, the data you send is included in the URL. For example, this command opens the search.php program and sends the value "John" for the query parameter:

```
ajaxreq.open("GET","search.php?query=John");
```

Sending the Request

You use the send() method of the XMLHttpRequest object to send the request to the server. If you are using the POST method, the data to send is the argument for send(). For a GET request, you can use the null value instead:

```
ajaxreq.send(null);
```

Awaiting a Response

After the request is sent, your script will continue without waiting for a result. Because the result could come at any time, you can detect it with an event handler. The XMLHttpRequest object has an onreadystatechange event handler for this purpose. You can create a function to deal with the response and set it as the handler for this event:

```
ajaxreq.onreadystatechange = MyFunc;
```

The request object has a property, readyState, that indicates its status, and this event is triggered whenever the readyState property changes. The values of readyState range from 0 for a new request to 4 for a complete request, so your event handling function usually needs to watch for a value of 4.

Although the request is complete, it may not have been successful. The status property is set to 200 if the request succeeded, or an error code if it failed. The statusText property stores a text explanation of the error, or "OK" for success.

> As usual with event handlers, be sure to specify the function name without parentheses. With parentheses, you're referring to the *result* of the function; without them, you're referring to the function itself.

Interpreting the Response Data

When the readyState property reaches 4 and the request is complete, the data returned from the server is available to your script in two properties: responseText is the response in raw text form, and responseXML is the response as an XML object. If the data was not in XML format, only the text property will be available.

JavaScript's DOM methods are meant to work on XML, so you can use them with the responseXML property. Later this hour, you'll use the getElementsByTagName() method to extract data from XML.

Creating a Simple AJAX Library

You should be aware by now that AJAX requests can be a bit complex. To make things easier, you can create an AJAX library. This is a JavaScript file that provides functions that handle making a request and receiving the result, which you can reuse any time you need AJAX functions.

This library will be used in the two examples later this hour. Listing 17.1 shows the complete AJAX library.

LISTING 17.1   The AJAX Library

```
// global variables to keep track of the request
// and the function to call when done
var ajaxreq=false, ajaxCallback;
// ajaxRequest: Sets up a request
function ajaxRequest(filename) {
   try {
    // Firefox / IE7 / Others
    ajaxreq= new XMLHttpRequest();
   } catch (error) {
    try {
      // IE 5 / IE 6
      ajaxreq = new ActiveXObject("Microsoft.XMLHTTP");
    } catch (error) {
      return false;
    }
   }
   ajaxreq.open("GET", filename);
   ajaxreq.onreadystatechange = ajaxResponse;
   ajaxreq.send(null);
}
// ajaxResponse: Waits for response and calls a function
function ajaxResponse() {
   if (ajaxreq.readyState !=4) return;
   if (ajaxreq.status==200) {
     // if the request succeeded...
     if (ajaxCallback) ajaxCallback();
   } else alert("Request failed: " + ajaxreq.statusText);
   return true;
}
```

The following sections explain how this library works and how to use it.

The `ajaxRequest()` Function

The `ajaxRequest()` function handles all of the steps necessary to create and send an `XMLHttpRequest`. First, it creates the `XMLHttpRequest` object. This requires a different command for different browsers, and will cause an error if the wrong one

executes, so `try` and `catch` are used to create the request. First the standard method is used, and if it causes an error, the ActiveX method is tried. If that also causes an error, the `ajaxreq` variable is set to `false` to indicate that AJAX is unsupported.

The `ajaxResponse()` Function

The `ajaxResponse()` function is used as the `onreadystatechange` event handler. This function first checks the `readyState` property for a value of 4. If it has a different value, the function returns without doing anything.

Next, it checks the `status` property for a value of `200`, which indicates the request was successful. If so, it runs the function stored in the `ajaxCallback` variable. If not, it displays the error message in an alert box.

Using the Library

To use this library, follow these steps:

1. Save the library file as `ajax.js` in the same folder as your HTML documents and scripts.

2. Include the script in your document with a `<script src>` tag. It should be included before any other scripts that use its features.

3. In your script, create a function to be called when the request is complete, and set the `ajaxCallback` variable to the function.

4. Call the `ajaxRequest()` function. Its parameter is the filename of the server-side program or file. (This library supports GET requests only, so you don't need to specify the method.)

5. Your function specified in `ajaxCallback` will be called when the request completes successfully, and the global variable `ajaxreq` will store the data in its `responseXML` and `responseText` properties.

The two remaining examples in this hour make use of this library to create AJAX applications.

Creating an AJAX Quiz Using the Library

Now that you have a reusable AJAX library, you can use it to create JavaScript applications that take advantage of remote scripting. This first example displays quiz questions on a page and prompts you for the answers.

Rather than including the questions in the script, this example reads the quiz questions and answers from an XML file on the server as a demonstration of AJAX.

> Unlike most of the scripts in this book, this example requires a web server. It will not work on a local machine due to browsers' security restrictions on remote scripting.

Watch Out!

The HTML File

The HTML for this example is straightforward. It defines a simple form with an Answer field and a Submit button, along with some hooks for the script. The HTML for this example is shown in Listing 17.2.

LISTING 17.2 The HTML File for the Quiz Example

```html
<html>
<head><title>Ajax Test</title>
<script language="JavaScript" type="text/javascript"
   src="ajax.js">
</script>
</head>
<body>
<h1>Ajax Quiz Example</h1>
<form>
<p><b>Question:</b>
<span id="question">...
</span>
</p>
<p><b>Answer:</b>
<input type="text" name="answer" id="answer">
<input type="button" value="Submit" id="submit">
</p>
<input type="button" value="Start the Quiz" id="startq">
</form>
<script language="JavaScript" type="text/javascript"
   src="quiz.js">
</script>
</body>
</html>
```

This HTML file includes the following elements:

▶ The <script> tag in the <head> section includes the AJAX library you created in the previous section from the ajax.js file.

▶ The <script> tag in the <body> section includes the quiz.js file, which will contain the quiz script.

▶ The <span id="question"> tag sets up a place for the question to be inserted by the script.

▶ The text field with the id value answer is where the user will answer the question.

▶ The button with the id value submit will submit an answer.

▶ The button with the id value startq will start the quiz.

You can test the HTML document at this time, but the buttons won't work until you add the script.

The XML File

The XML file for the quiz is shown in Listing 17.3. I've filled it with a few JavaScript questions, but it could easily be adapted for another purpose.

LISTING 17.3   The XML File Containing the Quiz Questions and Answers

```
<?xml version="1.0" ?>
<questions>
    <q>What DOM object contains URL information for the window?</q>
    <a>location</a>
    <q>Which method of the document object finds the object for an element?</q>
    <a>getElementById</a>
    <q>If you declare a variable outside a function, is it global or local?</q>
    <a>global</a>
    <q>What is the formal standard for the JavaScript language called?</q>
    <a>ECMAScript</a>
</questions>
```

The <questions> tag encloses the entire file, and each question and answer are enclosed in <q> and <a> tags. Remember, this is XML, not HTML—these are not standard HTML tags, but tags that were created for this example. Because this file will be used only by your script, it does not need to follow a standard format.

To use this file, save it as questions.xml in the same folder as the HTML document. It will be loaded by the script you create in the next section.

Of course, with a quiz this small, you could have made things easier by storing the questions and answers in a JavaScript array. But imagine a much larger quiz, with thousands of questions, or a server-side program that pulls questions from a database, or even a hundred different files with different quizzes to choose between, and you can see the benefit of using a separate XML file.

The JavaScript File

Because you have a separate library to handle the complexities of making an AJAX request and receiving the response, the script for this example only needs to deal with the action for the quiz itself. Listing 17.4 shows the JavaScript file for this example.

LISTING 17.4   The JavaScript File for the Quiz Example

```
// global variable qn is the current question number
var qn=0;
// load the questions from the XML file
function getQuestions() {
   obj=document.getElementById("question");
   obj.firstChild.nodeValue="(please wait)";
   ajaxCallback = nextQuestion;
   ajaxRequest("questions.xml");
}
// display the next question
function nextQuestion() {
   questions = ajaxreq.responseXML.getElementsByTagName("q");
   obj=document.getElementById("question");
   if (qn < questions.length) {
      q = questions[qn].firstChild.nodeValue;
      obj.firstChild.nodeValue=q;
   } else {
      obj.firstChild.nodeValue="(no more questions)";
   }
}
// check the user's answer
function checkAnswer() {
   answers = ajaxreq.responseXML.getElementsByTagName("a");
   a = answers[qn].firstChild.nodeValue;
   answerfield = document.getElementById("answer");
   if (a == answerfield.value) {
      alert("Correct!");
   }
   else {
      alert("Incorrect. The correct answer is: " + a);
   }
   qn = qn + 1;
   answerfield.value="";
   nextQuestion();
}
// Set up the event handlers for the buttons
obj=document.getElementById("startq");
obj.onclick=getQuestions;
ans=document.getElementById("submit");
ans.onclick=checkAnswer;
```

This script consists of the following:

▶ The first var statement defines a global variable, qn, which will keep track of which question is currently displayed. It is initially set to zero for the first question.

▶ The getQuestions() function is called when the user clicks the Start Quiz button. This function uses the AJAX library to request the contents of the questions.xml file. It sets the ajaxCallback variable to the nextQuestion() function.

▶ The nextQuestion() function is called when the AJAX request is complete. This function uses the getElementsByTagName() method on the responseXML property to find all of the questions (<q> tags) and store them in the ques-tions array.

▶ The checkAnswer() function is called when the user submits an answer. It uses getElementsByTagName() to store the answers (<a> tags) in the answers array, and then compares the answer for the current question with the user's answer and displays an alert indicating whether they were right or wrong.

▶ The script commands after this function set up two event handlers. One attaches the getQuestions() function to the Start Quiz button to set up the quiz; the other attaches the checkAnswer() function to the Submit button.

Testing the Quiz

To try this example, you'll need all four files in the same folder: ajax.js (the AJAX library), quiz.js (the quiz functions), questions.xml (the questions), and the HTML document. All but the HTML document need to have the correct filenames so they will work correctly. Also remember that because it uses AJAX, this example requires a web server.

Figure 17.1 shows the quiz in action. The second question has just been answered.

FIGURE 17.1
The quiz exam-ple as displayed by Internet Explorer.

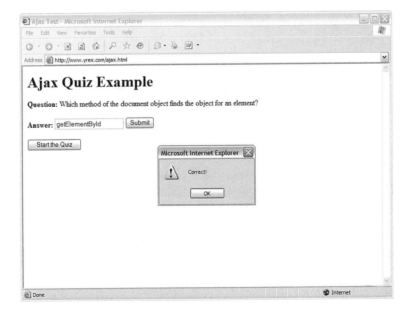

By the Way

This example should work on Internet Explorer 5–7, Mozilla 1.0 or later, any version of Firefox, or recent versions of Apple Safari. If you have trouble, try the latest Firefox.

Debugging AJAX Applications

Dealing with remote scripting means working with several languages at once—JavaScript, server-side languages such as PHP, XML, and of course HTML. Thus, when you find an error, it can be difficult to track down. Here are some tips for debugging AJAX applications:

▶ Be sure all filenames are correct, and that all files for your application are in the same folder on the server.

▶ If you are using a server-side language, test it without the script: Load it in the browser and make sure it works, and try passing variables to it in the URL and checking the results.

▶ Check the `statusText` property for the results of your request—an `alert` message is helpful here. It is often a clear message such as "File not found" that might explain the problem.

▶ If you're using a third-party AJAX library, check its documentation—many libraries have built-in debugging features you can enable to examine what's going on.

Did you Know?

Hour 16, "Debugging JavaScript Applications," includes more information on JavaScript debugging in general and includes descriptions of some useful debugging tools.

Try It Yourself ▼

Making a Live Search Form

One of the most impressive demonstrations of AJAX is *live search*: Whereas a normal search form requires that you click a button and wait for a page to load to see the results, a live search displays results within the page immediately as you type in the search field. As you type letters or press the backspace key, the results are updated instantly to make it easy to find the result you need.

Using the AJAX library you created earlier, live search is not too hard to implement. This example will use a PHP program on the server to provide the search results, and can be easily adapted to any search application.

> Once again, because it uses AJAX, this example requires a web server. You'll also need PHP version 3 or later, which is available on most servers.

The HTML Form

The HTML for this example simply defines a search field and leaves some room for the dynamic results. The HTML document is shown in Listing 17.5.

LISTING 17.5   The HTML File for the Live Search Example

```
<html>
<head>
<title>Live Search Ajax Example</title>
<script language="javascript" type="text/javascript"
    src="ajax.js">
</script>
</head>
<body>
<h1>Live Search: Ajax Example</h1>
<form>
<p>
<b>Search for:</b> <input type="text" size="40" id="searchlive">
</p>
<div id="results">
<ul id="list">
<li>Results will display here.</li>
</ul>
</div>
</form>
<script language="javascript" type="text/javascript"
    src="search.js">
</script>
</body>
</html>
```

This HTML document includes the following:

▶ The <script> tag in the <head> section includes the AJAX library, ajax.js.

▶ The <script> tag in the <body> section includes the search.js script, which you'll create next.

▶ The <input> element with the id value searchlive is where you'll type your search query.

▶ The <div> element with the id value results will act as a container for the dynamically fetched results. A bulleted list is created with a <ul> tag; this will be replaced with a list of results when you start typing.

The PHP Back End

Next, you'll need a server-side program to produce the search results. This PHP program includes a list of names stored in an array. It will respond to a JavaScript query with the names that match what the user has typed so far. The names will be returned in XML format. For example, here is the output of the PHP program when searching for "smith":

```
<names>
<name>John Smith</name>
<name>Jane Smith</name>
</names>
```

Although the list of names is stored within the PHP program here for simplicity, in a real application it would more likely be stored in a database—and this script could easily be adapted to work with a database containing thousands of names. The PHP program is shown in Listing 17.6.

LISTING 17.6   The PHP Code for the Live Search Example

```php
<?php
  header("Content-type: text/xml");
$names = array (
   "John Smith", "John Jones", "Jane Smith", "Jane Tillman",
   "Abraham Lincoln", "Sally Johnson", "Kilgore Trout",
   "Bob Atkinson","Joe Cool", "Dorothy Barnes",
   "Elizabeth Carlson", "Frank Dixon", "Gertrude East",
   "Harvey Frank", "Inigo Montoya", "Jeff Austin",
   "Lynn Arlington", "Michael Washington", "Nancy West" );
if (!$query) $query=$_GET['query'];
echo "<?xml version=\"1.0\" ?>\n";
echo "<names>\n";
while (list($k,$v)=each($names)) {
   if (stristr($v,$query))
      echo "<name>$v</name>\n";
}
echo "</names>\n";
?>
```

This hour is too small to teach you PHP, but here's a summary of how this program works:

▶ The header statement sends a header indicating that the output is in XML format. This is required for XMLHttpRequest to correctly use the responseXML property.

▶ The $names array stores the list of names. You can use a much longer list of names without changing the rest of the code.

▶ The program looks for a GET variable called query and uses a loop to output all of the names that match the query.

▶ Because PHP can be embedded in an HTML file, the <?php and ?> tags indicate that the code between them should be interpreted as PHP.

Did you Know?

The following books are good resources if you want to learn more on PHP quickly:

▶ *Sams Teach Yourself PHP in 10 Minutes*; ISBN: 0672327627

▶ *Sams Teach Yourself PHP in 24 Hours*; ISBN: 0672326191

Save the PHP program as search.php in the same folder as the HTML file. You can test it by typing a query such as search.php?query=John in the browser's URL field. Use the View Source command to view the XML result.

The JavaScript Front End

Finally, the JavaScript for this example is shown in Listing 17.7.

LISTING 17.7   The JavaScript File for the Live Search Example

```
// global variable to manage the timeout
var t;
// Start a timeout with each keypress
function StartSearch() {
   if (t) window.clearTimeout(t);
   t = window.setTimeout("LiveSearch()",200);
}
// Perform the search
function LiveSearch() {
   // assemble the PHP filename
   query = document.getElementById("searchlive").value;
   filename = "search.php?query=" + query;
   // DisplayResults will handle the Ajax response
   ajaxCallback = DisplayResults;
   // Send the Ajax request
   ajaxRequest(filename);
}
// Display search results
function DisplayResults() {
   // remove old list
   ul = document.getElementById("list");
   div = document.getElementById("results");
   div.removeChild(ul);
   // make a new list
   ul = document.createElement("UL");
   ul.id="list";
```

LISTING 17.7   Continued

```
    names = ajaxreq.responseXML.getElementsByTagName("name");
    for (i = 0; i < names.length; i++) {
        li = document.createElement("LI");
        name = names[i].firstChild.nodeValue;
        text = document.createTextNode(name);
        li.appendChild(text);
        ul.appendChild(li);
    }
    if (names.length==0) {
        li = document.createElement("LI");
        li.appendChild(document.createTextNode("No results"));
        ul.appendChild(li);
    }
    // display the new list
    div.appendChild(ul);
}
// set up event handler
obj=document.getElementById("searchlive");
obj.onkeydown = StartSearch;
```

This script includes the following components:

▶ A global variable, t, is defined. This will store a pointer to the timeout used later in the script.

▶ The StartSearch() function is called when the user presses a key. This function uses setTimeout() to call the LiveSearch() function after a 200-millisecond delay. The delay is necessary so that the key the user types has time to appear in the search field.

▶ The LiveSearch() function assembles a filename that combines search.php with the query in the search field, and launches an AJAX request using the library's ajaxRequest() function.

▶ The DisplayResults() function is called when the AJAX request is complete. It deletes the bulleted list from the <div id="results"> section, and then assembles a new list using the W3C DOM and the AJAX results. If there were no results, it displays a "No results" message in the list.

▶ The final lines of the script set the StartSearch() function up as an event handler for the onkeydown event of the search field.

Making It All Work

To try this example, you'll need three files on a web server: ajax.js (the library), search.js (the search script), and the HTML file. Figure 17.2 shows this example in action.

FIGURE 17.2
The live search example as displayed by Firefox.

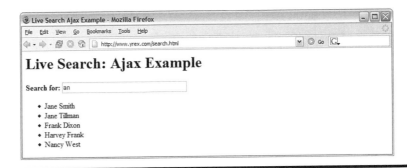

Summary

In this hour, you've learned how AJAX, otherwise known as remote scripting, can let JavaScript communicate with a web server. You created a reusable AJAX library that can be used to create any number of AJAX applications, and you created an example using an XML file. Finally, you created a live search form using AJAX and PHP.

You've nearly reached the end of Part IV. In the next hour, you'll learn about Greasemonkey, a Firefox extension that enables you to use JavaScript to enhance sites you visit, even those created by others.

Q&A

Q. *Why would I want to use* **POST** *instead of* **GET** *when making a request?*

A. Although GET is easy to use, it is limited to about 255 characters. If you are using a large amount of data, POST is the only way to send it to the server.

Q. *What happens if the server is slow, or never responds to the request?*

A. This is another reason you should use AJAX as an optional feature—whether caused by the server or by the user's connection, there will be times when a request is slow to respond or never responds. In this case, the callback function will be called late, or not at all. This can cause trouble with overlapping requests: for example, in the live search example, an erratic server might cause the responses for the first few characters typed to come in a few seconds apart, confusing the user. You can remedy this by checking the readyState property to make sure a request is not already in progress before you start another one.

Q. *In the live search example, why is the **onkeydown** event handler necessary? Wouldn't the **onchange** event be easier to use?*

A. Although onchange tells you when a form field has changed, it is not triggered until the user moves on to a different field—it doesn't work for "live" search, so you have to watch for key presses instead. The onkeypress handler would work, but in some browsers it doesn't detect the Backspace key, and it's nice to have the search update when you backspace to shorten the query.

Quiz Questions

Test your knowledge of AJAX by answering the following questions.

1. Which of the following is the *A* in *AJAX*?

    a. Advanced

    b. Asynchronous

    c. Application

2. Which property of an XMLHttpRequest object indicates whether the request was successful?

    a. status

    b. readyState

    c. success

3. Which browsers require ActiveX for remote scripting?

    a. Internet Explorer 5–7

    b. Firefox 1.0–1.5

    c. Internet Explorer 5–6

Quiz Answers

1. b. AJAX stands for Asynchronous JavaScript and XML.

2. a. The status property indicates whether the request was successful; readyState indicates whether the request is complete, but does not indicate success.

3. c. Internet Explorer 5 and 6 require ActiveX. Internet Explorer 7 supports the XMLHttpRequest object natively.

Exercises

If you want to gain more experience with AJAX, try the following exercises:

▶ Build your own XML file of questions and answers on your favorite topic and try it with the quiz example.

▶ Use the AJAX library to add an AJAX feature to your site, or create a simple example of your own.

HOUR 18

Greasemonkey: Enhancing the Web with JavaScript

What You'll Learn in This Hour:

▶ How Greasemonkey and user scripts can enhance your web browser
▶ How to install and configure Greasemonkey in Firefox
▶ Installing and managing user scripts
▶ Creating your own user scripts
▶ Defining metadata for scripts
▶ Using the Greasemonkey API
▶ Adding macros to web forms

One of the recent trends is that JavaScript is being used in new ways, both inside and outside web browsers. In this hour, you'll look at Greasemonkey, a Firefox extension that enables you to write scripts to modify the appearance and behavior of sites you visit. User scripts can also work in Internet Explorer, Opera, and Safari with the right add-ons.

Introducing Greasemonkey

So far in this book, you've been using JavaScript to work on your own sites. In this hour, you'll take a break from that and learn about a way to use JavaScript on *other people's sites*. Greasemonkey is an extension for the Firefox browser that enables *user scripts*. These are scripts that run as soon as you load a page and can make changes to the page's DOM.

A user script can be designed to work on all web pages, or only to affect particular sites. Here are some of the things user scripts can do:

▶ Change the appearance of one or more sites—colors, font size, and so on.
▶ Change the behavior of one or more sites with JavaScript.

▶ Fix a bug in a site before the site author does.

▶ Add a feature to your browser, such as text macros—see the Try It Yourself section of this hour for an example.

As a simple example, a user script called `Linkify` is provided with Greasemonkey. It affects all pages you visit and turns unlinked URLs into hyperlinks. In other words, the script looks for any string that resembles a URL in the page, and if it finds a URL that is not enclosed in an <a> tag, it modifies the DOM to add a link to the URL.

Greasemonkey scripts can range from simple ones such as `Linkify` to complex scripts that add a feature to the browser, rearrange a site to make it more usable, or eliminate annoying features of sites such as pop-up ads.

Keep in mind that Greasemonkey doesn't do anything to the websites you visit—it strictly affects your personal experience with the sites. In this way, it's similar to other browser customizations, such as personal style sheets and browser font settings.

By the Way

> Greasemonkey was created in 2004 by Aaron Boodman. Its official site is http://greasemonkey.mozdev.org/. At this writing, the current version of Greasemonkey is 0.6.4. The current developers are Aaron Boodman and Jeremy Dunck.

Installing Greasemonkey in Firefox

Greasemonkey works in Firefox for Windows, Macintosh, and Linux platforms. You can install it by visiting the Greasemonkey site and running the installer. Start at http://greasemonkey.mozdev.org/ and follow these steps:

1. Click the Install Greasemonkey link.

2. You will probably see a message in a yellow bar at the top of the window warning you about installing software. Click the Edit Options button within the yellow bar.

3. In the Allowed Sites dialog, shown in Figure 18.1, click the Allow button to allow the current site to install software, and then click Close.

4. Click the Install link again, and then click the Install button in the Software Installation dialog that appears.

5. Exit and restart Firefox. You should see a small monkey icon in the lower-right hand corner of the browser window if the extension was successfully installed.

FIGURE 18.1
Firefox prompts
you to allow a
site for installing
extensions.

> When you first install Greasemonkey, the extension doesn't do anything—you'll need to install one or more user scripts, as described in the next section, to make it useful.

By the Way

Turnabout for Internet Explorer

Greasemonkey was written as a Firefox extension, and does not work on other browsers. Fortunately, there's an alternative for those who prefer Internet Explorer: Turnabout, from Reify, is an open-source add-on for Internet Explorer that supports user scripts. Turnabout is available for free from its official site at http://www.reifysoft.com/turnabout.php. Two versions are available:

▶ Turnabout Basic, which only supports the scripts bundled with it

▶ Turnabout Advanced, which supports any user script, similar to Greasemonkey

Turnabout supports most of Greasemonkey's features, and user scripts for Greasemonkey often work with Turnabout Advanced without modification. The only potential problem is with differences in JavaScript and in the DOM between Internet Explorer and Firefox. If you follow the same cross-browser coding practices you learned throughout this book, there's a good chance you can make a user script that works on both platforms.

Other Browsers

Although Greasemonkey itself is still relatively new software, user script features have also appeared for other browsers. Along with Turnabout for IE, two other browsers can support user scripts:

▶ Opera, the cross-platform browser from Opera Software ASA, has built-in support for user scripts, and supports Greasemonkey scripts in many cases. See Opera's site for details at http://www.opera.com/.

▶ Creammonkey is a beta add-on for Apple's Safari browser to support user scripts. You can find it at http://8-p.info/Creammonkey/.

User Script Security

Before you get into user scripting, a word of warning: Don't install a script unless you understand what it's doing, or you've obtained it from a trustworthy source. Although the Greasemonkey developers have spent a great deal of time eliminating security holes, it's still possible for a malicious script to cause you trouble—at the very least, it could send information about which sites you visit to a third-party website.

To minimize security risks, be sure you're running the latest version of Greasemonkey or Turnabout. Only enable scripts you are actively using, and limit scripts you don't trust to specific pages so they don't run on every page you visit.

Working with User Scripts

User scripts are a whole new way of working with JavaScript—rather than uploading them for use on your website, you install them in the browser for your own personal use. The following sections show you how to find useful scripts, and install and manage them.

Finding Scripts

Anyone can write user scripts, and many people have. Greasemonkey sponsors a directory of user scripts at http://userscripts.org/. There you can browse or search for scripts, or submit scripts you've written.

The script archive has thousands of scripts available. Along with general-purpose scripts, many of the scripts are designed to add features to—or remove annoying features from—particular sites.

Installing a Script

After you've found a script you wish to install, you can install it from the Web:

▶ In Firefox with Greasemonkey, open the script in the browser and then select Tools, Install This User Script from the menu.

▶ In IE with Turnabout, right-click on a link to the script and select Turnabout, Install Script.

You can also install a script from a local file. You'll use this technique to install your own script later this hour.

Managing Scripts

After you've installed one or more scripts with Greasemonkey, you can manage them by selecting Tools, Manage User Scripts from the Firefox menu. The Manage User Scripts dialog is shown in Figure 18.2.

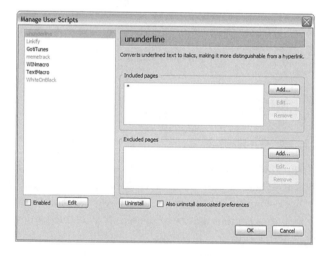

FIGURE 18.2
Managing user scripts in Greasemonkey.

The user scripts you have available are listed in the left column. Click on a script name to manage it:

▶ Use the Included Pages and Excluded Pages lists to control which pages the script works on. You can specify wildcards, such as * for all pages or *.google.com/* for all Google pages.

▶ Use the Enabled check box to enable or disable each script.

▶ Click the Uninstall button to remove a script.

▶ Click Edit to open a script in a text editor. When it is saved, it will immediately take effect on pages you load.

Turnabout for IE has a similar dialog. To access it, click the Reify button in the Turnabout toolbar and select Options. The dialog is similar to Greasemonkey's dialog, except that each script has a separate check box to enable or disable it. There is also an Install Feature button that prompts you for a new script to install. The Turnabout Options dialog is shown in Figure 18.3.

FIGURE 18.3
The Turnabout Options dialog.

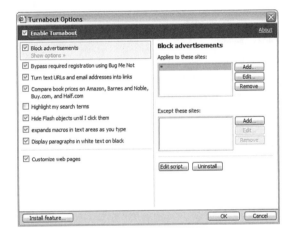

Testing User Scripts

If you have a script enabled, it will be activated as soon as you load a page that matches one of the Included Pages specified for the script. (The script is run after the page is loaded, but before the onLoad event.) If you want to make sure Greasemonkey is running, either try one of the scripts available for download, or type in the simple script in the next section.

Activating and Deactivating Greasemonkey or Turnabout

Sometimes you'll want to turn off Greasemonkey altogether, especially if one of the scripts you've installed is causing an error. To do this, right-click on the monkey icon in the lower-right corner of the browser window and select the Enabled option to deselect it. The monkey icon changes to a gray sad-faced monkey, and no user scripts will be run at all. You can re-enable it at any time using the same option.

With Turnabout for Internet Explorer, the procedure is similar: Click the Reify button in the Turnabout toolbar, and select the Enable Turnabout option. The icon changes to indicate that Turnabout is disabled. Choose Enable Turnabout again to re-enable it.

Creating Your Own User Scripts

You've already learned most of what you need to know to create user scripts since they're written in JavaScript. In this section, you'll create and test a simple script, and look at some features you'll use when creating more advanced scripts.

Creating a Simple User Script

One of the best uses for Greasemonkey is to solve annoyances with sites you visit. For example, a site might use green text on an orange background. Although you could contact the webmaster and beg for a color change, user scripting lets you deal with the problem quickly yourself.

As a simple demonstration of user scripting, you can create a user script that changes the text and background colors of paragraphs in sites you visit. Listing 18.1 shows this user script.

LISTING 18.1   A Simple User Script to Change Paragraph Colors

```
// Change the color of each paragraph
var zParagraphs = document.getElementsByTagName("p");
for (var i=0; i<zParagraphs.length; i++) {
   zParagraphs[i].style.backgroundColor="#000000";
   zParagraphs[i].style.color="#FFFFFF";
}
```

This script uses the `getElementsByTagName()` DOM method to find all of the paragraph tags in the current document and store their objects in the `zParagraphs` array. The `for` loop iterates through the array and changes the `style.color` and `style.backgroundColor` properties for each one.

Describing a User Script

Greasemonkey supports *metadata* at the beginning of your script. These are JavaScript comments that aren't executed by the script, but provide information to Greasemonkey. To use this feature, enclose your comments between `// ==UserScript==` and `// ==/UserScript` comments.

The metadata section can contain any of the following directives. All of these are optional, but using them will make your user script easier to install and use.

▶ @name—A short name for the script, displayed in Greasemonkey's list of scripts after installation.

▶ @namespace—An optional URL for the script author's site. This is used as a namespace for the script: Two scripts can have the same name as long as the namespace is different.

▶ @description—A one-line description of the script's purpose.

▶ @include—The URL of a site on which the script should be used. You can specify any number of URLs, each in its own @include line. You can also use the wildcard * to run the script on all sites, or a partial URL with a wildcard to run it on a group of sites.

▶ @exclude—The URL of a site on which the script should *not* be used. You can specify a wildcard for @include and then exclude one or more sites that the script is incompatible with. The @exclude directive can also use wildcards.

Listing 18.2 shows the color-changing example with a complete set of metadata comments added at the top.

LISTING 18.2   The Color-Changing Script with Metadata Comments

```
// ==UserScript==
// @name         WhiteOnBlack
// @namespace    http://www.jsworkshop.com/
// @description  Display paragraphs in white text on black
// @include      *
// ==/UserScript==
//
// Change the color of each paragraph
var zParagraphs = document.getElementsByTagName("p");
for (var i=0; i<zParagraphs.length; i++) {
   zParagraphs[i].style.backgroundColor="#000000";
   zParagraphs[i].style.color="#FFFFFF";
}
```

Testing Your Script

Now that you've added the metadata, installing your script is simple. Follow these steps to install the script in Firefox:

1. Save the script file as colors.user.js. The filename must end in .user.js to be recognized as a Greasemonkey script.

2. In Firefox, choose File, Open from the menu.

3. Select your script from the Open File dialog.

4. After the script is displayed in the browser, select Tools, Install This User Script.

5. An alert will display to inform you that the installation was successful. The new user script is now running on all sites.

If you're using Turnabout under Internet Explorer, click on the Turnabout toolbar and select Options, and then click the Install Feature button. Select the script and click Open to install it.

Both Greasemonkey and Turnabout for IE will use the metadata you specified to set the script's included pages, description, and other options when you install it.

After you've installed and enabled the script, any page you load will have its paragraphs displayed in white text on a black background. For example, Figure 18.4 shows the user script's effect on the Date and Time example from Hour 2, "Creating Simple Scripts." Because the date and time are within <p> tags, they are displayed in white on black.

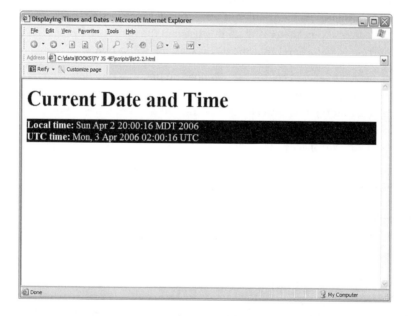

FIGURE 18.4
The Date and Time example altered by the color-changing user script.

> You probably don't want to make a change this drastic to *all* sites you visit. Instead, you can use @include to make this script affect only one or two sites whose colors you find hard to read. Don't forget that you can also change the colors in the script to your own preference.

By the Way

Greasemonkey API Functions

You can use all of the DOM methods covered in this book to work with pages in user scripts, along with JavaScript's built-in functions. In addition to these, Greasemonkey defines an API (Application Programmer's Interface) with a few functions that can be used exclusively in user scripts:

- ▶ `GM_log(message, level)`—Inserts a message into the JavaScript console. The `level` parameter indicates the severity of the message: 0 for information, 1 for a warning, and 2 for an error.

- ▶ `GM_setValue(variable, value)`—Sets a variable stored by Greasemonkey. These variables are stored on the local machine. They are specific to the script that set them, and can be used in the future by the same script. (These are similar to cookies, but are not sent to a server.)

- ▶ `GM_getValue(variable)`—Retrieves a value previously set with `GM_setValue`.

- ▶ `GM_registerMenuCommand(command, function)`—Adds a command to the browser menu. These commands appear under Tools, User Script Commands. The `command` parameter is the name listed in the menu, and `function` is a function in your script that the menu selection will activate.

- ▶ `GM_xmlhttpRequest(details)`—Requests a file from a remote server, similar to the AJAX features described in Hour 17, "AJAX: Remote Scripting." The `details` parameter is an object that can contain a number of properties to control the request. See the Greasemonkey documentation for all of the properties you can specify.

Turnabout for Internet Explorer also supports all of these API functions, so aside from the usual browser differences, scripts that use these functions should work in both browsers. Because Internet Explorer does not have a JavaScript console, Turnabout includes its own console, available from the menu, where log messages are displayed.

Creating a Site-Specific Script

You might want to use a user script to fix a problem or add a feature to a specific site. In addition to using `@include` to specify the site's URL, you'll need to know something about the site's DOM.

You can use the DOM Inspector in Firefox (or the similar feature in Internet Explorer's developer toolbar) to browse the DOM for the site and find the objects you want to work with. Depending on how they are marked up, you can access them through the DOM:

▶ If an element has an id attribute, you can simply use
document.getElementById() in your script to find its object.

▶ If a nearby element has an id defined, you can use DOM methods to find it—
for example, if the parent element has an id, you can use a method such as
firstChild() to find the object you need.

▶ If all else fails, you can use document.getElementsByTagName() to find all
objects of a certain type—for example, all paragraphs. If you need to refer to a
specific one, you can use a loop and check each one for a certain attribute.

> See Hour 16, "Debugging JavaScript Applications," for information about Firefox's
> DOM Inspector and IE's developer toolbar. See Hours 13, "Using the W3C DOM"
> and 14, "Using Advanced DOM Features," for information about DOM methods.

By the
Way

As an example, Listing 18.3 shows a simple user script you could use as a site-specific script to automatically fill out certain fields in forms.

LISTING 18.3 **A User Script to Fill Out Form Fields Automatically**

```
// ==UserScript==
// @name          AutoForm
// @namespace     http://www.jsworkshop.com/
// @description   Fills in forms automatically
// @include       *
// ==/UserScript==
// this function fills out form fields
//
var zTextFields = document.getElementsByTagName("input");
for (var i=0; i<zTextFields.length; i++) {
  thefield=zTextFields[i].name;
  if (!thefield) thefield=zTextFields[i].id;
  // Set up your auto-fill values here
  if (thefield == "yourname") zTextFields[i].value="Your Name Here";
  if (thefield == "phone") zTextFields[i].value="(xxx) xxx-xxxx";
  alert("field:" + thefield + " value: " + zTextFields[i].value);
}
```

This script uses getElementsByTagName() to find all of the <input> elements in a document, including text fields. It uses a for loop to examine each one. If it finds a field
with the name or id value "yourname" or "phone", it inserts the appropriate value.

To test this script, save it as autoform.user.js and install the user script as
described earlier in this hour. To test it, load Listing 11.1 from Hour 11, "Getting
Data with Forms," into the browser—it happens to have both of the field names the
script looks for. The yourname and phone fields will be automatically filled out, as
shown in Figure 18.5.

FIGURE 18.5
The form-filling
user script in
action.

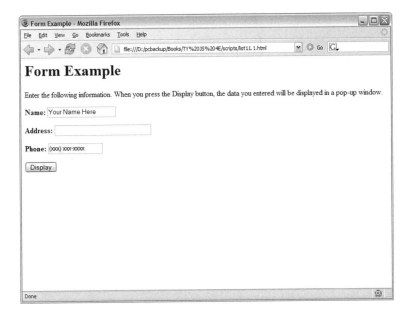

To make it easy to test, Listing 18.3 doesn't include specific sites in the @include line. To make a true site-specific script, you would need to find out the field names for a particular site, add if statements to the script to fill them out, and use @include to make sure the script only runs on the site.

Debugging User Scripts

Debugging a user script is much like debugging a regular JavaScript program—errors are displayed in the JavaScript Console in Firefox or in an error message in Internet Explorer. Here are a few debugging tips:

▶ As with regular scripts, you can also use the alert() method to display information about what's going on in your script.

▶ The browser may display a line number with an error message, but when you're working with user scripts, these line numbers are meaningless—they refer neither to lines in your user script nor to the page you're currently viewing.

▶ Use the GM_log() method described earlier in this hour to log information about your script, such as the contents of variables, to the JavaScript console.

▶ If you're trying to write a cross-browser user script, watch for methods that are browser specific. See Hour 15, "Unobtrusive Scripting," for information about cross-browser issues.

▶ Watch for conflicts with any existing scripts on the page.

▶ If you're using multiple user scripts, be sure they don't conflict. Use unique variable and function names in your scripts.

Most of the issues with user scripts are the same as for regular JavaScript. See Hour 16 for information on debugging tools, techniques, and common mistakes.

Try It Yourself ▼

Creating a User Script

Now that you've learned the basics of Greasemonkey, you can try a more complex—and more useful—example of a user script.

If you spend much time on the Web, you'll find yourself needing to fill out web forms often, and you probably type certain things—such as your name or URL—into forms over and over. The user script you create here will let you define macros for use in any text area. When you type a macro keyword (a period followed by a code) and then type another character, the macro keyword will be instantly replaced by the text you've defined. For example, you can define a macro so that every time you type .cu, it will expand into the text "See you later.".

> This script has been tested on Greasemonkey 0.6.4 for Firefox and Turnabout Advanced 0.31 b3 for Internet Explorer. Because browsers and extensions are always changing, it might stop working at some point—see this book's website for the latest updates.

Watch Out!

Listing 18.4 shows the text area macro user script.

LISTING 18.4 The Text Area Macro User Script

```
// ==UserScript==
// @name          TextMacro
// @namespace     http://www.jsworkshop.com/
// @description   expands macros in text areas as you type
// @include       *
// ==/UserScript==
// this function handles the macro replacements
function textmacro(e) {
   // define your macros here
   zmacros = [
     [".mm", "Michael Moncur"],
     [".js", "JavaScript"],
     [".cu", "See you later."]
   ];
   if (!e) var e = window.event;
```

LISTING 18.4   **Continued**

```
// which textarea are we in?
thisarea= (e.target) ? e.target : e.srcElement;
// replace text
for (i=0; i<zmacros.length; i++) {
    vv = thisarea.value;
    vv = vv.replace(zmacros[i][0],zmacros[i][1]);
    thisarea.value=vv;
}
}
// install the event handlers
var zTextAreas = document.getElementsByTagName("textarea");
for (var i=0; i<zTextAreas.length; i++) {
    if (zTextAreas[i].addEventListener)
        zTextAreas[i].addEventListener("keydown",textmacro,0);
    else if (zTextAreas[i].attachEvent)
        zTextAreas[i].attachEvent("onkeydown",textmacro);
}
```

How It Works

This user script begins with the usual comment metadata. The `@include` command specifies a wildcard, *, so the script will work on all sites. The actual work is done in the `textmacro()` function. This function begins by defining the macros that will be available:

```
zmacros = [
  [".mm", "Michael Moncur"],
  [".js", "JavaScript"],
  [".cu", "See you later."]
];
```

This example defines three macros using a two-dimensional array. To make the script useful to you, define your own. You can have any number of macros—just add a comma after the last macro line and add your items before the closing bracket.

Next, the function uses the `target` property to find the text area in which you're currently typing. Next, it uses a `for` loop to do a search and replace within the text area's `value` property for each of your macros.

The section of code after the `textmacro()` function sets up an event handler for each text area. First, it uses `getElementsByTagName()` to find all of the text areas, and then it uses a `for` loop to add an `onkeydown` event handler to each one.

By the Way

To avoid conflicts with existing event handlers within web pages, this example uses the `addEventListener()` method to add the event handler. This method defines an event handler without overwriting existing events. In Internet Explorer, it uses the similar `attachEvent()` method. See Hour 15 for more information.

Using This Script

To use this script, first make sure you've installed and enabled Greasemonkey as described earlier this hour. Save the script as `textmacro.user.js`. You can then install the user script.

After the script is installed, try loading any page with a text area. You should be able to type a macro, such as `.mm` or `.js`, followed by another character such as a space, within the text area and see it instantly expand into the correct text.

> This script runs on all sites by default. If you only want the macros to work on certain sites, you can change the `@include` directive to specify them. If the script causes trouble on some sites, you can exclude them with `@exclude`.

Did you Know?

▲

Summary

In this hour, you've learned how to use Greasemonkey—and its counterpart for Internet Explorer, Turnabout—to enable user scripting in your browser. You've learned how user scripts work and how to install and manage them. Finally, you created two examples of functioning user scripts.

Congratulations! You've reached the end of Part IV of this book, and you're well on your way to becoming a JavaScript expert. In Part V, you'll look at multimedia applications of JavaScript—graphics, animation, sound, and working with plug-ins. Hour 19, "Using Graphics and Animation," starts by helping you move beyond scripts that work with text.

Q&A

Q. *Is there any way to prevent users from using Greasemonkey while viewing my site?*

A. Because Greasemonkey only affects the user who installed it, it's usually harmless to allow it. If you still want to prevent its use, this is difficult but not impossible, and varies with different versions of Greasemonkey. Search the Web to find current solutions.

Q. *What if I want to do something more sophisticated, such as modifying Firefox's menu?*

A. This capability does not exist in Greasemonkey, but Firefox extensions are also written in JavaScript. In fact, you can compile a user script into a Firefox extension and then add more advanced features. See http://www.letitblog.com/greasemonkey-compiler/ for details.

Q. *What happens when a new version of Firefox or Internet Explorer is released?*

A. Although I have faith in the Greasemonkey developers, there's no guarantee that this extension will work in future browser versions. If you're concerned about this, you might want to write your own Firefox extension instead.

Q. *Are there limits to how much I can modify a page using Greasemonkey?*

A. No—in fact, you can yank the entire content of the page's DOM out and replace it with HTML of your choosing using the `innerHTML` property. You'd have to do quite a bit of work to make something as useful as the original page, of course.

Quiz Questions

Test your knowledge of Greasemonkey and user scripts by answering the following questions.

1. Which of the following offers user scripting for Microsoft Internet Explorer?

   a. Greasemonkey

   b. Microsoft Live Scripting Toolbar

   c. Turnabout

2. Which of the following is not a valid Greasemonkey API function?

   a. `GM_log()`

   b. `GM_alert()`

   c. `GM_setValue()`

3. Which is the correct @include directive to run a script on both www.google.com and google.com?

   a. `@include *.google.com`

   b. `@include www.google.com.*`

   c. `@include google.com`

Quiz Answers

1. c. Turnabout is a user script add-on for Internet Explorer.

2. b. There is no GM_alert() method, although the standard alert() method will work in a user script.

3. a. Using @include *.google.com will run the script on any page on any site within the google.com domain.

Exercises

If you want to gain more experience with user scripts, try the following exercises:

▶ Modify the color-changing user script in Listing 18.2 to use different colors, and add another style attribute—for example, use style.fontSize to change the font size.

▶ The color-changing example works on paragraphs, but text often appears in other places, such as bullet lists. Modify Listing 18.2 to make the changes to <li> tags as well as paragraphs.

▶ Currently, the macro example in the Try It Yourself section only works on text inputs that use <textarea> tags. Modify the script in Listing 18.3 to work on <input> tags also. (You'll need to add a second call to getElementsByTagName() and a loop to add the event handlers.)

PART V:

Building Multimedia Applications with JavaScript

HOUR 19

Using Graphics and Animation

What You'll Learn in This Hour:

▶ Using JavaScript to swap images within a page
▶ Using JavaScript rollovers
▶ Using CSS rollovers
▶ Creating an image slideshow
▶ Adding animation to the slideshow

Welcome to Part V! So far, you've used JavaScript to work with text and forms in web pages. In the next two hours, you'll look at how JavaScript can work with graphics, sounds, and plug-ins. This hour focuses on using JavaScript to manipulate graphics and create animated displays.

Using Dynamic Images

Long before the W3C DOM allowed JavaScript to change any part of a web page, a feature called *dynamic images* enabled you to swap one image for another with JavaScript. This technique is still supported by current browsers, and is still the most convenient (and compatible) way to work with images in JavaScript.

Working with `image` Objects

You can change images dynamically by using the `image` object associated with each one. The traditional way to do this is with the `document.images` array. This array contains an item for each of the images defined on the page. In the object hierarchy, each `image` object is a child of the `document` object.

With the W3C DOM, you can also assign an `id` attribute to an image within the `<img>` tag, and then use `document.getElementById` to find the object for that image. Each image object has the following properties:

▶ complete is a flag that tells you whether the image has been completely loaded. This is a Boolean value (true or false).

▶ height and width reflect the corresponding image attributes. This is for information only; you can't change an image's size dynamically.

▶ hspace and vspace represent the corresponding image attributes, which define the image's placement on the page. Again, this is a read-only attribute.

▶ name is the image's name. You can define this with the NAME attribute in the image definition.

▶ src is the image's source, or URL. You can change this value to change images dynamically.

For most purposes, the src attribute is the only one you'll use. The image object has no methods. It does have three event handlers you can use:

▶ The onLoad event occurs when the image finishes loading. (Because the onLoad event for the entire document is triggered when all images have finished loading, it's usually a better choice.)

▶ The onAbort event occurs if the user aborts the page before the image is loaded.

▶ The onError event occurs if the image file is not found or corrupt.

By the Way

Although changing image sources works fine, you can also use the W3C DOM to completely remove or replace image objects, or insert new ones, just like any other object.

Preloading Images

You can also create an independent image object. This enables you to specify an image that will be loaded and placed in the cache, but will not be displayed on the page.

This might sound useless, but it's a great way to work with modem-speed connections. After you've preloaded an image, you can replace any of the images on the page with that image—and because it's already cached, the change happens instantly. Even on a fast connection, this avoids flickering and makes animation smoother.

You can cache an image by creating a new `image` object, using the `new` keyword. Here's an example:

```
Image2 = new Image();
Image2.src = "arrow1.gif";
```

You learned about the new keyword and its other uses for object-oriented programming in Hour 6, "Using Functions and Objects."

By the Way

Creating Rollovers

One of the classic uses of JavaScript is to create *rollovers*—images that change when you move the mouse over them. They are typically used to create navigation links that give the user a bit of guidance by highlighting the one the mouse is over.

In this section, you'll learn how to use JavaScript's dynamic images to create rollovers—and then you'll learn why you shouldn't do this most of the time, and how to create rollovers with no scripting at all.

JavaScript Rollovers

First, let's take a quick look at how to create rollovers using JavaScript. To do this, you start with regular and highlighted versions of each rollover image. Figure 19.1 shows two examples of navigation buttons in both states.

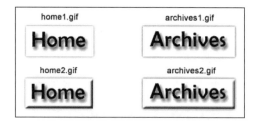

FIGURE 19.1
Regular and highlighted versions of two button images.

As you might guess, all this requires in JavaScript is to combine an `onMouseOver` event handler with a dynamic image. Adding `onMouseOut` allows your script to restore the original image when the mouse moves away. Listing 19.1 shows a simple way to do this with inline event handlers.

LISTING 19.1   Using Basic JavaScript Rollovers

```
<html>
<head>
<title>Rollovers - JavaScript</title>
</head>
<body>
<h1>JavaScript Rollovers</h1>
<a href="home.html"
    onmouseover="document.images[0].src='home2.gif';"
    onmouseout="document.images[0].src='home1.gif';">
    <image border="0" src="home1.gif">
</a>
<br>
<a href="archives.html"
    onmouseover="document.images[1].src='archives2.gif';"
    onmouseout="document.images[1].src='archives1.gif';">
    <image border="0" src="archives1.gif">
</a>
</body>
</html>
```

This is just a basic bit of inline JavaScript, so you can test it by simply loading the HTML file into a browser. The results are shown in Figure 19.2. In the figure, the mouse cursor is over the Archives button.

FIGURE 19.2
The rollover
example in
action.

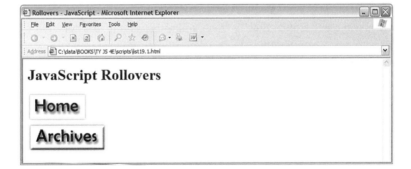

CSS Rollovers Without JavaScript

Although JavaScript rollovers work fine in today's browsers, the technique was developed in the days before CSS, and there is now a better way to accomplish the same thing. Using the :hover directive in CSS, you can create text links that change color when the mouse hovers over them. Listing 19.2 shows a simple example of CSS rollovers.

LISTING 19.2   JavaScript-Free Rollovers with CSS

```
<html>
<head>
<title>Rollovers - CSS</title>
<style>
#home,#archives {
    font-size: 30px;
    text-decoration: none;
}
#home:hover, #archives:hover {
    background-color: #AAAAAA;
}
</style>
</head>
<body>
<h1>JavaScript-Free Rollovers</h1>
<a id="home" href="home.html"><b>Home</b></a>
<br>
<a id="archives" href="archives.html"><b>Archives</b></a>
</body>
</html>
```

To try this example, simply load the HTML document into a browser. When you move the mouse over the links, their background color changes from white to gray. This example is shown in Figure 19.3.

FIGURE 19.3
Simple CSS-only rollovers.

This isn't as fancy as the JavaScript rollovers, but it has some advantages—first of all, it doesn't require JavaScript. Second, the links are actual text—this means they'll work even in text-based browsers, primitive mobile phone browsers, and voice-reading browsers for the blind, although the rollover effects won't work in these situations. Third, the page loads faster, and you can add more links without creating graphics.

Graphic CSS Rollovers

Suppose you're really attached to the nifty graphic look of the first rollover example. Before you do something like that, take a look at Listing 19.3. This listing uses CSS to implement graphic rollovers, which look and work exactly like Figure 19.2, with no JavaScript.

LISTING 19.3   Graphic Rollovers with CSS

```html
<html>
<head>
<title>Rollovers - CSS</title>
<style>
#home {
    display: block;
    height: 60px;
    width: 126px;
    background-image: url("home1.gif");
}
#home:hover {
    background-image: url("home2.gif");
}
#archives {
    display: block;
    height: 60px;
    width: 168px;
    background-image: url("archives1.gif");
}
#archives:hover {
    background-image: url("archives2.gif");
}
#home b, #archives b {
    display: none;
}
</style>
</head>
<body>
<h1>JavaScript-Free Rollovers</h1>
<a id="home" href="home.html"><b>Home</b></a>
<br>
<a id="archives" href="archives.html"><b>Archives</b></a>
</body>
</html>
```

Here's a summary of how the CSS works:

▶ The #home and #archives rules, which match the id attribute of the two links, set their display attribute to block and the width and height attributes to allow the links to be as large as their corresponding graphics. They then use the background-image property to display the unhighlighted graphics (home1.gif and archives1.gif).

▶ The #home:hover and #archives:hover rules change the background images to the highlighted versions (home2.gif and archives2.gif).

▶ The #home b and #archives b rule hides the text of the links within the <b> tags. This prevents the text from appearing on top of the graphics.

Notice that the HTML portion of this example is identical to the previous example, and it will work exactly the same on text-based browsers and browsers with JavaScript turned off. Users with modern browsers will see the graphic versions of the links instead. This gives you the look of graphic rollovers without JavaScript, and without compromising accessibility.

> Another reason to use this type of rollover: Because the links are still in the HTML as text, search engines see them as ordinary links, and can do a better job of indexing your site. See Hour 15, "Unobtrusive Scripting," for more information on accessibility and search engine optimization.

By the Way

A Simple JavaScript Slideshow

Suppose you wanted to create a simple picture slideshow using JavaScript: The page displays the first picture, and when you click on it the next picture replaces it. You can continue to click and view all of the pictures in the slideshow. The obvious way to do this is to change the `.src` attribute of an `image` object, and that will work fine—but here you'll take a look at a different approach that uses the W3C DOM to make a more flexible slideshow.

The HTML File

First, you'll need an HTML document that defines the page and where the images will appear. Before you start on the scripting, take a look at the HTML file in Listing 19.4.

LISTING 19.4   The HTML File for the Slideshow

```
<html>
<head>
  <title>Image Slideshow Test</title>
<script language="javascript" type="text/javascript"
   src="slideshow.js">
</script>
</head>
<body>
<h1>Image Slideshow Test</h1>
<img class="slide" src="pic1.jpg" width="400" height="300">
<img class="slide" src="pic2.jpg" width="400" height="300">
<img class="slide" src="pic3.jpg" width="400" height="300">
<img class="slide" src="pic4.jpg" width="400" height="300">
<img class="slide" src="pic5.jpg" width="400" height="300">
<p>Click the image to view the next slide.</p>
</body>
</html>
```

You might notice something peculiar about this document: All five of the images are included with <img> tags. If you load the document into a browser before you add the JavaScript file, you'll see all five images on the page at once.

The slideshow.js script is included with the <script> tag in the header. This script will hide all but the first image, and allow the images to be shown one at a time. This is an example of *unobtrusive scripting*—users without JavaScript can see the images just fine, although they'll have to scroll the page, and they'll miss the nifty slideshow feature.

Because the markup of this example uses ordinary <img> tags, we've used a special class="slide" attribute on the slide images. The script will check for this class to determine which images belong to the slideshow because there's a good chance you'll have other images on the page.

This is a flexible way to create a slideshow—you can change the order of the slides simply by rearranging the HTML, and you can add more slides just by adding more images with the right class value.

By the Way

> See Hour 15 for more information about keeping JavaScript unobtrusive and optional.

The JavaScript File

The script that brings the slideshow to life is shown in Listing 19.5. The script consists of two basic functions: MakeSlideShow(), which rearranges the images into a slideshow, and NextSlide(), which responds to a click and advances to the next image.

LISTING 19.5   The JavaScript File for the Slideshow

```
var numslides=0,currentslide=0;
var slides = new Array();
function MakeSlideShow() {
   // find all images with the class "slide"
   imgs=document.getElementsByTagName("img");
   for (i=0; i<imgs.length; i++) {
      if (imgs[i].className != "slide") continue;
      slides[numslides]=imgs[i];
      // hide all but first image
      if (numslides==0) {
         imgs[i].style.display="block";
      } else {
         imgs[i].style.display="none";
      }
      imgs[i].onclick=NextSlide;
      numslides++;
   } // end for loop
```

LISTING 19.5 Continued

```
} // end MakeSlideShow()
function NextSlide() {
   slides[currentslide].style.display="none";
   currentslide++;
   if (currentslide >= numslides) currentslide = 0;
   slides[currentslide].style.display="block";
}
// create the slideshow when the page loads
window.onload=MakeSlideShow;
```

Let's take a look at how this script works:

▶ The first lines define three global variables: numslides to store the current number of slides, currentslide to keep track of the current slide, and the slides array to store the image objects for each slide.

▶ The MakeSlides() function starts by using getElementsByTagName() to find all of the images on the page, and iterates through the array with a for loop. The first if statement in the loop checks the className attribute of the image, and if it does not belong to the slide class, the loop is continued without any action.

▶ The next statements store the image in the slides array, and then check numslides for a value of zero, meaning the first image in the array. For the first image, the display attribute is set to block; for all others, display is set to none so that only one image is visible at a time.

▶ The final statements in the loop set the image's onclick event handler to the NextSlide() function and increment the numslides variable.

▶ The NextSlide() function first hides the current slide by setting its display property to none. Next, it increments currentslide. The if statement resets currentslide to zero when the last slide is clicked on. Finally, the new slide is displayed by setting its display property to block.

▶ The final line of the script sets an onLoad event handler for the window to run the MakeSlideShow() function. This rearranges the images into a slideshow as soon as the page loads.

To test the script, save it as slideshow.js in the same folder as the HTML document you created previously, and load the HTML document into a browser. Figure 19.4 shows the script in action with the first image displayed.

FIGURE 19.4
The JavaScript slideshow shows the first image.

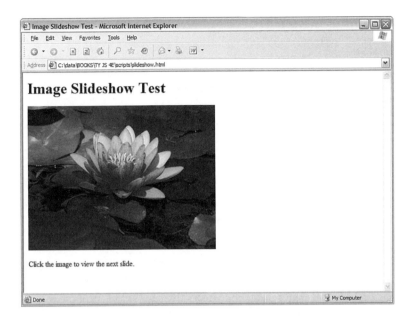

 Did you Know?

You might see a brief flicker when you load the page and the five images display before being hidden by the script. You can eliminate this by adding a `display:none` rule in CSS for the `slide` class, making all of the images invisible until the script displays the first one.

▼ **Try It Yourself**

Adding Animation to the Slideshow

Although the slideshow example works, the transitions between images are instantaneous—somewhat of a utilitarian effect. With a bit more code, you can use JavaScript and the CSS positioning properties to create an animated transition between the slides.

By the Way

See Hour 13, "Using the W3C DOM," for information about the CSS positioning properties used in this example.

The HTML File

The HTML for this example is similar to that of the basic slideshow, with two differences: First, the images are enclosed in a `<div>` element with the `id` attribute "slideshow". This element will be used to make the transition between slides work.

Second, a `<link>` tag in the header specifies a style sheet, slideshow2.css, because this example will require some CSS styles. The HTML document is shown in Listing 19.6.

LISTING 19.6   The HTML File for the Animated Slideshow

```
<html>
<head>
  <title>Animated Slideshow Test</title>
<script language="javascript" type="text/javascript"
  src="slideshow2.js">
</script>
<link rel="stylesheet" type="text/css" href="slideshow2.css">
</head>
<body>
<h1>Animated Slideshow Test</h1>
<div id="slideshow">
<img class="slide" src="pic1.jpg" width="400" height="300">
<img class="slide" src="pic2.jpg" width="400" height="300">
<img class="slide" src="pic3.jpg" width="400" height="300">
<img class="slide" src="pic4.jpg" width="400" height="300">
<img class="slide" src="pic5.jpg" width="400" height="300">
</div>
<p>Click the image to view the next slide.</p>
</body>
</html>
```

As before, if you load this document into a browser without the JavaScript or CSS files, it will display all five images on the page.

The CSS File

You'll need a bit of CSS to set things up for the slideshow. The style sheet will set the initial position of the images and set the positioning properties so that the animation will work. The CSS file for this example is shown in Listing 19.7. Save the file as slideshow2.css in the same folder as the HTML document you created previously.

LISTING 19.7   The CSS File for the Animated Slideshow

```
img.slide {
    position: absolute;
    left:0;
    top:0;
}
#slideshow {
    position: relative;
    overflow: hidden;
    width: 400;
    height: 300;
}
```

The #slideshow rule defines the styles for the <div> element that encloses the images. The position: relative rule enables positioning for the element and its children, while leaving it where it landed in the page by default. The overflow property hides the part of an image that lies outside the <div>, so the new image can "slide in" from the side. Finally, the width and height properties make the <div> as large as the images so that the slideshow is always one size.

The img.slide rule sets up the styles for the images themselves. The position property is set to absolute. In combination with the relative value on the <div>, this means that the image is positioned relative to its parent. It is set to left: 0 and top: 0, which positions each image at the upper-left corner of the <div>—to begin, all of the images will be on top of each other, so only one will be visible.

Instead of using the display property, the animated slideshow will use the z-index property (zIndex in JavaScript). This controls which of the overlapping images is "on top." To change slides, the script will set the new image to be on the top of the stack and position it off the right edge of the <div>, and then gradually slide both the old and new slides to the left until the new one is the only one visible.

The JavaScript File

Now that you have the HTML and CSS files, all that remains is the script. Listing 19.8 shows the JavaScript file for the animated slideshow.

LISTING 19.8   The JavaScript File for the Animated Slideshow

```
// Global variables
var numslides=0;
var currentslide=0,oldslide=4;
var x = 0;
var slides = new Array();
function MakeSlideShow() {
   // find all images with the class "slide"
   imgs=document.getElementsByTagName("img");
   for (i=0; i<imgs.length; i++) {
      if (imgs[i].className != "slide") continue;
      slides[numslides]=imgs[i];
      // stack images with first slide on top
      if (numslides==0) {
         imgs[i].style.zIndex=10;
      } else {
         imgs[i].style.zIndex=0;
      }
      imgs[i].onclick=NextSlide;
      numslides++;
   } // end for loop
} // end MakeSlideShow()
function NextSlide() {
   // Set current slide to be under the new top slide
   slides[currentslide].style.zIndex=9;
```

LISTING 19.8   Continued

```
    // Move older slide to the bottom of the stack
    slides[oldslide].style.zIndex=0;
    oldslide = currentslide;
    currentslide++;
    if (currentslide >= numslides) currentslide = 0;
    // start at the right edge
    slides[currentslide].style.left=400;
    x=400;
    // Move the new slide to the top
    slides[currentslide].style.zIndex=10;
    AnimateSlide();
}
function AnimateSlide() {
    // Lower moves slower, higher moves faster
    x = x - 25;
    slides[currentslide].style.left=x;
    // previous image moves off the left edge
    // (comment the next line for a different effect)
    slides[oldslide].style.left=x-400;
    // repeat until slide is at zero position
    if (x > 0) window.setTimeout("AnimateSlide();",10);
}
// create the slideshow when the page loads
window.onload=MakeSlideShow;
```

Here's how this script differs from the original slideshow script:

▶ An `oldslide` global variable has been added to keep track of the previous slide, so it can be moved out as the new slide moves in. Another global variable, `x`, will store the current horizontal position of the sliding image.

▶ Instead of using the `display` property, the `MakeSlideShow()` function sets the `zIndex` property to `10` for the first image and to zero for the others.

▶ The `NextSlide()` function works differently. First, it sets the current slide's `zIndex` property to 9, so it is the second one in the stack. (See the Did You Know? sidebar at the end of this section for the reason.) Next, it sets `zIndex` to zero for the old slide to move it to the bottom. It then assigns the `oldslide` value for next time, and increments the current slide as before.

▶ `NextSlide()` finishes by setting the new slide's `left` property to `400`, and the `x` variable to the same value. The slide will start off the right edge of the `<div>` and gradually become visible as it moves to the left. It then sets `zIndex` to 10 for the new slide to put it on top of the stack. Last, it calls the new `AnimateSlide()` function to make the transition.

▶ `AnimateSlide()` handles the animation. It starts by subtracting 25 from the value of `x` and setting the current slide's `left` property to that value. It also sets the position of the old slide 400 pixels to the left of the current one, so it slides out of the frame as the new one slides in.

▶ The last line in AnimateSlide() checks x, and if it has not yet reached zero, it uses setTimeout() to call itself after a brief (10 millisecond) delay. This function will be called repeatedly until the new slide reaches its final resting place on the left side.

Did you Know?

> The reason for setting the old slide's zIndex to 9 instead of 10 is to allow you to try a different transition effect. If you remove the slides[oldstyle].style.left assignment in AnimateSlide(), the old slide will stay in one place while the new slide moves over it.

Putting It All Together

To try out the animated slideshow, make sure you have all three files in the same folder: the HTML document, the style sheet (slideshow2.css), and the JavaScript file (slideshow2.js). Load the HTML document into a browser; then click on the image to advance the slideshow.

The AnimateSlide() function uses a lot of code, but on a reasonably fast machine, the transition will be very fast, taking about half a second. If you want to slow it down to see what's going on, change the 25 value in AnimateSlide() to a lower number—a value of 1 will make the transition extremely slow. Figure 19.5 shows the slideshow in action, halfway between the first slide and the second.

FIGURE 19.5
The animated slideshow in action.

Summary

In this hour, you learned some techniques for working with graphics in JavaScript. You learned how to use dynamic images to create rollovers, and how to use CSS for JavaScript-free rollovers. Finally, you created a script to turn any group of images on a page into an animated slideshow.

In the next hour, you'll look at how JavaScript works with plug-ins, particularly Flash, and learn how to add sounds to your scripts.

Q&A

Q. *Isn't it possible to make JavaScript rollovers unobtrusive?*

A. Yes, you could use a separate JavaScript file and do JavaScript rollovers "the right way." You would still have image links instead of text links, but aside from that it's arguably no worse than CSS rollovers. JavaScript rollovers can also go beyond what CSS can do—for example, the links could change in an animated way rather than simply changing graphics.

Q. *Can JavaScript work with any type of image?*

A. Yes, JavaScript's dynamic image features (and the W3C DOM features you used in the slideshow) will work fine with GIF, JPG, and PNG (Portable Network Graphics, the newest standard) images.

Q. *Why doesn't the slideshow example require preloading images for fast transitions?*

A. Because the images are all on the page in the HTML document, they are loaded with the page, although the JavaScript immediately hides them. Thus, they're available instantly when the slideshow switches them.

Q. *How do I speed up the transitions in the animated slideshow?*

A. There are two ways: Either increase the amount subtracted from x, or reduce the timeout in the setTimeout statement. Subtracting too much can make the transition jerky, and timeouts below 10 aren't handled well by browsers, so experiment with your changes to reach the best compromise.

Quiz Questions

Test your knowledge of JavaScript graphics by answering the following questions.

1. Which property of an `image` object stores the filename of the image?

   a. `href`

   b. `filename`

   c. `src`

2. Which of the following languages *cannot* be used to implement rollovers?

   a. HTML

   b. CSS

   c. JavaScript

3. If `image1` is the object for an image on the page, which of the following would you modify to change the image's horizontal position?

   a. `image1.left`

   b. `image1.style.left`

   c. `image1.style.xPosition`

Quiz Answers

1. c. The `src` property of the image stores its filename.

2. a. You can create rollovers using JavaScript or CSS, but it can't be done in plain HTML.

3. b. The `style.left` property controls the image's horizontal position.

Exercises

If you want to gain more experience working with graphics in JavaScript, try the following exercises:

▶ Change the animated slideshow example to move the slides downward instead of right to left to make the transition. You'll need to change the `style.top` property instead of `style.left`.

▶ Firefox and some other browsers support a CSS 3 property, `style.opacity`, which controls how opaque an element is, with a value of 100 being completely opaque and a value of 0 being completely transparent. Try changing the animated slideshow to fade the new slide in from 0 to 100 rather than slide it in from right to left.

HOUR 20

Working with Sound and Plug-Ins

What You'll Learn in This Hour:

- ▶ How browser plug-ins work
- ▶ How JavaScript works with plug-ins
- ▶ Scripting objects in plug-ins
- ▶ Integrating JavaScript and Flash
- ▶ Testing JavaScript's sound support
- ▶ Creating an application using sounds

Browser plug-ins enable the browser to work with sounds, printer-ready documents, and other formats instead of being limited to HTML. JavaScript can connect with some plug-ins to add interactive features. In this hour, you'll explore JavaScript's plug-in support and look specifically at playing sounds.

Introducing Plug-Ins

Plug-ins were introduced by Netscape in Navigator 3.0. Rather than adding support directly to the browser for media types such as formatted text, video, and audio, Netscape created a modular architecture that allows programmers to write their own browser add-ons for these features.

There are now hundreds of plug-ins available for Netscape, Firefox, and Internet Explorer. Here are a few of the most popular:

- ▶ Macromedia's Shockwave and Flash plug-ins support animation and video.
- ▶ Adobe's Acrobat plug-in supports precisely formatted, cross-platform text.

▶ Apple's QuickTime plug-in supports many audio and video formats.

▶ RealPlayer supports streaming audio and video.

Firefox and Internet Explorer use different plug-in formats and usually require different versions of a plug-in. Additionally, some plug-ins are available only for one platform, such as Windows or Macintosh.

The `<embed>` and `<object>` Tags

Browsers support two tags for plug-ins, `<embed>` and `<object>`. The following is an example of the `<embed>` tag that embeds a sound in a page:

```
<embed src="sound.wav" autostart="false" loop="false">
```

This example uses the `sound.wav` file. It sets two parameters: `autostart` controls whether the sound automatically plays when the page loads, and `loop` controls whether the sound repeats after it plays the first time. The parameters supported depend on the plug-in being used.

A more standard tag, `<object>`, is part of the HTML 4.0 specification. Here's the same sound file using `<object>`:

```
<object type="audio/x-wav" data="sound.wav" width="100" height="50">
  <param name="src" value="sound.wav">
  <param name="autostart" value="false">
</object>
```

Did you
Know?

Although `<object>` is a more standard way of embedding a file, most current browsers still support `<embed>`, which works better in some cases. Always try your pages that use plug-ins in different browsers to make sure they work.

Understanding MIME Types

Multipurpose Internet Mail Extensions types (MIME) is a standard for classifying different types of files and transmitting them over the Internet. The different types of files are known as *MIME types*.

You've already worked with a few MIME types: HTML (MIME type `text/html`), text (MIME type `text/plain`), and GIF images (MIME type `image/gif`). The `<script>` tag also uses a MIME type to indicate the language: `text/javascript`. Although web browsers don't normally support many more than these types, external applications and plug-ins can provide support for additional types.

When a web server sends a document to a browser, it includes that document's MIME type in the header. If the browser supports that MIME type, it displays the file. If not, you're asked what to do with the file (such as when you click on a .zip or .exe file to download it).

How JavaScript Works with Plug-Ins

Some plug-ins, such as the sound plug-ins you'll use later this hour, support scripting with JavaScript. Scripting plug-ins works just like scripting the DOM: You assign an id attribute to the <embed> or <object> tag, and then use document.getElementById() to find the object corresponding to the embedded item.

After you've found the object, what you can do with it depends on the file type and the plug-in. For example, most sound plug-ins support a Play() method. Here's an example that finds an embedded sound with the id attribute sound1 and plays the sound:

```
obj = document.getElementById("sound1");
obj.Play();
```

Because plug-in methods are not part of the standard DOM, you'll need to consult the plug-in's documentation to find out what methods are supported and what your script can do with the embedded object.

Plug-In Feature Sensing

Any time you work with plug-ins, it's important to remember that not all browsers will have the needed plug-in installed. Although both Firefox and Internet Explorer will attempt to notify users and let them know where to install the plug-in, expecting users to install software just to view your site is a bit optimistic.

Instead, you should use feature sensing to use the plug-in only when it is supported. For example, you could check for the Play() method like this:

```
if (obj.Play) {
  obj.Play();
} else alert("Can't Play.");
```

A more sophisticated method that handles errors as well as feature sensing is presented later in this hour.

> Feature sensing is the same technique you've used to make sure browsers support the W3C DOM. See Hour 15, "Unobtrusive Scripting," for information on feature sensing.

By the Way

JavaScript and Flash

Adobe (formerly Macromedia) Flash is the Web's most popular format for movies and interactive content that require a bit more graphical splendor than HTML and JavaScript can provide. Flash's programming language is similar to JavaScript, and JavaScript can work with Flash.

ActionScript

If you program scripts for a Flash movie, you use a language called ActionScript. You may find that ActionScript has a strong similarity to JavaScript, and for good reason—the version of ActionScript used in Flash 5.0 and later is based on the same ECMAScript standard that specifies the syntax for JavaScript.

Although the language is the same, Flash programming is quite different from writing JavaScript for the Web—you are scripting Flash objects rather than working with the DOM. However, you'll find that the basic syntax of the language is the same, which makes it easy for a JavaScript programmer to work with Flash when its capabilities are needed.

JavaScript and Flash Communication

JavaScript and Flash can communicate and work together. Adobe's Flash/JavaScript Integration Kit, available as a free download, enables JavaScript to call ActionScript functions within Flash objects, and also enables Flash scripts to call JavaScript functions within the page that contains them.

The Flash/JavaScript Integration Kit works best with Flash Player 6.0 or later, although it also includes basic support for earlier versions of Flash. If you are developing a Flash application and need it to communicate with JavaScript, you can download the kit from http://weblogs.macromedia.com/flashjavascript/.

If you're using an existing Flash object, the author might have already set it up to work with JavaScript, in which case it will have a list of methods available like other plug-in objects.

Embedding Flash with JavaScript

One other common use of JavaScript with Flash is to use JavaScript to generate the `<object>` or `<embed>` tag to embed a Flash object. Although you could use HTML directly, using JavaScript enables you to sidestep Internet Explorer's warning dialog that pops up whenever an embedded object is in use. JavaScript can also pass parameters, such as the user's screen size, to Flash by writing them into the `<embed>` or `<object>` tag.

Microsoft added the warning dialog for embedded objects in response to a patent dispute. See the Try It Yourself section later this hour for an example that uses JavaScript to embed objects in a page and avoid this warning.

Playing Sounds with JavaScript

Although the W3C DOM has made advanced effects and applications possible in JavaScript in a painless, cross-browser fashion, no standard has emerged to do the same for JavaScript's sound support. There are a few ways of making JavaScript play sounds, and none of them work consistently in all browsers all of the time. Nonetheless, with a bit of effort, you can play sounds in most browsers.

Because sound support in browsers is inconsistent, there's no guarantee your sounds will work for everyone. Be sure any sound you use in JavaScript applications is optional and that the script still works even on browsers that won't play the sounds.

Sound Formats

There are a wide variety of sound formats, usually identified by their file extensions. The following are some of the most common sound formats on the Web:

▶ .au (**Audio Unit**)—The earliest sound format supported by browsers, and still the most widely supported. Some browsers have built-in support for this format. In Firefox, the QuickTime plug-in supports .au files.

▶ .wav—The standard Windows sound format (usually played by Media Player on Windows machines).

▶ .mp3—A compressed format for larger files, such as music. MP3 plug-ins are not included with most browsers, but are often installed by users.

▶ .mid (**MIDI**)—Rather than audio, MIDI files store note information to re-create a song using a standard set of instruments. Most computers support MIDI music, although a browser plug-in might be required.

Any of these formats can be supported by most browsers, but unfortunately there is no format that is universally supported. If you're hoping as many visitors as possible will be able to hear your sounds, the best choice is .au if you're using standard audio plug-ins, or .mp3 if you're using Flash.

Sound-Playing Plug-Ins

Browsers almost always require a plug-in to play sounds. Fortunately, sound plug-ins are widely used and many of your site's visitors already have one or more of them installed. Here are the most common sound-playing plug-ins:

▶ **QuickTime**—Apple's sound and video player, installed by default on Macintosh systems. QuickTime plug-ins are also available for Internet Explorer for Windows and for Firefox on Windows and Macintosh.

▶ **Windows Media Player**—Microsoft's sound and video player, installed by default on Windows systems.

▶ **RealPlayer**—A popular third-party plug-in for playing music and video, available from http:// www.real.com.

▶ **Flash**—Although the Flash plug-in doesn't play standard embedded sounds, Flash animations and movies can play sounds, as you'll learn later in this section.

Embedding Sounds

The following is a simple example of an `<embed>` tag to embed a sound in a page:

```
<embed id="note_c1" src="c1.au"  width="0" height="0"
  autostart="false" enablejavascript="true"/>
```

This example works with the most common sound plug-ins. It specifies a source filename for the sound file (`c1.au`) and `autostart="false"` to prevent the sound from playing when the page loads. The `enablejavascript` parameter is required by some plug-ins to allow scripting.

The `width` and `height` parameters set the size of the embedded player. If they are not zero, the player will be visible with Play, Pause, and Stop buttons. Setting them to zero hides the player, useful when you intend to control it strictly with JavaScript. (A `hidden` parameter is supposed to hide the player, but this causes sounds not to play in some browsers.)

Controlling Sounds with JavaScript

After you've embedded a sound—assuming a browser plug-in supports it—you can use the following methods of the sound object to control the sound:

▶ `Play()` or `DoPlay()`—Starts playing the sound, and stops when the sound is finished. `DoPlay()` is supported by RealPlayer, and `Play()` is supported by most other sound plug-ins.

► Stop()—Stops the currently playing sound.

► Rewind()—Restarts the current sound at the beginning.

Depending on the audio plug-in in use, the methods supported might be different. Always use try and catch when attempting to control sounds to avoid errors.

Watch Out!

Detecting Sound Support

Because you can't count on sounds being supported by all browsers, it's a good practice to use try and catch to test the statements and display a message (or take another appropriate action) if sounds are not supported:

```
try {
  sound.DoPlay();
} catch (e) {
  try {
    sound.Play();
  } catch (e) {
    alert("No sound support.");
  }
}
```

This code first tries RealPlayer's DoPlay() method. If that doesn't work, it tries the Play() method. If neither approach works, it displays an error message.

The try and catch keywords are used to test a risky statement, find out whether it works, and suppress the browser's usual error messages. See Hour 16, "Debugging JavaScript Applications" for more information.

By the Way

Using Flash

If you are relying on sounds for an application, you might want to consider using Flash. You can create a simple Flash object that loads sound files and allows JavaScript to play them. This gives you scriptable sounds using one consistent plug-in that works on most platforms.

Scott Schiller's SoundManager provides an easy way to use Flash sounds from JavaScript. SoundManager uses a Flash object to play MP3-formatted sounds you specify in an XML file. After you've created the XML file and included SoundManager using a <script> tag, you can use its methods to control the sounds. More information and the download for SoundManager are available at http://www.schillmania.com/projects/soundmanager/.

Testing Sounds in JavaScript

You can now create a simple example that uses JavaScript to play a sound. Listing 20.1 shows an HTML document with an embedded script to play a sound when you click a button.

LISTING 20.1   **A Simple Example of Playing Sounds Using JavaScript**

```
<html>
<head>
<title>Sound Test</title>
<script language="JavaScript" type="text/javascript">
function PlaySound() {
  var sound = document.getElementById("note_c1");
  try {
    // RealPlayer
    sound.DoPlay();
  } catch (e) {
    try {
      // Windows Media / Quicktime
      sound.Play();
    } catch (e) {
      alert("No sound support.");
    }
  }
}
</script>
</head>
<body>
<h1>Sound Test</h1>
<embed id="note_c1" src="c1.au"  width="0" height="0"
  autostart="false" enablejavascript="true"/>
<input type="button" value="Play the Sound"
  onClick="PlaySound()">
</body>
</html>
```

To try the example, you'll need a sound file: the c1.au file is available at this book's website, or you can substitute the .au format sound of your choice. Load the document into a browser and click the button to play the sound.

If you don't hear a sound, or if the "No sound support" message is displayed, try looking at the JavaScript Console in Firefox or clicking the error icon in the lower-left corner of the window in Internet Explorer. You might need to install a plug-in to get it to work.

Internet Explorer might display an alert message when you load the page, as shown in Figure 20.1. Due to a patent dispute, Microsoft made their browser require you to click on something in order for embedded objects to work. Although this is only a minor annoyance in this example, it's possible to eliminate it by using JavaScript to write the <embed> tag. The Try It Yourself section of this hour includes an example of this technique.

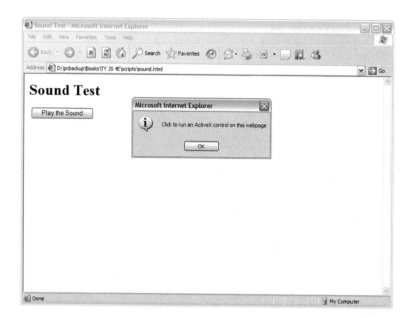

FIGURE 20.1
Internet Explorer warns you before enabling an embedded object.

Try It Yourself

Playing Music with the Mouse

As an example of scripting multiple embedded objects, you can create a simple demonstration that displays a piano keyboard and plays piano notes when you click on the keys. This example requires an .au sound file for each key, which you can download from this book's website.

The HTML Document

The HTML file for this document includes a series of <div> tags that will act as the black and white piano keys. A <link> tag is used to include a CSS file to style the keys, and a <script> tag includes a script you'll create later in this section. The complete HTML document is shown in Listing 20.2.

LISTING 20.2 The HTML Document for the Piano Example

```
<html>
<head>
<title>JavaScript Piano</title>
<link rel="stylesheet" type="text/css" href="piano.css">
</head>
<body>
<h1>JavaScript Piano</h1>
<div class="white" id="c1"> </div>
<div class="black" id="cs1"> </div>
<div class="white" id="d1"> </div>
```

LISTING 20.2   Continued

```
<div class="black" id="ds1"> </div>
<div class="white" id="e1"> </div>
<div class="white" id="f1"> </div>
<div class="black" id="fs1"> </div>
<div class="white" id="g1"> </div>
<div class="black" id="gs1"> </div>
<div class="white" id="a1"> </div>
<div class="black" id="as1"> </div>
<div class="white" id="b1"> </div>
<div class="white" id="c2"> </div>
<p style="clear:left">
Click the piano keys above to play sounds.
</p>
<script language="javascript" type="text/javascript"
  src="piano.js"> </script>
</body>
</html>
```

Type this document or download it from this book's website and store it in the same folder as the sound files. You'll also need the CSS and JavaScript files described in the next sections.

The CSS Style Sheet

Using CSS, you can make the browser display the series of <div> tags in the HTML document as something resembling piano keys. Listing 20.3 shows the CSS file for this example.

LISTING 20.3   The CSS File for the Piano Example

```
.white {
  float: left;
  background-color: white;
  height: 300px;
  width: 30px;
  border: 2px solid black;
}
.black {
  float: left;
  background-color: black;
  height: 225px;
  width: 25px;
}
```

This file defines two styles for the two classes used in the HTML document, white and black. The float attribute makes the keys appear as a horizontal set of boxes. The size of the keys is set using width and height attributes, and background-color sets the colors to differentiate the keys.

Playing the Sounds

The `PlaySound()` function will be called when a key is clicked to play a sound. The first lines of this function detect which key was clicked and use the `id` attribute of the key `<div>` element to construct the `id` attribute of the corresponding sound:

```
function PlaySound(e) {
  if (!e) var e = window.event;
  // which key was clicked?
  thiskey = (e.target) ? e.target: e.srcElement;
  var sound = document.getElementById("note_" + thiskey.id);
```

The remainder of `PlaySound()` will attempt to play the piano note using the `try` and `catch` routine described earlier in this hour.

Embedding the Sounds

This example will use JavaScript `document.write()` statements to write out an `<embed>` tag for each note. Although this is a roundabout way of doing things, it conveniently avoids Internet Explorer's warning dialog about embedded objects, which would otherwise pop up 13 times—once for each embedded sound. Here are the lines that write an `<embed>` tag:

```
    document.write('<embed id="' + 'note_' + divs[i].id + '"');
    document.write(' src="' + divs[i].id + '.au" width="0" height="0"');
    document.write(' autostart="false" enablejavascript="true">');
```

The `src` attribute of the `<embed>` tag is set using the `id` attribute of each `<div>` element to embed the corresponding sound file for each key.

Putting It All Together

To get the piano working, you can combine the techniques discussed previously with a bit more JavaScript. Listing 20.4 shows the JavaScript file for this example.

LISTING 20.4   The JavaScript File for the Piano Example

```
function Setup() {
  if (!document.getElementById) return;
  // Set up event handlers and embed the sounds
  divs = document.getElementsByTagName("div");
  for (i=0; i<divs.length; i++) {
    // embed the appropriate sound using document.write
    document.write('<embed id="' + 'note_' + divs[i].id + '"');
    document.write(' src="' + divs[i].id + '.au" width="0" height="0"');
    document.write(' autostart="false" enablejavascript="true">');
    // set up the event handler
    divs[i].onclick = PlaySound;
  }
}
```

LISTING 20.4   Continued

```
function PlaySound(e) {
  if (!e) var e = window.event;
  // which key was clicked?
  thiskey = (e.target) ? e.target: e.srcElement;
  var sound = document.getElementById("note_" + thiskey.id);
  try {
    // RealPlayer
    sound.DoPlay();
  } catch (e) {
    try {
      // Windows Media / Quicktime
      sound.Play();
    } catch (e) {
      alert("No sound support.");
    }
  }
}
// Run the setup routine when this script executes
Setup();
```

The Setup() function executes when the script loads. Because the <script> tag appears after the <div> elements in the HTML file, it can set event handlers for each <div> and write out the <embed> tags. Setup() uses document.getElementsByTagName and a for loop to do this for each of the keys.

To test the piano, make sure you have everything in one folder: The HTML document, the CSS file (piano.css), the JavaScript file (piano.js), and all 13 sound files. The complete example is shown in Figure 20.2.

FIGURE 20.2
The JavaScript piano example in action.

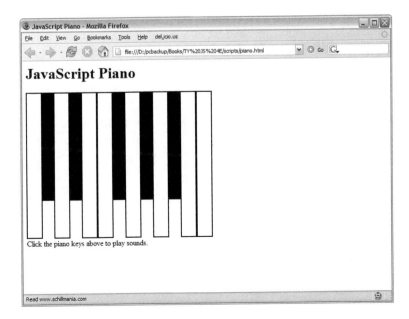

Summary

In this hour, you learned about browser plug-ins and how they work with JavaScript. You also learned about JavaScript's support for sound (or the lack there-of) and how you can use JavaScript to detect and work with common sound-playing plug-ins. Finally, you created a piano keyboard with audio using JavaScript.

Congratulations—you've reached the end of Part V of this book. In part VI, you'll apply your JavaScript knowledge to create some complex applications. This begins in Hour 21, "Building JavaScript Drop-Down Menus."

Q&A

Q. Is there a way to list all of the plug-ins installed in the browser?

A. Yes. Type about:plugins to display a list of plug-ins installed in Netscape or Firefox. These browsers also support a proprietary navigator.plugins object, an array that contains information about each installed plug-in, which you can access with JavaScript. Unfortunately, this is not a standard part of the DOM and is not supported by other browsers.

Q. Can I add sounds to a site's navigation bar or user interface?

A. Yes, this can be done using the techniques in this hour and onMouseOver or onClick event handlers. However, given the inconsistency of sound support in browsers, this is a lot of trouble for a feature that will probably annoy your visitors anyway.

Q. Can the browser play more than one sound at the same time?

A. This ultimately depends on the audio plug-in, but none of the current ones support playing more than one sound at a time.

Quiz Questions

Test your knowledge of JavaScript's sound and plug-in features by answering the following questions.

1. Which HTML tag is often used to include a plug-in object within a web page?

    a. <sound>

    b. <embed>

    c. <plugin>

2. Which of the following is not a sound-playing plug-in?

    a. RealPlayer

    b. QuickTime

    c. Acrobat

3. Which is the correct statement to play a sound?

    a. `sound.Go();`

    b. `sound.Play();`

    c. `sound.Submit();`

Quiz Answers

1. b. The <embed> tag embeds a plug-in object in a page.

2. c. The Acrobat plug-in displays PDF files.

3. b. The `Play()` method plays a sound.

Exercises

If you want to gain more experience working with sounds in JavaScript, try the following exercises:

▶ Expand the piano keyboard in Listing 20.2 to include more notes. (Additional sound files are available from this book's website.) You should only need to change the HTML file.

▶ Try adding one or more sounds to the animated slideshow in the previous hour (refer to Listing 19.8). You can adapt the `PlaySound()` function from this hour to play a specific sound as the slideshow advances.

PART VI:

Creating Complex Scripts

HOUR 21

Building JavaScript Drop-Down Menus

What You'll Learn in This Hour:

▶ How to create drop-down menus using JavaScript
▶ Defining menus using bullet lists
▶ Using CSS to lay out menus
▶ Using JavaScript to display and hide submenus
▶ Using CSS to improve the menu's appearance

Welcome to Part VI! Now that you've spent some time learning both beginning and advanced JavaScript techniques, it's time to put them into action with some more complicated examples. In this hour, you'll use HTML, CSS, and JavaScript to create a drop-down menu navigation system.

Designing Drop-Down Menus

One of the most common uses for JavaScript and the DOM is to create drop-down menus, similar to those used in Windows and MacOS, as a navigation system for a page. Figure 21.1 shows a drop-down menu in action.

Why use drop-down menus? Ideally, you should use them when a website or web application has too many options to conveniently fit on the page. Adding a drop-down menu to a site with only a few pages will just make it more confusing to visitors.

Another potential problem with drop-down menus is that they traditionally require some messy browser-specific code and some awkward HTML markup. Thanks to the now standard W3C DOM, you can create menus using simple markup and a script that works in all modern browsers.

FIGURE 21.1
A drop-down
menu.

Creating the HTML Markup

'There will always be browsers that don't support drop-down menus correctly—in particular, mobile phone browsers are unlikely to work with this script. You can avoid problems with compatibility by making an unobtrusive script using standard markup. The HTML document for this example, shown in Listing 21.1, uses bullet lists (<ul> and <li> tags) to organize the links into menus.

LISTING 21.1   The HTML for the Drop-Down Menu

```
<html>
<head>
<title>A DOM drop-down menu</title>
<link rel="stylesheet" type="text/css" href="dropdown.css">
<script language="javascript" type="text/javascript"
    src="dropdown.js">
</script>
</head>
<body>
<h1>Menu Test</h1>
<ul id="menu">
<li class="menu"><a href="#">Home</a></li>
<li class="menu"><a href="#">Products</a>
    <ul>
      <li><a href="#">Sub-item 1</a></li>
      <li><a href="#">Sub-item 2</a></li>
      <li><a href="#">Item 3</a></li>
    </ul>
</li>
<li class="menu"><a href="#">Support</a>
    <ul>
      <li><a href="#">Sub-item 1</a></li>
      <li><a href="#">Sub-item 2</a></li>
    </ul>
</li>
<li class="menu"><a href="#">Employment</a>
    <ul>
      <li><a href="#">Sub-item 1</a></li>
      <li><a href="#">Sub-item 2</a></li>
    </ul>
</li>
<li class="menu"><a href="#">Contact Us</a>
    <ul>
      <li><a href="#">Sub-item 1</a></li>
      <li><a href="#">Sub-item 2</a></li>
    </ul>
</li>
</ul>
</body>
</html>
```

The top-level links (Home, Products, Support, Employment, and Contact Us) are formatted as a bullet list. Most of the links have subitems, listed in a nested bullet list. These subitems will be displayed as drop-down menus using CSS formatting and JavaScript.

Although you have not yet created the CSS or JavaScript for this example, you can try the HTML document in a browser—it will be displayed as a simple bullet list, as shown in Figure 21.2.

Notice the class and id attributes in the HTML—these will be used by the CSS and JavaScript code to format the menu and add behavior. The main <ul> tag that encloses the top-level items has an id attribute of menu, and each top-level item's <li> tag has the class attribute menu.

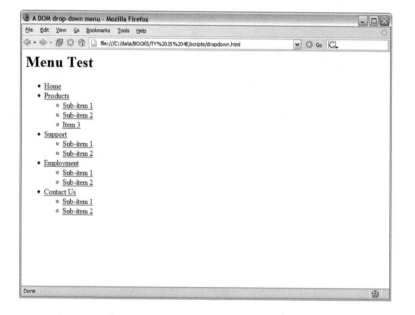

The links in this example all link to a nonexistent URL, #. To use the menu on your site, you'll need to replace them with actual links.

Watch Out!

Laying Out the Menu with CSS

As you can see in Figure 21.2, the list of links doesn't look much like a drop-down menu yet. You can now use CSS to format the links to appear in the right format.

The first step is to make the main list display in a horizontal format. This can be done with two CSS rules:

```
#menu li {
   float: left;
   list-style-type: none;
}
```

The selector, `#menu li`, looks for any list item directly under the `#menu` list. The `float: left` rule causes the items to display left to right instead of vertically, and `list-style-type: none` prevents a bullet from being displayed. Next, a couple of rules for the subitems:

```
#menu li ul li {
   float: none;
   list-style-type: none;
}
```

The selector here, `#menu li ul li`, looks for `<li>` items nested under the main `<li>` items. Once again, `list-style-type: none` is used to eliminate bullets. The `float: none` rule is necessary because we want the subitems to be listed vertically rather than inheriting the floating behavior of the main list.

Figure 21.3 shows what the list looks like with the styles so far. As you can see, the menu is beginning to take shape: The main links are displayed in a horizontal row, and each subitem list appears vertically underneath its corresponding item. The spacing and alignment needs work, but it's a start.

FIGURE 21.3
The list of links with some basic styles.

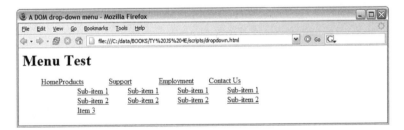

As you develop a complex layout using CSS, be sure to test in multiple browsers. Floats are one area where Internet Explorer shows its quirks, and you may need to adjust a few rules to make it work cross-browser.

To make the menu look more like a menu, you just need some padding, width, and other settings. Listing 21.2 shows the complete style sheet for the drop-down menu.

LISTING 21.2 The CSS File for the Drop-Down Menu

```
/* The whole menu */
#menu {
    position: absolute;
}
/* Each menu name */
#menu li {

    float: left;
    list-style-type: none;
    padding-right: 20px;
    width: 100px;
    background-color: silver;
}
/* The entire submenu */
#menu li ul {
    background-color: silver;
    margin: 0px;
    padding: 0px;
}
/* Each submenu item */
#menu li ul li {
    padding: 0px;
    margin: 0px;
    float: none;
    list-style-type: none;
    width: 80px;
}
```

This style sheet uses padding and width values to make sure the submenus line up with their headings. Some background-color attributes are applied to make the menu appear more solid.

The position: absolute rule is used so the menus can overlap the content of the page when they drop down. There's no content in the example, but on a real site you don't want to leave room for the menus—if you have that kind of room, you might as well just display the links all of the time.

Using position:absolute has a downside—because the menu isn't positioned in the normal flow of the page, the main menu can overlap part of your page unless you avoid it by positioning the other content around it. The ideal situation would be for the main menu to use relative positioning while the submenus use absolute positioning—unfortunately, this does not work consistently in Internet Explorer.

The styled menu is shown in Figure 21.4. As you can see, the entire menus are shown at this time—the submenus will be hidden by the script. This ensures that the menu will still be accessible to browsers that support CSS but not JavaScript.

FIGURE 21.4
The menu with
full CSS styling.

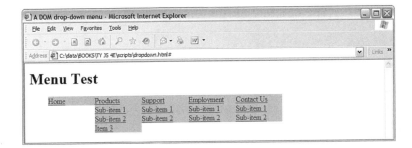

By the
Way

> When the script is added, the full menus will display for an instant before the
> script hides them. If you find this annoying, you can add a display:none rule to
> the CSS for the submenu <ul>. This eliminates the flicker, but makes the menu
> less useful to browsers without JavaScript support.

Scripting Drop-Down Menu Behavior

You now have a list of links that looks like a drop-down menu. All you need now is
a script to make it act like one. Your script will set up the menu when the page
loads, and respond to event handlers to show and hide the submenus.

Setting Up the Menu

The SetupMenu() function will run when the page loads, and then configure the
drop-down menu. This mainly consists of hiding the submenus and configuring
some event handlers. The function will use a loop to look at all of the <li> elements
in the page, and if they have a class attribute of menu, they're considered part of
the menu. The following lines set up the event handlers for the link and hide the
submenu:

```
thelink=findChild(items[i],"A");
thelink.onmouseover=ShowMenu;
thelink.onmouseout=StartTimer;
//is there a submenu?
if (ul=findChild(items[i],"UL")) {
    ul.style.display="none";
```

The findChild() function is used twice here. This function will also be defined in
your script, and will return the first child item of a particular type it finds for an
object. In the preceding lines, it is used to find the link (<a> tag) under the list item,
and to find the nested list of subitems (<ul> tag). The style.display property is
used to hide each submenu.

Showing a Submenu

The ShowMenu() function will be called by the onmouseover event handler when you move over a link. Here's an excerpt from this function that handles showing the submenu:

```
// find the submenu, if any
ul = findChild(thislink,"UL");
if (!ul) return;
ul.style.display="block";
```

Once again, findChild() is used to find the <ul> element under the current item, and the display property is set to block to display the menu.

Hiding Submenus

The logic for showing the submenus is simple—whenever the mouse pointer is over a menu heading, the corresponding submenu is displayed. Hiding a submenu is a bit more complicated—the menu needs to stay open while you select an item, but get out of the way quickly when you're not using it. The HideMenu() function will accomplish this:

```
function HideMenu(thelink) {
    // find the submenu, if any
    ul = findChild(thelink,"UL");
    if (!ul) return;
    ul.style.display="none";
}
```

One time you definitely want a menu to be hidden is when the user opens another menu, so the ShowMenu() function will call HideMenu() to hide the previous menu. You also want the menu to disappear if you move out of it, but a simple onmouse-out event handler won't work because the user could have moved off the menu heading and into the submenu. Instead, the onmouseout event calls the StartTimer() function:

```
function StartTimer() {
    t = window.setTimeout("HideMenu(current)",200);
}
```

This function sets a timeout to hide the menu in 200 milliseconds. If the user moves over any of the submenu items during the delay, the timer is reset with the ResetTimer() function:

```
function ResetTimer() {
    if (t) window.clearTimeout(t);
}
```

This function cancels the timeout using the `clearTimeout()` method, keeping the menu on the screen until the onmouseout event starts the timer again. Finally, some additional lines in the SetupMenu() function will set up event handlers to call StartTimer() and ResetTimer() for each subitem:

```
for (j=0; j<ul.childNodes.length; j++) {
    ul.childNodes[j].onmouseover=ResetTimer;
    ul.childNodes[j].onmouseout=StartTimer;
}
```

Completing the Script

You can now combine all of the functions discussed above to create working drop-down menus. The complete drop-down menu script is shown in Listing 21.3.

LISTING 21.3   The Complete JavaScript File for the Drop-Down Menus

```
// global variables for timeout and for current menu
var t=false,current;
function SetupMenu() {
    if (!document.getElementsByTagName) return;
    items=document.getElementsByTagName("li");
    for (i=0; i<items.length; i++) {
        if (items[i].className != "menu") continue;
        //set up event handlers
        thelink=findChild(items[i],"A");
        thelink.onmouseover=ShowMenu;
        thelink.onmouseout=StartTimer;
        //is there a submenu?
        if (ul=findChild(items[i],"UL")) {
            ul.style.display="none";
            for (j=0; j<ul.childNodes.length; j++) {
                ul.childNodes[j].onmouseover=ResetTimer;
                ul.childNodes[j].onmouseout=StartTimer;
            }
        }
    }
}
// find the first child object of a particular type
function findChild(obj,tag) {
    cn = obj.childNodes;
    for (k=0; k<cn.length; k++) {
        if (cn[k].nodeName==tag) return cn[k];
    }
    return false;
}
function ShowMenu(e) {
    if (!e) var e = window.event;
    // which link was the mouse over?
    thislink = (e.target) ? e.target: e.srcElement;
    ResetTimer();
    // hide the previous menu, if any
    if (current) HideMenu(current);
    // we want the LI, not the link
```

LISTING 21.3   The Complete JavaScript File for the Drop-Down Menus

```
/   thislink = thislink.parentNode;
    current=thislink;
    // find the submenu, if any
    ul = findChild(thislink,"UL");
    if (!ul) return;
    ul.style.display="block";
}
function HideMenu(thelink) {
    // find the submenu, if any
    ul = findChild(thelink,"UL");
    if (!ul) return;
    ul.style.display="none";
}
function ResetTimer() {
    if (t) window.clearTimeout(t);
}
function StartTimer() {
    t = window.setTimeout("HideMenu(current)",200);
}
// Set up the menu when the page loads
window.onload=SetupMenu;
```

Here's a summary of how the script works from top to bottom:

▶ The first line defines two global variables: t stores a reference to the timeout so that it can be canceled, and current is the object for the currently open menu.

▶ The SetupMenu() function sets up event handlers to call ShowMenu(), StartTimer(), and ResetTimer(), and hides the submenus.

▶ The findChild() function is used by several of the other functions to find a child object.

▶ The ShowMenu() function shows a menu.

▶ The HideMenu() function hides a menu when the timeout expires.

▶ The StartTimer() and ResetTimer() functions manage the timeout discussed earlier.

▶ The final line of the script sets the window's onload event handler to the SetupMenu() function to set up the menu when the page loads.

To try the menu, first be sure you have all three files in the same folder: the HTML document, the CSS file (dropdown.css), and the JavaScript file (dropdown.js). You can then load the HTML document into a browser. Figure 21.5 shows the drop-down menu in action.

FIGURE 21.5
The drop-down
menu in action.

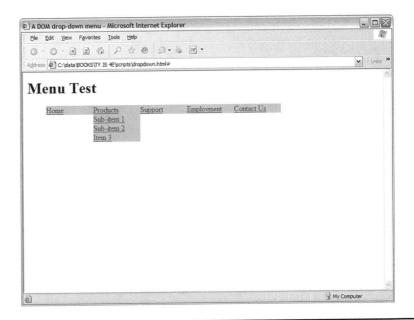

▼   **Try It Yourself**

Enhancing the Menu with CSS

Although the menu works as it is, the CSS could use some improvement. The menus
are not well delineated, and there are no rollover effects to let you know you're moving over menu items. Also, to make a menu appear, you have to move the mouse
over the *text* of the menu name—for this menu to work like users expect, the entire
block that contains the menu name should be active.

An improved CSS style sheet can solve these problems. You might also want to add
more CSS rules to fine-tune its formatting. Here are some suggestions:

▶ Change the fonts and colors to match your site.

▶ Add an a:hover selector to make the subitems change color as you move over
   them.

▶ Use border attributes to add borders around menus or subitems.

▶ Use margin attributes to add space between menu items.

Listing 21.4 shows a modified style sheet that makes the menu work as it should,
and implements several of these ideas to create a menu with a different style.

LISTING 21.4 A Style Sheet for a Different Style of Menu

```
/* The whole menu */
#menu {
    position: absolute;
    font-family: sans-serif;
    font-size: 100%;
}
/* Each menu name */
#menu li {
    float: left;
    list-style-type: none;
    width: 102px;
    background-color: silver;
    border: 1px solid black;
    text-indent: 0px;
    margin-left: 3px;
}
/* each main menu link */
#menu li a {
    color: black;
    text-decoration: none;
    width: 100%;
    display: block;
}
#menu li a:hover {
    color: white;
}
/* The entire submenu */
#menu li ul {
    background-color: silver;
    margin: 0px;
    padding: 0px;
}
/* Each submenu item */
#menu li ul li {
    padding: 0px;
    margin: 0px;
    float: none;
    list-style-type: none;
    width: 100px;
    text-indent: 0px;
    border: none;
}
#menu li ul li a{
    color: black;
    text-decoration: none;
}
#menu li ul li a:hover{
    color: black;
    background-color: aqua;
}
```

This style sheet has the following features:

▶ A sans-serif font is used for a more modern appearance.

▶ Borders and margins are used to make the menu names appear as separate boxes.

▶ An a:hover selector is used to make the menu names change color when the mouse is over them.

▶ The width: 100% and display: block rules for the menu names make the entire box active, not just the text.

▶ Another a:hover selector makes the submenu items change color when the mouse is over them.

▶ The width: 100% rule for submenu items makes the entire width of the submenu active, not just the text.

To use this style sheet, save it as dropdown2.css in the same folder as the HTML document, and change the <link> tag in the HTML document to refer to the new file. Figure 21.6 shows the drop-down menu with this style sheet.

FIGURE 21.6
The drop-down menu with an alternative style sheet.

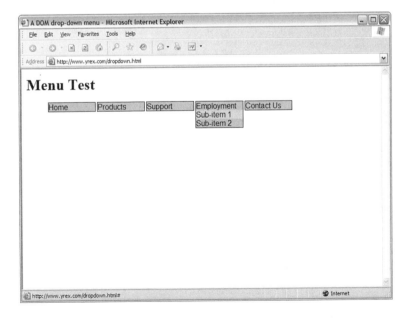

By the Way ▲

See Hour 12, "Working with Style Sheets," for more information about using CSS styles to format HTML elements.

Summary

In this hour, you've developed a complete application that uses HTML, CSS, and JavaScript to create drop-down menus for navigating a site. You learned how to create a simple HTML document using nested lists, and how to use CSS to format it as a horizontal menu with vertical drop-downs. You used JavaScript to make the drop-down menu work. Finally, you created an alternative style sheet to give the menu a different look.

In the next hour, you'll create another complex JavaScript application—a card game that uses JavaScript, images, and CSS to interact with the user.

Q&A

Q. *Can I make a vertical pop-out menu using the same script in Listing 21.3?*

A. Yes. You'll need a different style sheet that doesn't use `float` for the menu headings, but uses `float:left` for the submenu. The same script and HTML document can be used with a vertical menu.

Q. *Can I add some space before each menu heading?*

A. Yes, but be aware that Internet Explorer has some bugs involving margins and padding when `float` is in use. Be sure to test in multiple browsers.

Q. *Which browsers support the drop-down menus?*

A. The drop-down menus you created in this hour should work in Internet Explorer 5.0 and later, Netscape 6.0 and later, and all versions of Firefox. Most important, because it uses the standard W3C DOM, it should work in all standards-compliant browsers—but watch out for formatting quirks in different browsers when you change the styles.

Quiz Questions

Test your knowledge of the techniques used in this hour by answering the following questions.

1. Which of the following CSS rules makes the menu horizontal instead of vertical?

    a. `float: left`

    b. `position: absolute`

    c. `orientation: horizontal`

2. Which of the following CSS selectors refers to an `<li>` element directly under the `<ul>` element with the id value menu?

   a. `#menu ul li`

   b. `#menu li`

   c. `ul #menu li`

3. Which of the following is the correct command to cancel a timeout set with the command `t=window.timeout("HideMenu(current)",500);`?

   a. `t = window.clearTimeout();`

   b. `window.clearTimeout(t);`

   c. `window.setTimeout("HideMenu(current)",0);`

Quiz Answers

1. a. The drop-down menu uses `float:left` to make a horizontal menu.

2. b. The correct selector is `#menu li`.

3. b. The correct command is `window.clearTimeout(t)`.

Exercises

If you want to gain more experience working with JavaScript drop-down menus, try the following exercises:

▶ Change the drop-down menu to contain the appropriate links for your site, or for an imaginary site. (You only need to change the HTML file, but each menu item needs the `class` value of `menu`.)

▶ Modify the CSS file for the drop-down menu to use colors, borders, or other attributes of your choice.

HOUR 22

Creating a JavaScript Game

What You'll Learn in This Hour:

▶ How to design a JavaScript Game
▶ Creating game graphics
▶ Laying out the game board in HTML
▶ Using CSS to style the board
▶ Creating gameplay scripts
▶ Finalizing and testing the game

In this hour, you'll look at another complex application of JavaScript: a Poker Solitaire game that uses the W3C DOM, graphics, and some JavaScript logic to interact with the user quickly and responsively.

About the Game

Although it's possible to create just about any game with JavaScript, a card game is a simple choice because the graphics are easy to create and the gameplay is relatively simple. In this hour, you'll create a Poker Solitaire game using HTML, JavaScript, and a bit of CSS.

How to Play

Poker Solitaire is played on a five by five board. The deck of cards is shuffled, and you draw one card from the deck at a time and place it anywhere on the board. Your goal is to make each column, row, and diagonal row form the best possible poker hand. For example, in Figure 22.1, several cards have been placed on the board and the score for the completed column and row is shown.

FIGURE 22.1
Playing Poker
Solitaire.

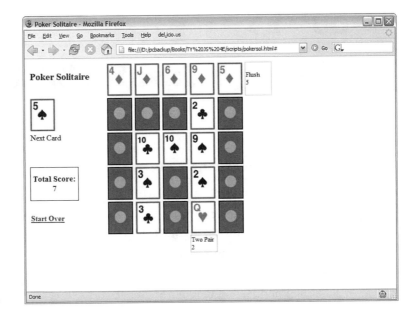

Scoring

Because there are no other players, the game will be scored. The script will calculate the score for each column, row, and diagonal on the board, and combine them for a total score. Points are awarded for poker hands, with more difficult (and less likely) combinations scoring higher:

- ▶ **Pair**—1 point (Two cards of the same number and different suits)

- ▶ **Two pair**—2 points (Two pairs)

- ▶ **Three of a kind**—3 points (Three cards of the same number)

- ▶ **Straight**—4 points (Five cards in numeric sequence)

- ▶ **Full house**—8 points (One pair plus three of a kind)

- ▶ **Four of a kind**—25 points (All four cards of the same number)

- ▶ **Flush**—5 points (Five cards of the same suit)

- ▶ **Straight flush**—50 points (Five cards of the same suit, in sequence)

- ▶ **Royal flush**—250 points (10, Jack, Queen, King, and Ace of the same suit)

In the JavaScript version of the game, the score for each row or column will be displayed as you complete it, and the total score will be updated in real time as you place each card on the board.

Creating Graphics

This game will require some graphics—you'll need 52 images, one for each card in a standard deck. One more image, blank.gif, will be used to mark the spaces on the board that don't yet contain cards. You can download all of the graphics for the game from this book's website.

All of the graphics will be the same size, including the blank space image. The board will consist entirely of blanks at the start of a game, and images will be switched to the appropriate card when the user clicks to place a card. The images I used in the example are all 53 × 68 pixels.

When you're working with a large number of graphics, filenames become important. It will make coding easier if you decide in advance on a naming scheme for the images. In this case, the filenames will include a number for the card's rank (1–13, with 1 representing Ace, and 11, 12, and 13 representing Jack, Queen, and King) and a letter for the suit. For example, the Seven of Hearts image would be 7h.gif, and the Queen of Spades would be 12s.gif.

Creating the HTML Document

The HTML document for the game is straightforward. In keeping with the unobtrusive scripting strategies you've learned in previous hours, it contains no JavaScript—just a <script> tag that imports a script that will handle the game. Similarly, a separate CSS file will be used for styles. Listing 22.1 shows the HTML document.

LISTING 22.1   The HTML Document for the Poker Solitaire Game

```html
<html>
<head>
<title>Poker Solitaire</title>
<script language="JavaScript" type="text/javascript"
   src="pokersol.js">
</script>
<link rel="stylesheet" type="text/css" href="pokersol.css">
</head>
<body>
<table>
<tr>
  <td colspan="2"><h1>Poker Solitaire</h1></td>
  <td> <img id="card1" src="blank.gif" height="68" width="53"> </td>
  <td> <img id="card2" src="blank.gif" height="68" width="53"> </td>
  <td> <img id="card3" src="blank.gif" height="68" width="53"> </td>
  <td> <img id="card4" src="blank.gif" height="68" width="53"> </td>
  <td> <img id="card5" src="blank.gif" height="68" width="53"></td>
  <td class="score" id="row0">  </td>
</tr>
<tr>
  <td> <img id="dcard" border="0"
```

LISTING 22.1   Continued

```
         src="blank.gif" height="68" width="53"></td>
   <td> </td>
   <td> <img id="card6" src="blank.gif" height="68" width="53"></td>
   <td> <img id="card7" src="blank.gif" height="68" width="53"></td>
   <td> <img id="card8" src="blank.gif" height="68" width="53"></td>
   <td> <img id="card9" src="blank.gif" height="68" width="53"></td>
   <td> <img id="card10" src="blank.gif" height="68" width="53"></td>
   <td class="score" id="row1"> </td>
 </tr>
 <tr>
   <td valign="top" id="status"> Next Card</td>
   <td> </td>
   <td> <img id="card11" src="blank.gif" height="68" width="53"></td>
   <td> <img id="card12" src="blank.gif" height="68" width="53"></td>
   <td> <img id="card13" src="blank.gif" height="68" width="53"></td>
   <td> <img id="card14" src="blank.gif" height="68" width="53"></td>
   <td> <img id="card15" src="blank.gif" height="68" width="53"></td>
   <td class="score" id="row2"> </td>
 </tr>
 <tr>
   <td id="total"> <b>Total Score:</b>
      <div id="totalscore">0</div></td>
   <td> </td>
   <td> <img id="card16" src="blank.gif" height="68" width="53"></td>
   <td> <img id="card17" src="blank.gif" height="68" width="53"></td>
   <td> <img id="card18" src="blank.gif" height="68" width="53"></td>
   <td> <img id="card19" src="blank.gif" height="68" width="53"></td>
   <td> <img id="card20" src="blank.gif" height="68" width="53"></td>
   <td class="score" id="row3"> </td>
 </tr>
 <tr>
   <td> <a id="newgame" href="#"><b>Start Over</b></a></td>
   <td> </td>
   <td> <img id="card21" border=0 src="blank.gif" height=68 width=53></td>
   <td> <img id="card22" border=0 src="blank.gif" height=68 width=53></td>
   <td> <img id="card23" border=0 src="blank.gif" height=68 width=53></td>
   <td> <img id="card24" border=0 src="blank.gif" height=68 width=53></td>
   <td> <img id="card25" border=0 src="blank.gif" height=68 width=53></td>
   <td class="score" id="row4"> </td>
 </tr>
 <tr>
   <td> </td>
   <td class="score" id="diag1"> </td>
   <td class="score" id="col0"> </td>
   <td class="score" id="col1"> </td>
   <td class="score" id="col2"> </td>
   <td class="score" id="col3"> </td>
   <td class="score" id="col4"> </td>
   <td class="score" id="diag2"> </td>
 </tr>
</table>
</body>
</html>
```

The game board is laid out using an HTML table. Although the game board is five by five squares, the table contains eight columns and six rows. The leftmost column

will be used for displaying the next card and the score, as well as a Start Over link. The remaining columns and rows will be used to display the score for each column and row as they are filled with cards.

The 25 spaces on the board are given unique id values, card1 through card25. These will be used by the script to determine which card the user clicks on, and also to replace the appropriate image when a card is placed. The table cells for displaying scores are given the id values row0-4, col0-4, diag1, and diag2.

Save the HTML document in a folder, or download it from this book's website. You can load it into a browser to see the game layout, as shown in Figure 22.2. The game won't be playable until you add the script you'll develop in the next section.

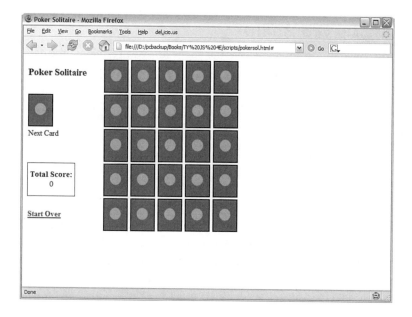

FIGURE 22.2
The Poker Solitaire game layout.

Creating the Script

Because this is the longest script in this book, it will be easier to understand if you look at some of its key functions before the entire script. The following sections discuss how the script will manage the game.

Using Objects to Store Cards

Because JavaScript is designed to work with numbers but not specifically with playing cards, you can create a custom object to make it easier to manage the card game. The following code is the constructor for a Card object:

```
// make a filename for an image, given Card object
function fname() {
   return this.num + this.suit + ".gif";
}
// constructor for Card objects
function Card(num,suit) {
   this.num = num;
   this.suit = suit;
   this.fname = fname;
}
```

Each Card object will represent a space on the board. It has two properties, num and suit, and an fname() method that returns the filename for the graphic representing the card.

Setting Up the Board

Along with the graphics on the screen, the board array will represent the game board by storing 25 Card objects, one for each space. Here's the code that will set up the board:

```
// array for board contents
   board = new Array(26);
   for (i=1; i<26; i++) {
      board[i] = new Card(0,"x");
      obj=document.getElementById("card"+i);
      obj.src = "blank.gif";
      obj.onclick = PlaceCard;
   }
```

The first line creates the board array. The for loop then sets up each space on the board. First, it places a blank card in the array. Next, it finds the object for the corresponding space on the screen. It makes sure blank.gif is displayed in each space, and sets an event handler for onClick events to call the PlaceCard() function, which will handle the user's clicks on the board.

Shuffling the Deck

The deck array will be used to simulate a deck of cards. The following code fills the array with Card objects:

```
   deck = new Array(53);
   for (i=1; i<14; i++) {
     deck[i] = new Card(i,"c");
     deck[i+13] = new Card(i,"h");
     deck[i+26] = new Card(i,"s");
     deck[i+39] = new Card(i,"d");
   }
```

To save time, the statements in the `for` loop insert cards of each of the four suits into the deck. At this point, the cards are in order. The next step is to shuffle the deck:

```
n = Math.floor(100 * Math.random() + 200);
for (i=1; i<n; i++) {
    c1 = Math.floor(52*Math.random() + 1);
    c2 = Math.floor(52*Math.random() + 1);
    temp = deck[c2];
    deck[c2] = deck[c1];
    deck[c1] = temp;
}
```

This code starts by choosing a random number, n, ranging from 200 to 299. It then loops n times using a `for` loop. Each iteration of the loop chooses two random cards in the deck and swaps their positions. This ensures a reasonably random deck that still contains exactly 52 unique cards.

Placing Cards on the Board

The `PlaceCard()` function will be called by an event handler when the user clicks on a space on the board. This function begins by determining which space was clicked:

```
function PlaceCard(e) {
    if (!e) var e = window.event;
    // which space on the board was clicked?
    thiscard = (e.target) ? e.target: e.srcElement;
    pos = thiscard.id.substring(4);
    if (board[pos].suit != "x") {
        return;
    }
}
```

These statements use the `target` or `srcElement` property to determine which space was clicked. The pos variable stores the numeric position on the board (1–25), calculated by removing "card" from the id value using the `substring()` method. The final `if` statement checks whether a card is already in place, and returns to prevent placing a card over an existing card.

The next section of `PlaceCard()` does the actual card placement:

```
drawcard=document.getElementById("dcard");
thiscard.src = deck[nextcard].fname();
drawcard.src = "blank.gif";
board[pos] = deck[nextcard];
nextcard++;
Score();
```

The `nextcard` variable keeps track of the next card in the deck, starting at one for the top card. This function uses `getElementById()` to find the object for the "next

card" display, and then uses the `fname()` method to assign the appropriate filename to the `src` property of the `image` object. The `board` array is updated with the new card, `nextcard` is incremented, and the `Score()` function is called to update the scores.

The next task for `PlaceCard()` is to check whether the game is over:

```
// Game over?
if (nextcard > 25) {
    EndGame();
}
else {
    drawcard.src = deck[nextcard].fname();
// cache next image for draw pile
    nexti = new Image(53,68);
    nexti.src = deck[nextcard+1].fname();
}
}
```

If 25 cards have been placed, the `EndGame()` function is called to end the game. Otherwise, the next card is displayed in the display. The next card image (not yet displayed) is also preloaded so the game will respond quickly.

Scoring Columns, Rows, and Diagonals

The `Score()` function will update the scores for each column, row, and diagonal each time a card is placed. Here is the code for the `Score()` function:

```
function Score() {
    score=document.getElementById("totalscore");
    totscore = 0;
// rows
    for (x=0; x<5; x++) {
        r = x * 5 + 1;
        a =
AddScore(board[r],board[r+1],board[r+2],board[r+3],board[r+4],"row"+x);
        totscore += a;
    }
// columns
    for (x=0; x<5; x++) {
        r = x + 1;
        a =
AddScore(board[r],board[r+5],board[r+10],board[r+15],board[r+20],"col"+x);
        totscore += a;
    }
// diagonals
        a = AddScore(board[5],board[9],board[13],board[17],board[21],"diag1");
        totscore += a;
        a = AddScore(board[1],board[7],board[13],board[19],board[25],"diag2");
        totscore += a;
        score.firstChild.nodeValue = totscore;
}
```

This function uses for loops to process each row and each column. It then handles the diagonals. A separate function, AddScore(), will handle the actual detection of poker hands in each of these.

The totscore variable stores a total of all of the scores. Each time a card is placed, the updated total score is displayed in the left column.

Adding Up Scores

The AddScore() function is called by Score() for each column, row, and diagonal. This function determines which poker hand, if any, is represented by the cards passed to it. It then updates the appropriate score box on the board with the row's score, and returns the numeric value to be used by Score(). The AddScore() function begins by setting up some variables:

```
function AddScore(c1,c2,c3,c4,c5,scorebox) {
    obj=document.getElementById(scorebox);
    straight = false;
    flush = false;
    royal = false;
    pairs = 0;
    three = false;
// sorted array for convenience
    nums = new Array(5);
    nums[0] = c1.num;
    nums[1] = c2.num;
    nums[2] = c3.num;
    nums[3] = c4.num;
    nums[4] = c5.num;
    nums.sort(numsort);
```

The function first sets up a number of flag variables, such as straight and flush, to keep track of which poker hand it finds. It then stores the five card values in an array and sorts it to make it easy to detect straights. The function continues by testing for each hand, one at a time. For example, this if statement tests for a flush by comparing card suits:

```
// flush
    if (c1.suit == c2.suit && c2.suit == c3.suit
        && c3.suit == c4.suit && c4.suit == c5.suit) {
        flush = true;
    }
```

After doing each test, AddScore() updates the board with a description of the poker hand and score for the row and returns a numeric score:

```
    if (flush) {
        obj.innerHTML="Flush<br>5"
        return 5;
    }
```

Ending the Game

The game ends when all 25 spaces on the board have been filled with cards and the `EndGame()` function is called. Because the score is updated in real time and no moves can be made after all cards are placed, the only thing left for this function to do is to display a "Game Over" message:

```
function EndGame() {
    stat=document.getElementById("status");
    stat.innerHTML="<b>Game Over</b>";
}
```

This uses `innerHTML` to display a message in the `status` element, which normally displays "Next Card" to label the draw card.

Adding Style with CSS

The game will also need a small CSS file to define the appearance of some of the game elements. Listing 22.2 shows the CSS file for the Poker Solitaire game.

LISTING 22.2   The CSS File for the Poker Solitaire Game

```
h1 {
    font-size: 125%;
}
td.score {
    font-size: 80%;
    border: 1px solid silver;
    width: 53px;
}
#total {
    border: 1px solid black;
    font-size: 105%;
    padding: 5px;
}
#totalscore {
    text-align: center;
}
```

The CSS rules set the size of H1 headers, and then define a border, width, and font size for td elements in the `score` class, which will display each row's score. Finally, a border, font size, and padding are defined for the "Total Score" display, and the numeric score is centered.

Try It Yourself

Putting It All Together

To get the game working, you'll need to use the complete JavaScript file that incorporates the functions you learned about earlier in this hour. Listing 22.3 shows the JavaScript file for the game.

LISTING 22.3   The Complete JavaScript File for the Poker Solitaire Game

```javascript
// global variables
var tally = new Array(14)
var nextcard = 1;
var nexti = new Image(53,68);
// numeric comparison for sort()
function numsort(a, b) {
  return a - b;
}
function InitGame() {
  if (!document.getElementById) return;
  stat=document.getElementById("status");
  stat.innerHTML="Next Card";
  nextcard = 1;
// array for board contents
  board = new Array(26);
  for (i=1; i<26; i++) {
    board[i] = new Card(0,"x");
    obj=document.getElementById("card"+i);
    obj.src = "blank.gif";
    obj.onclick = PlaceCard;
  }
  // fill the deck (in order, for now)
  deck = new Array(53);
  for (i=1; i<14; i++) {
    deck[i] = new Card(i,"c");
    deck[i+13] = new Card(i,"h");
    deck[i+26] = new Card(i,"s");
    deck[i+39] = new Card(i,"d");
  }
  // Clear the scores
  Score();
  // shuffle the deck
  n = Math.floor(100 * Math.random() + 200);
  for (i=1; i<n; i++) {
    c1 = Math.floor(52*Math.random() + 1);
    c2 = Math.floor(52*Math.random() + 1);
    temp = deck[c2];
    deck[c2] = deck[c1];
    deck[c1] = temp;
  }
  // draw the first card on screen
  next=document.getElementById("dcard");
  next.src = deck[nextcard].fname();
  // preload the next image
  nexti.src = deck[nextcard+1].fname();
```

LISTING 22.3   Continued

```
   obj=document.getElementById("newgame")
   obj.onclick=InitGame;
} // end InitGame
// place the draw card on the board where clicked
function PlaceCard(e) {
   if (!e) var e = window.event;
   // which space on the board was clicked?
   thiscard = (e.target) ? e.target: e.srcElement;
   pos = thiscard.id.substring(4);
   if (board[pos].suit != "x") {
      return;
   }
   drawcard=document.getElementById("dcard");
   thiscard.src = deck[nextcard].fname();
   drawcard.src = "blank.gif";
   board[pos] = deck[nextcard];
   nextcard++;
   Score();
   // Game over?
   if (nextcard > 25) {
      EndGame();
   }
   else {
      drawcard.src = deck[nextcard].fname();
   // cache next image for draw pile
      nexti = new Image(53,68);
      nexti.src = deck[nextcard+1].fname();
   }
}
// check for completed rows and display row scores
function Score() {
   score=document.getElementById("totalscore");
   totscore = 0;
// rows
   for (x=0; x<5; x++) {
      r = x * 5 + 1;
      a =
AddScore(board[r],board[r+1],board[r+2],board[r+3],board[r+4],"row"+x);
      totscore += a;
   }
// columns
   for (x=0; x<5; x++) {
      r = x + 1;
      a =
AddScore(board[r],board[r+5],board[r+10],board[r+15],board[r+20],"col"+x);
      totscore += a;
   }
// diagonals
      a = AddScore(board[5],board[9],board[13],board[17],board[21],"diag1")
      totscore += a;
      a = AddScore(board[1],board[7],board[13],board[19],board[25],"diag2")
      totscore += a;
      score.firstChild.nodeValue = totscore;
}
// check for poker hands
function AddScore(c1,c2,c3,c4,c5,scorebox) {
```

LISTING 22.3 Continued

```
    obj=document.getElementById(scorebox);
    straight = false;
    flush = false;
    royal = false;
    pairs = 0;
    three = false;
// sorted array for convenience
    nums = new Array(5);
    nums[0] = c1.num;
    nums[1] = c2.num;
    nums[2] = c3.num;
    nums[3] = c4.num;
    nums[4] = c5.num;
    nums.sort(numsort);
// no score if row is not filled
    if (c1.num == 0 || c2.num == 0 || c3.num == 0
        || c4.num == 0 || c5.num == 0) {
        obj.innerHTML="";
        return 0;
    }
// flush
    if (c1.suit == c2.suit && c2.suit == c3.suit
        && c3.suit == c4.suit && c4.suit == c5.suit) {
        flush = true;
    }
// straight
    if (nums[4] - nums[3] == 1
      && nums[3] - nums[2] == 1
      && nums[2] - nums[1] == 1
      && nums[1] - nums[0] == 1) {
        straight = true;
    }
// royal straight (10, J, Q, K, A)
    if (nums[1] == 10 && nums[2] == 11 && nums[3] == 12
      && nums[4] == 13 && nums[0] == 1) {
        straight = true;
        royal = true;
    }
// royal flush, straight flush, straight, flush
    if (straight && flush && royal) {
        obj.innerHTML="Royal Flush<br>250";
        return 250;
    }
    if (straight && flush) {
        obj.innerHTML="Straight Flush<br>50";
        return 50;
    }
    if (straight) {
        obj.innerHTML="Straight<br>4";
        return 4;
    }
    if (flush) {
        obj.innerHTML="Flush<br>5"
        return 5;
    }
// tally array is a count for each card value
```

LISTING 22.3   **Continued**

```javascript
   for (i=1; i<14; i++) {
      tally[i] = 0;
   }
   for (i=0; i<5; i++) {
      tally[nums[i]] += 1;
   }
   for (i=1; i<14; i++) {
// four of a kind
      if (tally[i] == 4) {
         obj.innerHTML="Four of a Kind<br>25";
         return 25;
      }
      if (tally[i] == 3) three = true;
      if (tally[i] == 2) pairs += 1;
   }
// full house
   if (three && pairs == 1) {
      obj.innerHTML="Full House<br>8";
      return 8;
   }
// two pair
   if (pairs == 2) {
      obj.innerHTML="Two Pair<br>2";
      return 2;
   }
// three of a kind
   if (three) {
      obj.innerHTML="Three of a Kind<br>3";
      return 3;
   }
// just a pair
   if (pairs == 1) {
      obj.innerHTML="Pair<br>1";
      return 1;
   }
// nothing
   obj.innerHTML="No Score<br>0";
   return 0;
// end AddScore()
}
// game over - final score
function EndGame() {
   stat=document.getElementById("status");
   stat.innerHTML="<b>Game Over</b>";
}
// make a filename for an image, given Card object
function fname() {
   return this.num + this.suit + ".gif";
}
// constructor for Card objects
function Card(num,suit) {
   this.num = num;
   this.suit = suit;
   this.fname = fname;
}
// event handlers to start game
window.onload=InitGame;
```

Because this is the longest code listing in this book, I recommend you download the files from this book's website rather than type it all in. You'll need the card graphics to make it work anyway.

To try the game, make sure you have everything you need in one folder:

▶ The HTML document

▶ The CSS file (pokersol.css)

▶ The JavaScript file (pokersol.js)

▶ All 53 graphics (52 cards plus blank.gif)

You can now load the HTML file to test the game. Figure 22.3 shows the Poker Solitaire game after a complete game—it shouldn't take you long to beat my score.

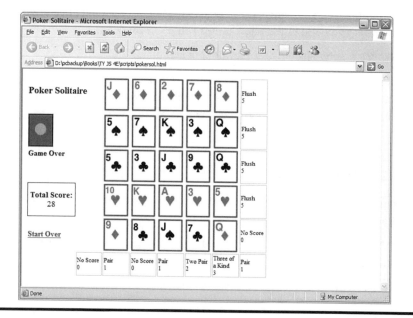

FIGURE 22.3
The Poker Solitaire example at the end of a game.

Summary

In this hour, you've applied your JavaScript knowledge to create a complete application—a playable game. Along the way, you've used objects to represent playing cards, used graphics and the W3C DOM to display the game, and learned some of the issues involved in a complex application.

In the next hour, you'll return to practical applications of JavaScript with some advanced examples using the W3C DOM.

Q&A

Q. *Because the spaces on the board aren't links, is there a way to make the cursor indicate that they can be clicked on?*

A. Yes. You can do this with an `onMouseOver` event handler that changes the `style.cursor` property to `pointer` for the spaces on the board. You could also use a rollover effect that changes the graphic, as demonstrated in Hour 19, "Using Graphics and Animation."

Q. *Can I add images or other HTML to the page without messing up the script?*

A. Yes. Because the game script works with `id` attributes rather than making any assumptions about which `image` objects to change, it shouldn't be affected by anything you add to the page, unless you use a conflicting `id` value.

Q. *What's a good strategy for playing this game?*

A. A simple approach is to dedicate each of the first four rows to a suit, so you have very good odds of scoring a flush on each row. As you do this, try to place cards where they'll form pairs with cards in other columns.

Quiz Questions

Test your knowledge of the JavaScript techniques you used in this hour by answering the following questions.

1. Which property of an `image` object do you change to display a different image?

   a. `href`

   b. `src`

   c. `fname`

2. Which of the following statements converts the text "card21" to the number 21?

   a. `pos = thiscard.id.substring(4);`

   b. `pos = thiscard.id.numValue;`

   c. `pos = 1 * thiscard.id;`

3. Assuming Card objects have been defined as in this hour, which statement creates a new Card object?

    a. `c = Card(12,"s");`

    b. `c = new Card(12,"s");`

    c. `var c (Card);`

Quiz Answers

1. b. You change the `src` property to display a different image.

2. a. The `substring()` method removes the first four letters of the string.

3. b. The `new` keyword is used to create a new instance of an object.

Exercises

If you want to gain more experience creating games in JavaScript, try the following exercises:

▶ Spend some time playing the game and see if you find any bugs in the script. Notice how difficult it can be to fully test an application like this—you won't know for certain that it scores a royal flush correctly until you get one.

▶ Using the techniques described in Hour 19, try adding a rollover effect that changes the `blank.gif` appearance when you move over a square where you can drop the current card. Make sure the image does not change if there is already a card placed on the space.

HOUR 23

Creating JavaScript Applications

What You'll Learn in This Hour:

▶ Using the DOM to create a scrolling window
▶ Switching between CSS style sheets using JavaScript
▶ Using the DOM to create dynamic forms

You've learned quite a bit about JavaScript in the last 22 hours. In this hour, you'll apply this knowledge to create three quick, practical examples of JavaScript applications that could be useful for just about any website.

Creating a Scrolling Window

One of the most common, and the most unfortunate, early uses of JavaScript was for scrolling messages, which crept across the browser's status line giving you information one letter at a time rather than making use of the whole page.

In this section, you'll create a different kind of scrolling message. This one scrolls a large block of text vertically within a window, similar to the credits at the end of a movie. This type of scrolling message is easier to read, is standards compliant, and can include links or other HTML features.

This example uses the same techniques as the animated slideshow in Hour 19, "Using Graphics and Animation." The only difference is that the animated text is only visible within a box, making it appear to scroll.

By the Way

The HTML Document

The HTML document for this example includes a link to the script, a link to a CSS style sheet, the text displayed on the page, and the text that will be scrolled within the box. Listing 23.1 shows the HTML for this example.

LISTING 23.1   The HTML Document for the Scrolling Window

```
<html>
<head>
<title>A DOM Scrolling Window</title>
<script language="JavaScript" type="text/javascript"
   src="scroll.js">
</script>
<link rel="stylesheet" type="text/css" href="scroll.css">
</head>
<body>
<h1>Scrolling Window Example</h1>
<p>This example shows a scrolling window created using JavaScript and
the W3C DOM. The red-bordered window below is actually a layer that
shows a clipped portion of a larger layer.</p>
<div id="thewindow">
<div id="thetext">
<p>This is the first paragraph of the scrolling message. The message
is created with ordinary HTML.</p>
<p>Entries within the scrolling area can use any HTML tags. They can
contain <a href="http://www.jsworkshop.com/">Links</a>.</p>
<p>There's no limit on the number of paragraphs that you can include
here. They don't even need to be formatted as paragraphs.</p>
<ul>
    <li>For example, you could format items using a bulleted list.</li>
</ul>
<p>The scrolling ends when the last part of the scrolling text
is on the screen. You've reached the end.</p>
</div>
</div>
</body>
</html>
```

The `<div>` tags in this document create two nested layers: One, `thewindow`, will form the small window for text to display in. The other, `thetext`, contains the text to scroll. You can use any HTML here, although it should be able to wrap to the small window.

The CSS File

The CSS file for this example, shown in Listing 23.2, sets margins and borders for the two `<div>` elements. The box's `position` property is set to `relative`, so it will be laid out normally within the document, and the `position` property for the scrolling text is set to `absolute` so it can be repositioned by the script.

LISTING 23.2 The CSS Style Sheet for the Scrolling Window

```
#thewindow {
    position:relative;
    width:180;
    height:150;
    overflow:hidden;
    border: 2px solid red;
}
#thetext {
    position: absolute;
    width: 170;
    left: 5;
    top: 100;
}
```

Because the text doesn't all fit in the small window, you'll only see part of it at a time. The overflow property on the window layer prevents the rest of the content from showing. Your script will manipulate the scrolling text's style.top property to move it relative to the window, creating a scrolling effect.

> The text layer is actually 10 pixels narrower than the window layer. This, along with the left property, creates a small margin of white space on either side of the window, preventing any of the text from being obstructed.

By the Way

The JavaScript File

The JavaScript code for this example uses a function, Scroll(), that is called repeatedly by a timeout. Listing 23.3 shows the JavaScript file for this example.

LISTING 23.3 The JavaScript File for the Scrolling Window

```
// global variable for position of the scrolling window
var pos=100;
function Scroll() {
  if (!document.getElementById) return;
  obj=document.getElementById("thetext");
  pos -=1;
  if (pos < 0-obj.offsetHeight+130) return;
  obj.style.top=pos;
  window.setTimeout("Scroll();",30);
}
// Start scrolling when the page loads
window.onload = Scroll;
```

The first line defines a global variable, pos, to store the current scroll position. The Scroll() function subtracts 1 from pos and checks its value. If the scrolling has reached the end, the function exits; otherwise, it sets the object position and calls the Scroll() function again using a timeout.

Did you
Know?

> Notice the `if` statement at the beginning of the function. This is a simple example of feature sensing, described in Hour 15, "Unobtrusive Scripting"—if the browser doesn't support the `getElementById()` method, the function exits rather than cause errors.

To try this example, make sure you have all three files in the same folder: the HTML document, the CSS file (`scroll.css`), and the JavaScript file (`scroll.js`) and load the HTML document into a browser. Figure 23.1 shows this example in action, after the scrolling text has reached the end.

FIGURE 23.1
The scrolling text box example in action.

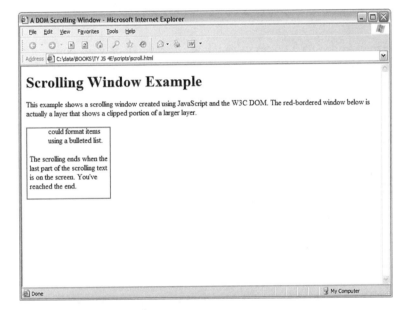

Style Sheet Switching with JavaScript

Suppose you want to offer your visitors a choice of different ways of viewing your site—for example, a choice of large or small fonts, or different background colors. Although you can use the `style` properties of elements within a page to make these changes individually, it would take a lot of code to change a page between drastically different styles.

One alternative is to create two or more completely separate style sheets, and use JavaScript to switch between them. This allows the user to have a large amount of control over the site's appearance without using a large and complex script.

Creating the HTML Document

First, you can create a basic HTML document for the style-switching example. This document will include a <script> tag for the script you'll create later, as well as links to two different style sheets. The HTML document for this example is shown in Listing 23.4.

LISTING 23.4   The HTML Document for the Style-Switching Example

```
<html>
<head>
<title>Style Sheet Example</title>
<link rel="stylesheet" type="text/css" href="style1.css">
<link rel="stylesheet" type="text/css" href="style2.css" disabled>
<script language="javascript" type="text/javascript"
   src="styleswitch.js">
</script>
</head>
<body>
<h1>multiple-choice styles</h1>
<p>This is a standard paragraph of text. Its font, margins,
colors, justification, and other attributes depend on the style
sheet you select. This paragraph includes some text in
<b>bold</b> and <i>italics</i>.
</p>
<p>You can select one of three styles for this document:
</p>
<ul>
<li><a href="#" onclick="Style(0,true);">Style sheet # 1</a></li>
<li><a href="#" onclick="Style(1,true);">Style sheet # 2</a></li>
<li><a href="#" onclick="Style(0,false);">No style sheet</a></li>
</ul>
<p>These links call a short JavaScript function that enables one
of this document's two linked external style sheets. You can edit
the style sheets to style this document in two different ways,
without changing any HTML.</p>
</body>
</html>
```

Although most of the document is just sample text to show off the styles of the different style sheets, it has several important components to make this technique work:

▶ The <script> tag uses the src attribute to include a script, styleswitch.js.

▶ There are two <link> tags to attach two external style sheets, style1.css and style2.css. The second tag includes the disabled attribute, so the document will be styled using only style1.css by default.

▶ The three links within the <li> list items have event handlers that call the Style() function to switch styles.

By the Way

Some browsers don't correctly support the `disabled` attribute in HTML. The script you create later will use JavaScript to disable the second style sheet by default to ensure that only one style sheet is used, regardless of the browser.

Save the HTML document in a folder. You'll be adding two style sheets and a script file to the folder to complete the example. If you load the document into a browser before creating the style sheets, it will be displayed without styles. Figure 23.2 shows how the document looks with no styles applied.

FIGURE 23.2
The style-switching example displayed without styles.

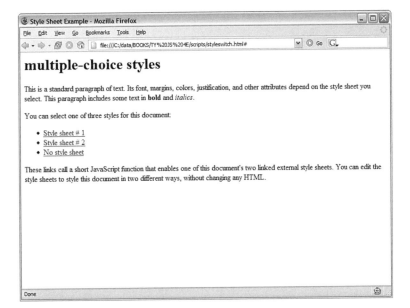

Creating the First Style Sheet

Next, you can create the first of the two style sheets. Listing 23.5 shows the complete style sheet `style1.css`.

LISTING 23.5   The First Style Sheet for the Style-Switching Example (`style1.css`)

```
body {
    font-family: Arial, Helvetica, sans-serif;
    font-size: 12pt;
}
P {
    margin-left: 10%;
    margin-right: 10%;
    text-align: justify;
    text-indent: 3%;
}
```

LISTING 23.5   Continued

```
B { color: red; }
I { color: DarkViolet; }
H1 {
    font-size: 300%;
    text-align: center;
    text-transform: capitalize;
}
UL {
    margin-left: 20%;
    margin-right: 20%;
}
LI { margin-top: 10px;}
```

Save this style sheet as `style1.css` in the same folder as the HTML document. This style sheet assigns some basic styles to the body, and to specific tags: <p>, <h1>, and so on. Because this is the default style sheet, it will be used if you load the HTML document now. Figure 23.3 shows the document as styled by this style sheet.

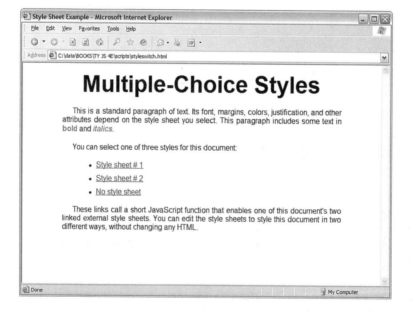

FIGURE 23.3 The style-switching example using the first style sheet.

Creating the Second Style Sheet

The second style sheet, `style2.css`, uses some more dramatic styles and is unlikely to be suited to all viewers. This sheet is disabled by default. Listing 23.6 shows the second style sheet.

LISTING 23.6   The Second Style Sheet for the Style-Switching Example
(style2.css)

```css
body {
    font-family: Times, "Times New Roman", sans-serif;
    font-size: 14pt;
}
P {
    margin-left: 20%;
    margin-right: 20%;
    text-align: left;
    text-indent: 0%;
}
B {
    color: black;
    background-color: aqua;
}
I { color: red;}
H1 {
    font-size: 200%;
    text-align: right;
    text-transform: uppercase;
}
UL {
    margin-left: 30%;
    margin-right: 30%;
    background-color: yellow;
}
LI { margin-top: 20px;}
```

Save this style sheet as `style2.css` in the same folder as the HTML document.

Creating the Script

You can use JavaScript to enable or disable style sheets. The `<link>` elements that
you used to attach the two style sheets to the HTML document are objects in the
DOM, and you can manipulate them using DOM methods. In this example, you
will use the `getElementsByTagName()` method to find all of the `<link>` elements,
and then enable one and disable the other. Listing 23.7 shows the complete
JavaScript file.

LISTING 23.7   The JavaScript File for the Style-Switching Example
(styleswitch.js)

```javascript
function Style(n,enable) {
    if (!document.getElementsByTagName) return;
    links = document.getElementsByTagName("link");
    links[n].disabled=!enable;
    links[1-n].disabled=true;
}
Style(0,true);
```

This script defines the Style() function, which accepts two parameters. The first, n, specifies the style sheet to activate. The second parameter, enable, specifies whether to enable the new style sheet (true) or to disable all style sheets (false). This feature is used by the No Style Sheet link.

> This example uses getElementsByTagName, but you could also assign an id attribute to each <link> tag and then use document.getElementById to find the object for each one individually.

The script enables (or disables, depending on the parameter) the chosen style sheet, and always disables the other sheet. The last line of the script calls the Style() function to select the first style sheet, just in case the browser doesn't support the disabled attribute.

To try the example, make sure you have all four files in the same folder: The HTML document, the two style sheets (style1.css and style2.css), and the script file (styleswitch.js). Load the HTML document into a browser and try clicking the links to change styles. Figure 23.4 shows the document after the second style sheet has been selected.

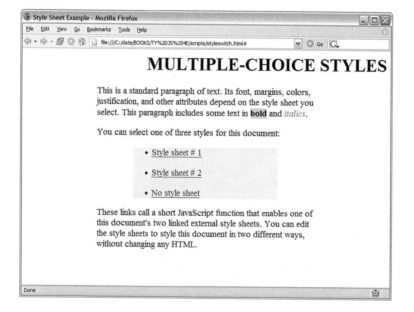

FIGURE 23.4
The style-switching example with the second style sheet selected.

▼ **Try It Yourself**

Creating a Dynamic Form

In Hour 11, "Getting Data with Forms," you learned how JavaScript can work with data from HTML forms, and change form elements. Using the W3C DOM, you can take this one step further, creating a script that can add elements to a form or show or hide sections of a form.

Creating the HTML Document

Listing 23.8 shows the HTML document for this example, which defines an order form. The form will have two dynamic features: first, the Ship To address fields aren't shown unless they're needed, and second, a button enables you to add additional item fields to the form.

LISTING 23.8   The HTML Document for the Dynamic Form Example

```
<html>
<head>
<title>Dynamic Order Form</title>
<script language="JavaScript" type="text/javascript"
   src="dform.js">
</script>
</head>
<body>
<h1>Order Form</h1>
<hr>
<form name="form1">
<b>Bill to:</b><br>
<b>Name:</b> <input type="text" name="customer" size="20"><br>
<b>Address 1:</b> <input type="text" name="addr1" size="20"><br>
<b>Address 2:</b> <input type="text" name="addr2" size="20"><br>
<b>City:</b> <input type="text" name="city" size="15">
<b>State:</b> <input type="text" name="state" size="4">
<b>Zip:</b> <input type="text" name="zip" size="9">
<hr>
<b>Ship to:</b><br>
<input type="radio" name="shipopt" value="same" checked onClick="Show(0);">
<b>Same Address</b>
<input type="radio" name="shipopt" value="other" onClick="Show(1);">
<b>Other Address</b>
<div ID="shipto" style="display: none;">
<br>
<b>Name:</b> <input type="text" name="shipname" size="20"><br>
<b>Address 1:</b> <input type="text" name="shipaddr1" size="20"><br>
<b>Address 2:</b> <input type="text" name="shipaddr2" size="20"><br>
<b>City:</b> <input type="text" name="shipcity" size="15">
<b>State:</b> <input type="text" name="shipstate" size="4">
<b>Zip:</b> <input type="text" name="shipzip" size="9">
</div>
<hr>
<div ID="items">
<b>Qty:</b>
```

LISTING 23.8 Continued

```
<input type="text" name="qty1" size="3">
<b>Item:</b>
<input type="text" name="item1" size="45">
<br>
<input type="button" value="Add an Item"
onClick="AddItem();" ID="add">
</div>
<hr>
<input type="submit" value="Continue...">
</form>
</body>
</html>
```

Save this HTML document in a folder. If you load it into a browser, you'll see the form's default appearance, but the dynamic features won't work yet. Figure 23.5 shows the default look of the form.

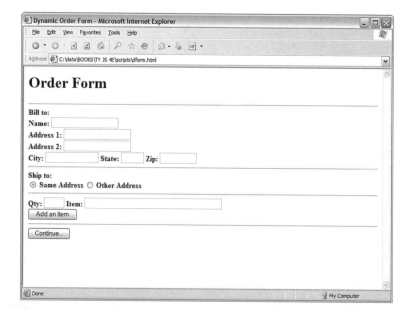

FIGURE 23.5
The dynamic form before the script is added.

Adding the Script

The script for this example will include two functions: AddItem(), for adding items to the form, and Show(), for showing or hiding the ship-to address. Listing 23.9 shows the script file.

LISTING 23.9   The JavaScript File for the Dynamic Form Example

```
// global variable
var items=1;
function AddItem() {
  if (!document.getElementById) return;
  // Add an item to the form
  div=document.getElementById("items");
  button=document.getElementById("add");
  items++;
  newitem="<b>Qty: </b>";
  newitem+="<input type=\"text\" name=\"qty" + items;
  newitem+="\" size=\"3\"> ";
  newitem+="<b>Item: </b>";
  newitem+="<input type=\"text\" name=\"item" + items;
  newitem+="\" size=\"45\"><br>";
  newnode=document.createElement("span");
  newnode.innerHTML=newitem;
  div.insertBefore(newnode,button);
}
function Show(a) {
  if (!document.getElementById) return;
  //Hide or show ship-to address
  obj=document.getElementById("shipto");
  if (a) obj.style.display="block";
    else obj.style.display="none";
}
```

Here's a breakdown of how this script works:

▶ The first line defines a global variable, items, to keep track of the number of items. This is used to assign a unique name attribute to each <input> tag as they are added.

▶ The AddItem() function adds additional Quantity and Item fields to the form using the insertBefore() DOM method.

▶ The Show() function uses the style.display property to either show or hide the section with the id value shipto.

To try the script, save it as dform.js (or download the files from this book's website) and load the HTML document into a browser. Figure 23.6 shows the document with two additional item fields added and the ship-to address displayed.

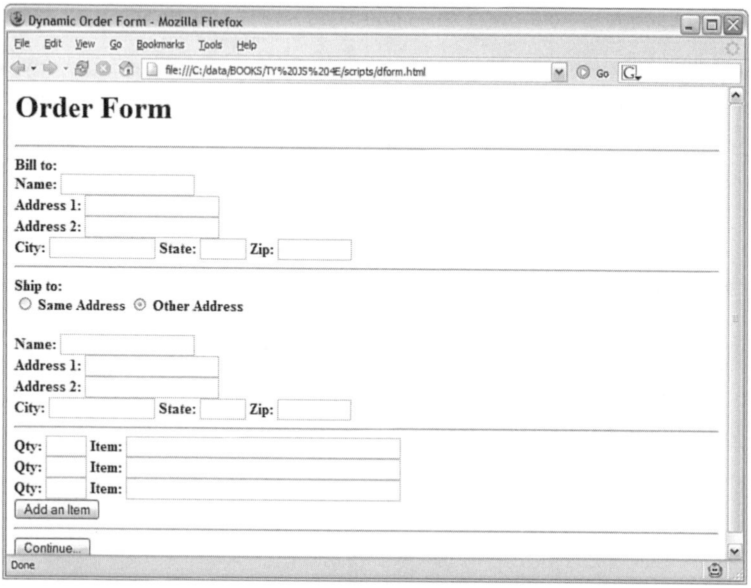

FIGURE 23.6
The dynamic form in action.

Summary

In this hour, you put your knowledge of JavaScript and the DOM to work with three examples: a scrolling text box, a page with user-selectable styles, and a dynamic form. Each of these could serve as the basis for a much more sophisticated feature for a site.

Your 24-hour tour of JavaScript is nearly over. In the final hour of this book, you'll learn about the future of JavaScript, learn what other web languages and disciplines you might want to learn next, and create one final code example.

Q&A

Q. *Can I make text scroll horizontally rather than vertically?*

A. Yes, the scrolling text example could easily work horizontally by changing the left property rather than the top property. However, this will be confusing unless the text is designed for horizontal scrolling—a single line would work fine.

Q. *Why don't more sites use dynamic forms?*

A. There are some usability and accessibility issues with a dynamic form—for starters, if JavaScript is disabled, the form in this hour would be limited to ordering a single item. You could compensate for this with some server-side code to allow adding additional items (slowly), but it would be far more complex than a simple form.

> **Q.** *Can my script enable more than one style sheet at a time?*
>
> **A.** Yes, you can have any number of <link> tags for style sheets, and any or all of them can be enabled. One obvious approach is to have one common style sheet that is always enabled, and use the script to enable or disable additional style sheets for user preferences.

Quiz Questions

Test your knowledge of the DOM by answering the following questions.

1. In the scrolling-text example, which CSS rule prevents the scrolling text from being visible outside the box?

   a. `overflow: hidden;`

   b. `position: relative;`

   c. `position: absolute;`

2. Which property of a <link> element determines whether the style sheet affects the document?

   a. `enabled`

   b. `disabled`

   c. `active`

3. In the dynamic forms example, which DOM method is used to add additional fields to the form?

   a. `insertAfter`

   b. `addItem`

   c. `insertBefore`

Quiz Answers

1. a. The `overflow: hidden;` rule prevents the text from being visible outside the box.

2. b. The `disabled` property controls whether the style sheet affects the document.

3. c. The `insertBefore` method is used to add additional items before the Add an Item button.

Exercises

If you want to gain more experience working with the techniques you explored in this hour, try the following exercises:

▶ Create your own text for the scrolling text box, and try modifying the HTML document (refer to Listing 23.1) to scroll your text.

▶ Create a third style sheet for the style-switching example, and modify the HTML document and the script (refer to Listings 23.4 and 23.7) to allow switching between three different style sheets.

▶ Right now, the dynamic forms example in Listings 23.8 and 23.9 will never display the Ship To address if JavaScript is disabled. To improve the accessibility of the form, make the script hide the Ship To section rather than having it hidden by default in the HTML document.

HOUR 24

Your Future with JavaScript

What You'll Learn in This Hour:

▶ Where to go to learn more about JavaScript
▶ How future versions of JavaScript might affect your scripts
▶ An introduction to XML (Extensible Markup Language)
▶ XHTML (Extensible Hypertext Markup Language)
▶ How to be sure you're ready for future web technologies
▶ How to move on to other web languages
▶ Implementing drag-and-drop using JavaScript

You've reached the last hour of this book. In this final hour, you'll find some ideas of where to go next—whether you want to learn more about JavaScript or move on to other languages and technologies. You'll also learn some tips for future-proofing your scripts, and you'll create a drag-and-drop script as a final example.

Learning Advanced JavaScript Techniques

Although you've now learned all of the essentials of the JavaScript language, there is still much to learn. JavaScript can be used to script environments other than the Web, and you can move beyond simple scripts to develop entire applications that combine JavaScript with server-side programming.

Here are some ways you can further your JavaScript education:

▶ See Appendix A, "Other JavaScript Resources," for a list of JavaScript books and web pages with further information.

▶ While the core JavaScript language is in place, be sure to follow the latest developments. The websites in Appendix A and this book's site will let you know when changes are on the way.

▶ Be sure to spend some time practicing the JavaScript techniques you've learned throughout this book. You can use them to create much more complex applications than those you've worked with so far.

One advanced technique that is becoming popular is AJAX (Asynchronous JavaScript and XML), which allows JavaScript to communicate with a server without reloading pages. You learned the basics of AJAX in Hour 17, "AJAX: Remote Scripting".

Because this is one of the most exciting features of JavaScript, it's a good one to learn more about. Try using the AJAX library you created in Hour 17 to add remote scripting to a site, or explore the Web's AJAX sites to learn more sophisticated techniques.

Future Web Technologies

The Web has changed dramatically in the last 10 years, and is continually changing. In the following sections, you will explore some of the upcoming—and already developed—technologies that will affect your pages and scripts.

Future Versions of JavaScript

JavaScript has gone through several versions to reach its current one, 1.6. Fortunately, the core language hasn't changed much through these version changes, and nearly all scripts written for older versions will work on the latest one.

The next version of JavaScript, 2.0, is currently being developed by the Mozilla Foundation and ECMA. Version 2.0's main change will be the addition of true object-oriented features, such as classes and inheritance.

As with previous versions, 2.0 should be backward compatible with older versions. To be sure your scripts will work under version 2.0, follow the standard language features and do not rely on any undocumented or browser-specific features.

Future DOM Versions

Currently, the W3C DOM level 1 is an official specification, whereas level 2 is only a recommendation. Level 2 adds features such as event handling and better style sheet support, and is already partially supported by the latest browsers.

Hour 15, "Unobtrusive Scripting," introduces the event-handling features of DOM level 2, and describes how to implement the same techniques in Internet Explorer, which does not support them yet.

In the future, expect better browser support for the DOM, and less compatibility issues between browsers.

XML (Extensible Markup Language)

HTML was originally created as a language for the Web, and was based on an older standard for documentation called SGML (Standard Generalized Markup Language). HTML is a much-simplified version of SGML, specifically designed for web documents.

A relatively new language on the scene is XML (Extensible Markup Language). XML is also a simplified version of SGML, but it isn't nearly as simple as HTML. Although HTML has a specific purpose, XML can be used for virtually any purpose.

> The W3C (World Wide Web Consortium) developed XML, and has published a specification to standardize the language.

By the Way

Strictly speaking, XML isn't a language in itself—there is no concise list of XML tags because XML has no set list of tags. Instead, XML enables you to create your own markup languages for whatever purpose you choose.

So what use is a language without any specific commands? Well, XML enables you to define tags, similar to HTML tags, for any purpose. If you were storing recipes, for example, you could create tags for ingredients, ingredient quantities, and instructions.

XML uses a DTD (Document Type Definition) to define the tags used in a particular document. The DTD can be in a separate file or built into the document, and specifies which tags are allowed, their attributes, and what they can contain.

XML is already in use today. Although it isn't directly supported by web browsers, you can use a program on the server to parse XML documents into HTML documents before sending them to the browser.

To return to the recipe example, an XML processor could convert each recipe into HTML. The reason for doing this is simple: By changing the rules in the parser, you could change the entire format of all of the recipes—a difficult task to perform manually if you had thousands of recipes.

XHTML (Extensible Hypertext Markup Language)

The HTML specification, at version 4.01, is still considered valid, but the W3C has been working on the successor to HTML, XHTML, now at version 1.1. XHTML is a reformulated version of HTML that fits the strict rules of XML and can be processed with software designed to work with XML.

In practice, XHTML looks very similar to HTML. Here are some of the most obvious changes you will need to make to adapt a page to XHTML:

▶ All tags should be lowercase: <p>, <body>, and so forth.

▶ Most tags require closing tags: </p>, and so forth.

▶ For standalone tags that don't enclose other elements, such as <img> and <br>, a special syntax combines opening and closing tags with a slash before the closing brace: <br/>.

▶ The document must follow strict rules of structure and tags must be nested correctly.

▶ A <!DOCTYPE> tag is required to specify the XML DTD used for the document. The following specifies the XHTML Transitional DTD:

```
<!DOCTYPE html PUBLIC "-//W3C//DTD XHTML 1.0 Transitional//EN"
  "http://www.w3.org/TR/xhtml1/DTD/xhtml1-transitional.dtd">
```

The transitional DTD allows some deprecated HTML tags, such as <center>, for compatibility. There is also an XHTML Strict DTD that does not allow any deprecated tags.

By the Way

> Browser support for XHTML isn't perfect, especially when it comes to the Strict DTD. It's also difficult to meet XHTML's strict validation requirements while dealing with issues such as user-generated content and scripts. For these reasons, most webmasters use either XHTML Transitional or the still-valid HTML 4.01.

XSL (Extensible Stylesheet Language)

XML documents focus strictly on the meaning of the tags—content—and ignore presentation. The presentation of XML can be determined by creating an XSL (Extensible Stylesheet Language) style sheet.

XSL is based on XML, but specifies presentation—parameters such as font size, margins, and table formatting—for an XML document. When you use an XML processing program to create HTML output, it uses an XSL style sheet to determine the HTML formatting of the output.

By the Way

> XSL documents are actually XML documents, using their own DTD that specifies style sheet tags. XSL is a newer W3C specification.

Planning for the Future

In the history of JavaScript, there has never been such a major change to the language that a great number of scripts written using the older version have stopped working. Nevertheless, many scripts have been crippled by new browser releases—chiefly those that used browser-specific features.

The following sections offer some guidelines you can follow in writing scripts to ensure that the impact of future JavaScript versions and browser releases will be minimal.

Keeping Scripts Compatible

Years ago, Netscape and Microsoft introduced separate and incompatible versions of DHTML (Dynamic HTML), which allowed scripts to modify any element of a page for the first time. Early adopters jumped in to write many scripts, some of which you can still find online today. These scripts made some serious mistakes:

▶ Browser detection was used to separately support browsers, or in some cases a specific browser was required.

▶ Scripts were written to work around bugs in browsers, or sometimes even take advantage of them.

▶ The process of writing scripts often involved trial and error rather than consulting official documentation.

This messy scripting gave DHTML—and JavaScript—a bad name among serious programmers. Fortunately, the standardized W3C DOM has now replaced the proprietary browser DHTML features, and it's easier than ever to create scripts the right way—but as time goes by, there will undoubtedly be cutting-edge features that aren't quite standard.

One obvious example is AJAX (Asynchronous JavaScript and XML), which is only now being developed as a standard by the W3C, despite working (in sometimes confusingly different ways) in the major browsers.

There's nothing wrong with using these cutting-edge features—but if you do, you should be aware that you're going to need to test the scripts on several different browsers. You should use feature sensing rather than detecting (or expecting) particular browsers. Finally, you should be prepared to do a bit of rewriting when the standard arrives.

Staying HTML Compliant

One trend as browsers advance is that newer browsers tend to do a better job of following the W3C standard for HTML—and, often, relying on it. This means that although a page that uses completely standard HTML will likely work in future browsers, one that uses browser-specific features or workarounds is bound to have problems eventually.

By the Way

> In particular, the first release of Netscape 6.0 received many complaints about "breaking" previously working pages. In most cases, the page used bad HTML, and previous browsers happened to handle the error more gracefully.

To avoid these problems, try to use completely valid HTML whenever possible. This means not only using standard tags and attributes, but following certain formatting rules: For example, always using both opening and closing <p> tags, and enclosing numbers for table widths and other parameters in quotation marks.

To be sure your documents follow the HTML standard, see Appendix B, "Tools for JavaScript Developers," for suggested HTML validation programs and services. These will examine your document and point out any areas that do not comply with the HTML standard.

Document Everything

Last but not least, be sure you understand everything your scripts are doing. Document your scripts using comments, and particularly document any statements that might look cryptic or are particularly hard to get working correctly.

If your scripts are properly documented, it will be a much easier process if you have to modify them to be compatible with a future browser, JavaScript, or DOM version.

Did you Know?

> See Hour 15 for more tips on future-proofing your scripts by using unobtrusive scripting techniques.

Moving on to Other Languages

Assuming you've spent the last 24 hours learning JavaScript to further your career (or hobby) as a web developer, where will you go next? As you should know by now, JavaScript can't do everything, and there are many other languages that work on the Web. Here are some you might want to explore:

▶ **Java** is useful for more complex client-side programs. Although Java applets aren't as integrated with web pages as JavaScript, you can build applications that go beyond JavaScript's capabilities. Java's syntax is similar to JavaScript, although the language is more complicated. See http://java.sun.com/ for more information.

▶ **Flash** is also a popular choice for more sophisticated client-side programs, and is an especially good choice if you want to create games or applications that work with video. Flash's ActionScript is based on the same ECMAScript standard as JavaScript, so you have a headstart. See http://www.adobe.com/products/flash/flashpro/ for more information.

▶ **Ruby** is a relatively new server-side language that has taken the web development world by storm, particularly thanks to the Ruby on Rails framework. Ruby on Rails includes features for easily integrating JavaScript and AJAX features into sites. See http://www.ruby-lang.org/en/ and http://www.rubyonrails.org/ for details.

▶ **PHP** is the workhorse of server-side languages, and a popular choice for back-end development, whether with basic HTML or JavaScript and AJAX front ends. See http://www.php.net/ for details.

▶ **Python** is another popular server-side language, noted for its simple coding style and the excellent libraries available for adapting it to various purposes. See http://www.python.org/ for more information.

There are many other languages on the Web, but these are five popular choices. It's worth taking the time to learn a bit about these languages and others even if you don't plan on making them your primary development tool.

Try It Yourself   ▼

Creating Drag-and-Drop Objects

Just to prove JavaScript can do many things beyond what you've learned so far, here is a final example. Although desktop operating systems support drag-and-drop actions (for example, moving a file into the trash can), web pages have traditionally lacked this feature. Using JavaScript and the DOM, you can unobtrusively create objects that the user can pick up, drag, and drop.

> This is a simple implementation of drag-and-drop. Full-featured dragging and dropping leads to a very complex script. Fortunately, you can use JavaScript libraries such as Script.aculo.us to add drag-and-drop to your pages without any scripting. See Hour 8, "Using Built-in Functions and Libraries," for more details.

Did you Know?

The HTML Document

The HTML document for this example exists mainly to define four draggable objects with <div> tags. Listing 24.1 shows the complete HTML document.

LISTING 24.1   The HTML Document for the Drag-and-Drop Example

```
<html>
<head>
<title>Drag and Drop</title>
<link rel="stylesheet" type="text/css" href="dragdrop.css">
<script language="javascript" type="text/javascript"
   src="dragdrop.js">
</script>
</head>
<body>
<h1>Drag and Drop in JavaScript</h1>
<div class="drag" id="drag1">
<h3>Box #1</h3>
<p>Click one of these boxes and hold the
mouse button down to move it to a new location.</p>
</div>
<div class="drag" id="drag2">
<h3>Box #2</h3>
<p>This is another box you can drag and drop.</p>
</div>
<div class="drag" id="drag3">
<h3>Box #3</h3>
<p>This is yet another box you can drag and drop.</p>
</div>
<div class="drag" id="drag4">
<h3>Box #4</h3>
<p>This is the fourth and final draggable box.</p>
</div>
</body>
</html>
```

Each of the <div> tags with the class="drag" attribute will be a draggable object. The document also includes a <script> tag to attach a script and a <link> tag for a style sheet.

The CSS Style Sheet

The style sheet sets up the four positionable objects with an initial position as well as a distinctive border. Listing 24.2 shows the CSS file for this example.

LISTING 24.2   The CSS File for the Drag-and-Drop Example

```
.drag {
   position: absolute;
   width: 150px;
   border: 2px solid black;
   border-top: 20px solid black;
```

LISTING 24.2 Continued

```
    top: 100px;
    padding: 5px;
}
#drag1 { left: 20px; }
#drag2 { left: 190px; }
#drag3 { left: 360px; }
#drag4 { left: 530px; }
```

The position: absolute rule makes the elements positionable. The top property sets the vertical position of all four elements, and the left property is set for each one to space them across the page. The width and border properties make the <div> elements look like boxes, and the border-top property creates a thick top border for dragging.

Save this file as dragdrop.css in the same folder as the HTML document. If you load the HTML document into a browser at this point, you can see the styled boxes, but they won't be movable until you add the script. Figure 24.1 shows this example before adding the script.

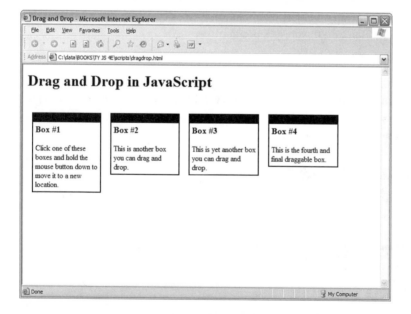

FIGURE 24.1
The initial display of the draggable objects.

Implementing Drag-and-Drop

Because drag-and-drop isn't built in to the DOM, your script will have to do it the hard way. When the user clicks on an element, an onmousedown event handler will begin dragging the object. After that starts, an onmousemove event handler will update the object's position, and onmousedown will "drop" the object.

One tricky part is determining the mouse position in the onmousemove event handler. This is stored as a property of the event object, but Netscape and Firefox use the pageX and pageY properties, whereas Internet Explorer uses the clientX and clientY properties. A series of if statements finds the x and y values, regardless of the browser:

```
if (!e) var e = window.event;
if (e.pageX) {
  x = e.pageX;
  y = e.pageY;
} else if (e.clientX) {
  x = e.clientX;
  y = e.clientY;
} else return;
```

By the Way

> See Hour 9, "Responding to Events," for more information on event handlers and the event object.

One more issue: Objects are positioned based on their top-left corner, but you can click anywhere on the object with the mouse. This will result in a "jump" effect when you pick up an object. The solution is to calculate an offset between the mouse position and the object's position:

```
dx = x - obj.offsetLeft;
dy = y - obj.offsetTop;
```

When the object is moved, these offsets will be subtracted from the mouse position. This way, the object is anchored to the mouse pointer wherever you click it, and does not jump to a new position.

The JavaScript File

Now all you need is the JavaScript file to add the drag-and-drop feature to the document. Listing 24.3 shows the complete script.

LISTING 24.3 The JavaScript File for the Drag-and-Drop Example

```
// global variables
var obj,x,y,dx,dy;
// set up draggable elements
function Setup() {
  // exit if the browser doesn't support the DOM
  if (!document.getElementsByTagName) return;
  divs = document.getElementsByTagName("DIV");
  for (i=0; i<divs.length; i++) {
    if (divs[i].className != "drag") continue;
    // set event handler for each div with class="drag"
    divs[i].onmousedown = Drag;
  }
```

LISTING 24.3 Continued

```
}
function Drag(e) {
  // Start dragging an object
  if (!e) var e = window.event;
  // which object was clicked?
  obj = (e.target) ? e.target: e.srcElement;
  obj.style.borderColor="red";
  // calculate object offsets from mouse position
  dx = x - obj.offsetLeft;
  dy = y - obj.offsetTop;
}
function Move(e) {
  // track mouse movements
  if (!e) var e = window.event;
  if (e.pageX) {
    x = e.pageX;
    y = e.pageY;
  } else if (e.clientX) {
    x = e.clientX;
    y = e.clientY;
  } else return;
  if (obj) {
    obj.style.left = x - dx;
    obj.style.top = y - dy;
  }
}
function Drop() {
  // let go!
  if (!obj) return;
  obj.style.borderColor="black";
  obj = false;
}
// Detect mouse movement
document.onmousemove = Move;
// drop current object on mouse up
document.onmouseup = Drop;
// Set up when the page loads
window.onload = Setup;
```

Here's a rundown of how this script works:

▶ The first line declares five global variables: obj to keep track of the current object being dragged, x and y for the mouse position, and dx and dy for the object's offset from the mouse position.

▶ The Setup() function runs when the page loads. This function uses getElementsByTagName to find all of the <div> elements in the page. For each one with the class="drag" attribute, it sets up an onmousedown event handler to call the Drag() function.

▶ The Drag() function sets obj to the correct object, sets the object's border color to red to indicate it's being dragged, and calculates the dx and dy offsets.

▶ The Move() function is where the action happens. After calculating the mouse pointer's x and y position, it sets the object's left and top properties to move it to follow the mouse.

▶ The Drop() function ends the process by setting the object's border color back to black, and then setting obj to false, so mouse movements won't move any object.

▶ The final lines set some global event handlers: onmousemove to call the Move() function, onmouseup to call the Drop() function, and onload to call Setup().

Save this file as dragdrop.js. To try the example, make sure you have all three files in the same folder: the HTML document, the CSS file (dragdrop.css), and the JavaScript file (dragdrop.js). Load the HTML document into a browser. Figure 24.2 shows the example after all four objects have been dragged to new positions.

FIGURE 24.2
The drag-and-drop example in action.

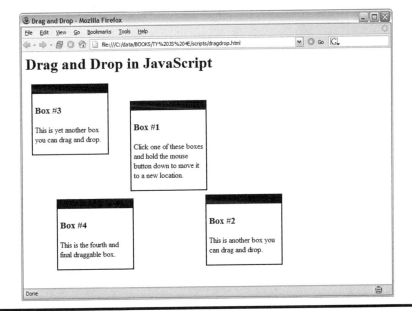

Summary

In this hour, you've learned how the future of JavaScript and the Web might affect your web pages and scripts, and learned some of the upcoming technologies that might change the way you work with the Web. Finally, you learned how to create drag-and-drop effects using JavaScript.

Time's up—you've reached the end of this book. I hope you've enjoyed spending 24 hours learning JavaScript, and that you'll continue to learn more about it on your own. See Appendix A for starting points to further your knowledge.

Q&A

Q. *Besides parsing documents into HTML, what other practical uses are there for XML?*

A. XML is a great way to store any type of marked-up text in a standardized way. Developers of many software applications, including popular word processors, are considering using XML-based files.

Q. *In the drag-and-drop example, the objects overlap each other. Is there a way to avoid this?*

A. Yes, if you set a background-color property for the objects in the style sheet, they won't overlap. However, you'll notice that sometimes you're dragging the current object behind the others. To avoid this, you can set the style.zIndex property for the current object in the script to keep it on top.

Q. *What if I have a JavaScript question that isn't answered in this book?*

A. Start with the resources in Appendix A. You should also stop by the author's website (www.jsworkshop.com) for a list of updates to the book, frequently asked questions, and a forum where you can discuss JavaScript with the author and other users.

Quiz Questions

Test your knowledge of JavaScript's future by answering the following questions.

1. Which of the following is the latest DOM recommendation from the W3C?

   a. DOM 1.5

   b. DOM level 1

   c. DOM level 2

2. When should you use a new JavaScript feature?

   a. Immediately

   b. As soon as it's supported by browsers

   c. As soon as it's part of a standard, and browsers that support it are widely available

3. Which of the following is an important way of making sure your scripts will work with future browsers?

  a. Follow HTML, JavaScript, and DOM standards.

  b. Spend an hour a day downloading the newest browsers and testing your scripts.

  c. Wait until the very last browsers are released before writing any scripts.

Quiz Answers

1. c. DOM level 2 is the latest W3C recommendation.

2. c. Wait until JavaScript features are standardized and widely available before implementing them.

3. a. Following HTML, JavaScript, and DOM standards is an important way of making sure your scripts will work with future browsers.

Exercises

If you want to gain more experience working with JavaScript, try the following exercises:

▶ Try adding another <div> element to the drag-and-drop example and make the appropriate changes to the style sheet so it will respond correctly.

▶ Try changing the drag-and-drop example to move a different type of element, such as paragraphs of text.

PART VII:

Appendixes

APPENDIX A

Other JavaScript Resources

Although you've learned a lot about JavaScript in 24 hours, there's still a lot to know. If you'd like to move on to advanced features of JavaScript or learn more, the resources listed in this appendix will be helpful.

Other Books

The following books, also from Sams.net, discuss JavaScript and DHTML in more detail:

- ▶ *Sams Teach Yourself JavaScript in 21 Days* by Jinjer Simon, Andrew Watt, Jonathan Watt. ISBN 0672322978.

- ▶ *JavaScript Unleashed, Fourth Edition* by Jason D. Gilliam, R. Allen Wyke ISBN 0672324318.

- ▶ *JavaScript Developer's Dictionary* by Alexander J. Vincent. ISBN 0672322013.

- ▶ *Sams Teach Yourself DHTML in 24 Hours* by Michael Moncur. ISBN 0672323028.

JavaScript Websites

The following websites will help you learn more about JavaScript:

- ▶ The JavaScript Workshop is a weblog about JavaScript written by Michael Moncur, the author of this book. There you'll find updates on the JavaScript language and the DOM, as well as detailed tutorials on beginning and advanced tasks.

  http://www.jsworkshop.com/

- ▶ The DOM Scripting Task Force, part of the Web Standards Project, works toward better use of standards in scripting, and has an informative weblog with the latest on JavaScript and DOM standards.

  http://domscripting.webstandards.org/

- ▶ The Mozilla Project's JavaScript section has information on the latest updates to the JavaScript language, as well as documentation, links to resources, and information about JavaScript implementations.

  http://www.mozilla.org/js/

Web Development Sites

The following sites have news and information about web technologies, including JavaScript, XML, and the DOM, as well as basic HTML:

▶ The W3C (World Wide Web Consortium) is the definitive source for information about the HTML and CSS standards.

http://www.w3.org/

▶ WebReference.com has information and articles about web technologies ranging from Java to plug-ins.

http://www.webreference.com/

▶ *Digital Web Magazine* features regular online articles on everything from JavaScript and web design to running a web business.

http://www.digital-web.com/

This Book's Website

Be sure to register your book at www.samspublishing.com/register by entering this book's ISBN number. You'll find updates to the book, information on new browsers and new JavaScript features, and other useful resources there, as well as a place to download all of this book's examples and the files you will need to try them out.

APPENDIX B

Tools for JavaScript Developers

One of the best things about JavaScript is that it requires no specialized tools—all you need to start scripting is a web browser and a simple text editor. Nonetheless, tools are available that will make scripting easier. Some of these are described in this appendix.

HTML and Text Editors

Although they aren't specifically intended for scripting, a wide variety of HTML editors are available. These allow you to easily create web documents, either by automating the process of entering tags, or by presenting you with an environment for directly creating styled text.

HomeSite

HomeSite, from Adobe, is a full-featured HTML editor. It is similar to a text editor, but includes features to automatically add HTML tags, and to easily create complicated HTML elements such as tables.

HomeSite also includes a number of JavaScript features, such as creating tags automatically and coloring script commands to make them easy to follow.

A demo version of HomeSite is available for download from Macromedia's site:

http://www.macromedia.com/software/homesite/

TopStyle

TopStyle, from NewsGator Technologies, Inc., is a CSS and HTML editor written by Nick Bradbury, who originally created HomeSite. It specializes in CSS editing and includes powerful tools for editing style sheets, but it also works as an editor for HTML and JavaScript:

http://www.newsgator.com/

FrontPage

Microsoft FrontPage is a popular WYSIWYG (What You See Is What You Get) HTML editor that allows you to easily create HTML documents. The latest version, FrontPage 2000, includes a component to create simple scripts automatically.

You can download FrontPage from Microsoft's site:

http://www.microsoft.com/frontpage/

BBEdit

For Macintosh users, BBEdit is a great HTML editor that also includes JavaScript features. You can download it from Bare Bones Software's website:

http://www.bbedit.com/

Text Editors

Often, a simple text editor is all you need to work on an HTML document or script. Here are some editors that are available for download:

▶ TextPad, from Helios Software Solutions, is a Windows text editor intended as a replacement for the basic Notepad accessory. It's a fast, useful editor, and also includes a number of features for working with HTML. TextPad is shareware, and a fully working version can be downloaded from its official site:

http://www.textpad.com/

▶ UltraEdit-32, from IDM Computer Solutions, is another good Windows text editor, with support for hexadecimal editing for binary files as well as simple text editing. The shareware version is available for download here:

http://www.ultraedit.com/

▶ SlickEdit, from MicroEdge, is a sophisticated programmer's editor for Windows and UNIX platforms:

http://www.slickedit.com/

▶ TextWrangler, from Bare Bones Software (the developers of BBEdit) is a text editor for the Macintosh that works great for general text files, HTML, and JavaScript:

http://www.barebones.com/products/textwrangler/

HTML Validators

Writing web pages that comply with the HTML specifications is one way to avoid JavaScript errors, as well as to ensure that your pages will work with future browser versions. Here are some automated ways of checking the HTML compliance of your pages:

▶ CSE HTML Validator, from AI Internet Solutions, is an excellent standalone utility for Windows that checks HTML documents against your choice of HTML versions. It can also be integrated with HomeSite, TextPad, and several other HTML and text editors. Although the Pro version of this product is commercial, a Lite version is available for free download. Visit their website:

http://www.htmlvalidator.com/

▶ The W3C's HTML Validation Service is a web-based HTML validator. Just enter your URL, and it will be immediately checked for HTML compliance. Access this service at this URL:

http://validator.w3.org/

▶ The WDG HTML Validator offers a different perspective, and is also an easy-to-use web-based service. Access it at this URL:

http://www.htmlhelp.com/tools/validator/

Debugging Tools

You might find the following tools useful in debugging your JavaScript applications:

▶ The Web Developer Extension for Firefox includes several helpful features for debugging JavaScript and for analyzing pages. (See Hour 16, "Debugging JavaScript Applications," for more information.)

http://chrispederick.com/work/webdeveloper/

▶ The Mozilla project's Venkman is a sophisticated debugger for JavaScript in Mozilla or Firefox. Find out more here:

http://www.mozilla.org/projects/venkman/

▶ Microsoft Script Debugger works with JavaScript and VBScript in Internet Explorer:

http://msdn.microsoft.com/library/en-us/sdbug/html/sdbug_1.asp

APPENDIX C

Glossary

The following are some terms relating to JavaScript and web development that are used throughout this book. Although most of them are explained in the text of the book, this section can serve as a useful quick reference while reading the book, or while reading other sources of JavaScript information.

ActiveX   A technology developed by Microsoft to allow components to be created, primarily for Windows computers. ActiveX components, or controls, can be embedded in web pages.

AJAX (Asynchronous JavaScript and XML)   a combination of technologies that allows JavaScript to send requests to a server, receive responses, and update sections of a page without loading a new page.

anchor   In HTML, a named location within a document, specified using the <a> tag. Anchors can also act as links.

applet   A Java program that is designed to be embedded in a web page.

argument   A parameter that is passed to a function when it is called. Arguments are specified within parentheses in the function call.

array   A set of variables that can be referred to with the same name and a number, called an index.

attribute   A property value that can be defined within an HTML tag. Attributes specify style, alignment, and other aspects of the element defined by the tag.

Boolean   A type of variable that can store only two values: `true` and `false`.

browser sensing   A scripting technique that detects the specific browser in use by clients to provide compatibility for multiple browsers.

Cascading Style Sheets (CSS)   The W3C's standard for applying styles to HTML documents. CSS can control fonts, colors, margins, borders, and positioning.

concatenate   The act of combining two strings into a single, longer string.

conditional   A JavaScript statement that performs an action if a particular condition is true, typically using the `if` statement.

debug   The act of finding errors, or bugs, in a program or script.

decrement   To decrease the value of a variable by one. In JavaScript, this can be done with the decrement operator, - -.

deprecated   A term the W3C applies to HTML tags or other items that are no longer recommended for use, and may not be supported in the future. For example, the <font> tag is deprecated in HTML 4.0 because style sheets can provide the same capability.

Document Object Model (DOM)   The set of objects that JavaScript can use to refer to the browser window and portions of the HTML document. The W3C (World Wide Web Consortium) DOM is a standardized version supported by the latest browsers, and allows access to every object within a web page.

Dynamic HTML (DHTML)   The combination of HTML, JavaScript, CSS, and the DOM, which allows dynamic web pages to be created. DHTML is not a W3C standard or a version of HTML.

element   A single member of an array, referred to with an index. In the DOM, an element is a single node defined by an HTML tag.

event   A condition, often the result of a user's action, that can be detected by a script.

event handler   A JavaScript statement or function that will be executed when an event occurs.

expression   A combination of variables, constants, and operators that can be evaluated to a single value.

feature sensing   A scripting technique that detects whether a feature, such as a DOM method, is supported before using it to avoid browser incompatibilities.

function   A group of JavaScript statements that can be referred to using a function name and arguments.

global variable   A variable that is available to all JavaScript code in a web page. It is declared (first used) outside any function.

Greasemonkey   An extension for the Firefox browser that allows user scripts to modify the appearance and behavior of web pages.

Hypertext Markup Language (HTML)   The language used in web documents. JavaScript statements are not HTML, but can be included within an HTML document.

increment   To increase the value of a variable by one. In JavaScript, this is done with the increment operator, ++.

interpreter The browser component that interprets JavaScript statements and acts on them.

Java An object-oriented language developed by Sun Microsystems. Java applets can be embedded within a web page. JavaScript has similar syntax, but is not the same as Java.

JavaScript A scripting language for web documents, loosely based on Java's syntax, developed by Netscape. JavaScript is now supported by the most popular browsers.

layer An area of a web page that can be positioned and can overlap other sections in defined ways. Layers are also known as positionable elements.

local variable A variable that is available to only one function. It is declared (first used) within the function.

loop A set of JavaScript statements that are executed a number of times, or until a certain condition is met.

method A specialized type of function that can be stored in an object, and acts on the object's properties.

Navigator A browser developed by Netscape, and the first to support JavaScript.

node In the DOM, an individual container or element within a web document. Each HTML tag defines a node.

object A type of variable that can store multiple values, called properties, and functions, called methods.

operator A character used to divide variables or constants used in an expression.

parameter A variable sent to a function when it is called, also known as an argument.

progressive enhancement The approach of building a basic page that works on all browsers, and then adding features such as scripting that will work on newer browsers without compromising the basic functionality of the page.

property A variable that is stored as part of an object. Each object can have any number of properties.

rule In CSS, an individual element of a style block that specifies the style for an HTML tag, class, or identifier.

scope The part of a JavaScript program that a variable was declared in and is available to.

selector   In a CSS rule, the first portion of the rule that specifies the HTML tag, class, or identifier that the rule will affect.

statement   A single line of a script or program.

string   A group of text characters that can be stored in a variable.

tag   In HTML, an individual element within a web document. HTML tags are contained within angle brackets, as in <body> and <p>.

text node   In the DOM, a node that stores a text value rather than an HTML element. Nodes that contain text, such as paragraphs, have a text node as a child node.

unobtrusive scripting   A set of techniques that make JavaScript accessible and avoid trouble with browsers by separating content, presentation, and behavior.

variable   A container, referred to with a name, that can store a number, a string, or an object.

VBScript   A scripting language developed by Microsoft, with syntax based on Visual Basic. VBScript is supported only by Microsoft Internet Explorer.

World Wide Web Consortium (W3C)   An international organization that develops and maintains the standards for HTML, CSS, and other key web technologies.

XHTML (Extensible Hypertext Markup Language)   A new version of HTML developed by the W3C. XHTML is similar to HTML, but conforms to the XML specification.

XML (Extensible Markup Language)   A generic language developed by the W3C (World Wide Web Consortium) that allows the creation of standardized HTML-like languages, using a DTD (Document Type Definition) to specify tags and attributes.

APPENDIX D

JavaScript Quick Reference

This appendix is a quick reference for the JavaScript language. It includes the built-in objects and the objects in the basic object hierarchy, JavaScript statements, and built-in functions.

Built-in Objects

The following objects are built in to JavaScript. Some can be used to create objects of your own; others can only be used as they are. Each is detailed in the following sections.

Array

You can create a new array object to define an array—a numbered list of variables. (Unlike other variables, arrays must be declared.) Use the new keyword to define an array, as in this example:

```
students = new Array(30)
```

Items in the array are indexed beginning with 0. Refer to items in the array with brackets:

```
fifth = students[4];
```

Arrays have a single property, length, which gives the current number of elements in the array. They have the following methods:

- ▶ join quickly joins all of the array's elements together, resulting in a string. The elements are separated by commas, or by the separator you specify.

- ▶ reverse returns a reversed version of the array.

- ▶ sort returns a sorted version of the array. Normally this is an alphabetical sort; however, you can use a custom sort method by specifying a comparison routine.

String

Any string of characters in JavaScript is a string object. The following statement assigns a variable to a string value:

```
text = "This is a test."
```

Because strings are objects, you can also create a new string with the new keyword:

```
text = new String("This is a test.");
```

String objects have a single property, length, which reflects the current length of the string. There are a variety of methods available to work with strings:

▶ substring returns a portion of the string.

▶ toUpperCase converts all characters in the string to uppercase.

▶ toLowerCase converts all characters in the string to lowercase.

▶ indexOf finds an occurrence of a string within the string.

▶ lastIndexOf finds an occurrence of a string within the string, starting at the end of the string.

▶ link creates an HTML link using the string's text.

▶ anchor creates an HTML anchor within the current page.

There are also a few methods that allow you to change a string's appearance when it appears in an HTML document:

▶ string.big displays big text using the <big> tag in HTML 3.0.

▶ string.blink displays blinking text using the <blink> tag in Netscape.

▶ string.bold displays bold text using the <b> tag.

▶ string.fixed displays fixed-font text using the <tt> tag.

▶ string.fontcolor displays the string in a colored font, equivalent to the <fontcolor> tag in Netscape.

▶ string.fontsize changes the font size using the <fontsize> tag in Netscape.

▶ string.italics displays the string in italics using the <i> tag.

▶ string.small displays the string in small letters using the <small> tag in HTML 3.0.

▶ string.strike displays the string in a strike-through font using the <strike> tag.

▶ string.sub displays subscript text, equivalent to the <sub> tag in HTML 3.0.

▶ string.sup displays superscript text, equivalent to the <sup> tag in HTML 3.0.

Math

The Math object is not a "real" object because you can't use it to create your own objects. A variety of mathematical constants are also available as properties of the Math object:

▶ Math.E is the base of natural logarithms (approximately 2.718).

▶ Math.LN2 is the natural logarithm of two (approximately 0.693).

▶ Math.LN10 is the natural logarithm of 10 (approximately 2.302).

▶ Math.LOG2E is the base 2 logarithm of *e* (approximately 1.442).

▶ Math.LOG10E is the base 10 logarithm of *e* (approximately 0.434).

▶ Math.PI is the ratio of a circle's circumference to its diameter (approximately 3.14159).

▶ Math.SQRT1_2 is the square root of one half (approximately 0.707).

▶ Math.SQRT2 is the square root of two (approximately 1.4142).

The methods of the Math object allow you to perform mathematical functions. The methods are listed in the following categories.

Algebraic Functions

▶ Math.acos calculates the arc cosine of a number in radians.

▶ Math.asin calculates the arc sine of a number.

▶ Math.atan calculates the arc tangent of a number.

▶ Math.cos calculates the cosine of a number.

▶ Math.sin returns the sine of a number.

▶ Math.tan calculates the tangent of a number.

Statistical and Logarithmic Functions

▶ Math.exp returns *e* (the base of natural logarithms) raised to a power.

▶ Math.log returns the natural logarithm of a number.

▶ Math.max accepts two numbers and returns whichever is greater.

▶ Math.min accepts two numbers and returns the smaller of the two.

Basic Math and Rounding

▶ Math.abs calculates the absolute value of a number.

▶ Math.ceil rounds a number up to the nearest integer.

▶ Math.floor rounds a number down to the nearest integer.

▶ Math.pow calculates one number to the power of another.

▶ `Math.round` rounds a number to the nearest integer.

▶ `Math.sqrt` calculates the square root of a number.

Random Numbers

▶ `Math.random` returns a random number between 0 and 1.

Date

The `Date` object is a built-in JavaScript object that allows you to conveniently work with dates and times. You can create a `Date` object any time you need to store a date, and use the object's methods to work with the date:

▶ `setDate` sets the day of the month.

▶ `setMonth` sets the month. JavaScript numbers the months from 0 to 11, starting with January (0).

▶ `setYear` sets the year. `SetFullYear` is a four-digit, Y2K-compliant version.

▶ `setTime` sets the time (and the date) by specifying the number of milliseconds since January 1, 1970.

▶ `setHours`, `setMinutes`, and `setSeconds` set the time.

▶ `getDate` gets the day of the month.

▶ `getMonth` gets the month.

▶ `getYear` gets the year.

▶ `getTime` gets the time (and the date) as the number of milliseconds since January 1, 1970.

▶ `getHours`, `getMinutes`, and `getSeconds` get the time.

▶ `getTimeZoneOffset` gives you the local time zone's offset from GMT.

▶ `toGMTString` converts the date object's time value to text using GMT (Greenwich Mean Time, also known as UTC).

▶ `toLocalString` converts the `Date` object's time value to text using local time.

▶ `Date.parse` converts a date string, such as "June 20, 2003" to a `Date` object (number of milliseconds since 1/1/1970).

▶ `Date.UTC` converts a `Date` object value (number of milliseconds) to a UTC (GMT) time.

Creating and Customizing Objects

This is a brief summary of the keywords you can use to create your own objects and customize existing objects. These are documented in detail in Hour 6, "Using Functions and Objects."

Creating Objects

There are three JavaScript keywords used to create and refer to objects:

- ▶ new is used to create a new object.

- ▶ this is used to refer to the current object. This can be used in an object's constructor function or in an event handler.

- ▶ with makes an object the default for a group of statements. Properties without complete object references will refer to this object.

To create a new object, you need an object constructor function. This simply assigns values to the object's properties using this:

```
function Name(first,last) {
   this.first = first;
   this.last = last;
}
```

You can then create a new object using new:

```
Fred = new Name("Fred","Smith");
```

Customizing Objects

You can add additional properties to an object you have created just by assigning them:

```
Fred.middle = "Clarence";
```

Properties you add this way apply only to that instance of the object, not to all objects of the type. A more permanent approach is to use the prototype keyword, which adds a property to an object's prototype (definition). This means that any future object of the type will include this property. You can include a default value:

```
Name.prototype.title = "Citizen";
```

You can use this technique to add properties to the definitions of built-in objects as well. For example, this statement adds a property called num to all existing and future string objects, with a default value of 10:

```
string.prototype.num = 10;
```

JavaScript Statements

This is an alphabetical listing of the statements available in JavaScript and their syntax.

Comments

Comments are used to include a note within a JavaScript program, and are ignored by the interpreter. There are two different types of comment syntax:

```
//this is a comment
/* this is also a comment */
```

Only the second syntax can be used for multiple-line comments; the first must be repeated on each line.

break

This statement is used to break out of the current `for` or `while` loop. Control resumes after the loop, as if it had finished.

continue

This statement continues a `for` or `while` loop without executing the rest of the loop. Control resumes at the next iteration of the loop.

for

This statement defines a loop, usually to count from one number to another using an index variable. In this example, the variable i counts from 1 to 9:

```
for (i=1;i<10;i++;) { statements }
```

for...in

This is a different type of loop, used to iterate through the properties of an object, or the elements of an array. This statement loops through the properties of the `Scores` object, using the variable x to hold each property in turn:

```
for (x in Scores) { statements }
```

function

This statement defines a JavaScript function that can be used anywhere within the current document. Functions can optionally return a value with the `return` statement. This example defines a function to add two numbers and return the result:

```
function add(n1,n2) {
    result = n1 + n2;
    return result;
}
```

if...else

This is a conditional statement. If the condition is true, the statements after the `if` statement are executed; otherwise, the statements after the `else` statement (if present) are executed. This example prints a message stating whether a number is less than or greater than 10:

```
if (a > 10) {
    document.write("Greater than 10");
}
else {
    document.write("10 or less");
}
```

A shorthand method, known as the "hook and colon" conditional, can also be used for these types of statements, where ? indicates the `if` portion and : indicates the `else` portion. This statement is equivalent to the previous example:

```
document.write((a > 10) ? "Greater than 10" : "10 or less");
```

Conditional statements are explained further in Hour 7, "Controlling Flow with Conditions and Loops."

return

This statement ends a function, and optionally returns a value. The `return` statement is necessary only if a value is returned.

var

This statement is used to declare a variable. If you use it within a function, the variable is guaranteed to be local to that function. If you use it outside the function, the variable is considered global. Here's an example:

```
var students = 30;
```

Because JavaScript is a loosely typed language, you do not need to specify the type when you declare the variable. A variable is also automatically declared the first time you assign it a value:

```
students = 30;
```

Using var will help avoid conflicts between local and global variables. Note that arrays are not considered ordinary JavaScript variables; they are objects. See Hour 5, "Using Variables, Strings, and Arrays," for details.

while

The while statement defines a loop that iterates as long as a condition remains true. This example waits until the value of a text field is "go":

```
while (document.form1.text1.value != "go") {statements }
```

JavaScript Built-in Functions

The functions in the following sections are built in to JavaScript, rather than being methods of a particular object.

eval

This function evaluates a string as a JavaScript statement or expression, and either executes it or returns the resulting value. In the following example, a function is called using variables as an argument:

```
a = eval("add(x,y);");
```

eval is typically used to evaluate an expression or a statement entered by the user.

parseInt

This function finds an integer value at the beginning of a string and returns it. If there is no number at the beginning of the string, "NaN" (not a number) is returned.

parseFloat

Finds a floating-point value at the beginning of a string and returns it. If there is no number at the beginning of the string, "NaN" (not a number) is returned.

APPENDIX E

DOM Quick Reference

This appendix presents a quick overview of the DOM objects available, including the basic level 0 DOM and the W3C level 1 DOM.

DOM Level 0

The level 0 DOM includes objects that represent the browser window, the current document, and its contents. The following is a basic summary of level 0 DOM objects.

> The level 0 DOM was an informal standard developed by Netscape when JavaScript was introduced. Its objects and properties are now formalized in the W3C DOM level 1 recommendation.

window

The window object represents the current browser window. If multiple windows are open or frames are used, there might be more than one window object. These are given aliases to distinguish them:

- ▶ self represents the current window, as does window. This is the window containing the current JavaScript document.

- ▶ top is the window currently on top (active) on the screen.

- ▶ parent is the window that contains the current frame.

- ▶ The frames array contains the window object for each frame in a framed document.

The window object has three child objects:

- ▶ location stores the location (URL) of the document displayed in the window.

- ▶ document stores information about the current web page.

- ▶ history contains a list of sites visited before or after the current site in the window.

location

The `location` object contains information about the current URL being displayed by the window. It has a set of properties to hold the different components of the URL:

▶ `location.hash` is the name of an anchor within the document, if specified.

▶ `location.host` is a combination of the host name and port.

▶ `location.hostname` specifies the host name.

▶ `location.href` is the entire URL.

▶ `location.pathname` is the directory to find the document on the host, and the name of the file.

▶ `location.port` specifies the communication port.

▶ `location.protocol` is the protocol (or method) of the URL.

▶ `location.query` specifies a query string.

▶ `location.target` specifies the `TARGET` attribute of the link that was used to reach the current location.

history

The `history` object holds information about the URLs that have been visited before and after the current one in the window, and includes methods to go to previous or next locations:

▶ `history.back` goes back to the previous location.

▶ `history.forward` goes forward to the next location.

▶ `history.go` goes to a specified offset in the history list.

document

The `document` object represents the current document in the window. It includes the following child objects:

▶ `document.forms` is a collection with an element for each form in the document.

▶ `document.links` is a collection containing elements for each of the links in the document.

▶ `document.anchors` is a collection with elements for each of the anchors in the document.

▶ document.images contains an element for each of the images in the current document.

▶ document.applets is a collection with references to each embedded Java applet in the document.

navigator

The navigator object includes information about the current browser version:

▶ appCodeName is the browser's code name, usually "Mozilla."

▶ appName is the browser's full name.

▶ appVersion is the version number of the browser. (Example: "4.0(Win95;I).")

▶ userAgent is the user-agent header, which is sent to the host when requesting a web page. It includes the entire version information, such as "Mozilla/4.5(Win95;I)."

▶ plugIns is a collection, which contains information about each currently available plug-in (Netscape and Firefox only).

▶ mimeTypes is a collection containing an element for each of the available MIME types (Netscape and Firefox only).

DOM Level 1

The level 1 DOM is the first cross-browser DOM standardized by the W3C. Its objects are stored under the document object of the level 0 DOM.

Basic Node Properties

Each object has certain common properties:

▶ nodeName is the name of the node (not the ID). The name is the tag name for HTML tag nodes, #document for the document node, and #text for text nodes.

▶ nodeType is a number describing the node's type: 1 for HTML tags, 3 for text nodes, and 9 for the document.

▶ nodeValue is the text contained within a text node.

▶ innerHTML is the HTML contents of a container node.

▶ id is the value of the ID attribute for the node.

▶ classname is the value of the class attribute for the node.

Relationship Properties

The following properties describe an object's relationship with others in the hierarchy:

▶ firstChild is the first child node for the current node.

▶ lastChild is the last child object for the current node.

▶ childNodes is an array of all the child nodes under a node.

▶ previousSibling is the sibling before the current node.

▶ nextSibling is the sibling after the current node.

▶ parentNode is the object that contains the current node.

Offset Properties

Although not part of the W3C DOM, both Netscape and Internet Explorer support the following properties that provide information about a node's position:

▶ offsetLeft is the distance from the left side of the browser window or containing object to the left edge of the node object.

▶ offsetTop is the distance from the top of the browser window or containing object to the top of the node object.

▶ offsetHeight is the height of the node object.

▶ offsetWidth is the width of the node object.

Style Properties

The style child object under each DOM object includes its style sheet properties. These are based on attributes of a style attribute, <style> tag, or external style sheet. See Hour 12, "Working with Style Sheets," for details on these properties.

Node Methods

The following methods are available for all DOM nodes:

▶ appendChild(node) adds a new child node to the node after all its existing children.

▶ insertBefore(node,oldnode) inserts a new node before the specified existing child node.

▶ replaceChild(node,oldnode) replaces the specified old child node with a new node.

▶ removeChild(node) removes an existing child node.

▶ hasChildNodes() returns a Boolean value of true if the node has one or more children, or false if it has none.

▶ cloneNode() returns a copy of the current node.

▶ getAttribute(attribute_name) gets the value of the attribute you specify and stores it in a variable.

▶ setAttribute(attribute_name, value) sets the value of an attribute.

▶ removeAttribute(attribute_name) removes the attribute you specify.

▶ hasAttributes() simply returns true if the node has attributes, and false if it has none.

Document Object Methods and Properties

The following are methods and properties of the document object:

▶ document.getElementById(ID) returns the element with the specified ID attribute.

▶ document.getElementsByTagName(tag) returns an array of the elements with the specified tag name. You can use the asterisk (*) as a wildcard to return an array containing all of the nodes in the document.

▶ document.createElement(tag) creates a new element with the specified tag name.

▶ document.createTextNode(text) creates a new text node containing the specified text.

▶ document.documentElement is an object that represents the document itself, and can be used to find information about the document.

Index

How can we make this index more useful? Email us at indexes@samspublishing.com

How can we make this index more useful? Email us at indexes@samspublishing.com

How can we make this index more useful? Email us at indexes@samspublishing.com

Sams Teach Yourself JavaScript in 24 Hours

International Standard Book Number: 0-672-32879-8

Library of Congress Catalog Card Number: 2005909315

Printed in the United States of America

Fifth Printing: December 2009

13 12 11 10   10 9 8 7 6 5

Trademarks

All terms mentioned in this book that are known to be trademarks or service marks have been appropriately capitalized. Sams Publishing cannot attest to the accuracy of this information. Use of a term in this book should not be regarded as affecting the validity of any trademark or service mark.

Warning and Disclaimer

Every effort has been made to make this book as complete and as accurate as possible, but no warranty or fitness is implied. The information provided is on an "as is" basis. The author and the publisher shall have neither liability nor responsibility to any person or entity with respect to any loss or damages arising from the information contained in this book.

Bulk Sales

Sams Publishing offers excellent discounts on this book when ordered in quantity for bulk purchases or special sales. For more information, please contact

    U.S. Corporate and Government Sales
    1-800-382-3419
    corpsales@pearsontechgroup.com

For sales outside of the U.S., please contact

    International Sales
    international@pearsoned.com

Acquisitions Editor
Betsy Brown

Development Editor
Songlin Qiu

Managing Editor
Patrick Kanouse

Senior Project Editor
Matthew Purcell

Copy Editor
Jessica McCarty

Indexer
Tim Wright

Proofreader
Carla Lewis

Technical Editor
Jim O'Donnell

Publishing Coordinator
Vanessa Evans

Book Designer
Gary Adair

Page Layout
TnT Design, Inc.

SAMS
Teach
Yourself

JavaScript

in 24 Hours

Michael Moncur

SAMS   800 East 96th Street, Indianapolis, Indiana, 46240 USA